Past and Present Publications

A
MEDIEVAL
SOCIETY

Past and Present Publications

General Editor: T. H. ASTON, *Corpus Christi College, Oxford*

Past and Present Publications comprise books similar in character to the articles in the journal *Past and Present*. Whether the volumes in the series are collections of essays – some previously published, others new studies – or monographs, they encompass a wide variety of scholarly and original works primarily concerned with social, economic and cultural changes, and their causes and consequences. They will appeal to both specialists and non-specialists and will endeavour to communicate the results of historical and allied research in readable and lively form. This new series continues and expands in its aims the volumes previously published elsewhere.

Family and Inheritance: Rural Society in Western Europe 1200–1800, edited by Jack Goody, Joan Thirsk and E. P. Thompson*

French Society and the Revolution, edited by Douglas Johnson

Peasants, Knights and Heretics: Studies in Medieval English Social History, edited by R. H. Hilton*

Towns in Societies: Essays in Economic History and Historical Sociology, edited by Philip Abrams and E. A. Wrigley*

Desolation of a City: Coventry and the Urban Crisis of the Late Middle Ages, Charles Phythian-Adams

Puritanism and Theatre: Thomas Middleton and Opposition Drama under the Early Stuarts, Margot Heinemann* ·

Lords and Peasants in a Changing Society: The Estates of the Bishopric of Worcester, 680–1540, Christopher Dyer

Life, Marriage and Death in a Medieval Parish: Economy, Society and Demography in Halesowen 1270–1400, Zvi Razi

Biology, Medicine and Society 1840–1940, edited by Charles Webster

The Invention of Tradition, edited by Eric Hobsbawm and Terence Ranger

Industrialization before Industrialization: Rural Industry and the Genesis of Capitalism, Peter Kriedte, Hans Medick and Jürgen Schlumbohm*
Co-published with the Maison des Sciences de l'Homme, Paris

The Republic in the Village: The People of the Var from the French Revolution to the Second Republic, Maurice Agulhon*
Co-published with the Maison des Sciences de l'Homme, Paris

Social Relations and Ideas: Essays in Honour of R. H. Hilton, edited by T. H. Aston, P. R. Coss, Christopher Dyer and Joan Thirsk

A Medieval Society: The West Midlands at the End of the Thirteenth Century, R. H. Hilton

Winstanley: 'The Law of Freedom' and Other Essays, edited by Christopher Hill

* *Also issued as a paperback*

A
MEDIEVAL
SOCIETY

*The West Midlands at the End of
the Thirteenth Century*

R. H. HILTON

CAMBRIDGE UNIVERSITY PRESS

Cambridge
London   New York   New Rochelle
Melbourne   Sydney

Published by the Press Syndicate of the University of.Cambridge
The Pitt Building, Trumpington Street, Cambridge CB2 1RP
32 East 57th Street, New York, NY 10022, USA
296 Beaconsfield Parade, Middle Park, Melbourne 3206, Australia

First published by Weidenfeld and Nicolson 1966
Reissued by Cambridge University Press 1983

Printed in Great Britain at the
University Press, Cambridge

Library of Congress catalogue card number: 82-19732

British Library Cataloguing in Publication Data

Hilton, R. H.
A medieval society. – (Past and Present publications)
1. Midlands – Social life and customs
I. Title   II. Series
942.4′03′4   HN398.M/

ISBN 0 521 25374 8

CONTENTS

MAPS AND PLANS

ACKNOWLEDGEMENTS

I wish to thank the following for their kind permission to repro-
duce material in their possession: Mr F. W. B. Charles for
drawings of Noakes Court, Defford; Mr P. A. Rahtz for the
Upton plans; Dr Cyril Hart for information from his unpublished
'Forest of Dean as a Timber Producing Area' (Leicester University
PhD thesis) on which the map of the Forest of Dean is based;*
Mr J. West for the map of Feckenham Forest, the Birmingham and
Midland Archaeological Society for Mr F. T. S. Houghton's map
of the saltways (TBAS liv).
I also wish to thank Mr J. Hogan for the maps.
The following friends and colleagues have also helped me with
their comments: Dr K. R. Andrews, Miss J. R. Birrell, Mr
F. W. B. Charles, Professor H. A. Cronne and Mr P. A. Rahtz. I
am very grateful to them and absolve them from all responsibility
for what I have written.

R. H. H.

* Now published as *Royal Forest*, 1966.

FOREWORD TO THE
1983 REISSUE

Much work has been done on the history of late medieval English society since this book was first published. Only minor corrections have been possible for this reissue, but I do not think that I would have wished to make major alterations.

Three important subsequent studies relating to the West Midlands should be mentioned: Christopher Dyer, *Lords and Peasants in a Changing Society: the Estates of the Bishopric of Worcester 680–1540*, 1980; Zvi Razi, *Life, Marriage and Death in a Medieval Parish: Economy, Society and Demography in Halesowen, 1240–1400*, 1980; Nigel Saul, *Knights and Esquires: the Gloucestershire Gentry in the Fourteenth Century*, 1981. This last work suggests some modifications to figures I had calculated.

I rashly promised to follow this study with another book dealing with the fourteenth and fifteenth centuries. To some extent I have fulfilled this promise with my Ford Lectures, *The English Peasantry in the Later Middle Ages*, 1975. I hope to be able to reinforce this with another work on urban society.

Apart from reviewers of the original edition, I have had help in making corrections from Christopher Dyer, Richard Holt and Simon Penn, to whom I am very grateful.

Owing to the loss of plates, the photographs which were included in the original edition have regretfully had to be omitted.

R.H.H.

INTRODUCTION

This book is about the society of peasants, townsmen, knights, barons and clergy who inhabited a part of the English midlands. It is a description of this society at the end of the thirteenth and the beginning of the fourteenth century, roughly the period covered by the reign of Edward I (1272–1307). It is one of the difficulties of writing about a period when documentary evidence is, if not exactly scanty, at any rate unevenly distributed, that one must take one's evidence over this rather long span of time on the assumption that the various social classes and the relationships between them did not substantially change during this period. This may well be an unjustified assumption, but in this case my study of this society is intended to set the stage for a later work covering the fourteenth and fifteenth centuries in which I will attempt to show how things changed during that longer period.

As the reader will see, I have not hesitated to use evidence from the twelfth century or earlier in order to explain how a situation, which I attempt to describe in more detail as it was at the end of the thirteenth century, came about. On the other hand, I have attempted to keep my use of evidence later than the 1320s to a minimum. The changes of the mid-fourteenth century were so great that it is very misleading to use examples from, say, about the year 1400 to illustrate any aspect of social life a century earlier. Only when an aspect of the earlier period is a complete blank (as in the case of the building of the houses of the peasants) have I risked using the later evidence.

There was probably a certain (quite relative) stability of social and economic conditions in the last two or three decades of the thirteenth and the first decade of the fourteenth century. This was the period when the rising curve of population growth was flattening

1

out, when almost all land capable of use with the techniques available was under cultivation or used for pasture. In fact, such was the demand for foodstuffs that the area under the plough had encroached so dangerously on the land (such as meadow, pasture and wood) which was needed for keeping livestock, that there was a serious shortage of animals. Since the animals not only provided meat and pulling power but the only good manure that was known to the medieval agriculturalist, this shortage was one of the most serious weaknesses of the economy.

The late thirteenth century was also the period when urban industry and commerce were reaching the limit of a major phase of expansion. European towns and merchants, above all those of Italy and the Low Countries, achieved during this period a degree of wealth and social and political influence which makes one compare this phase of the urbanization of western and central Europe with that of the early Roman Empire. Merchants were not rulers, however, and governments had enough power to be able to divert a considerable proportion of the cash which was in circulation, thanks to the vigour of local and international trade, into their own coffers. It was then spent almost entirely on war. But wealthy warring states also needed, besides soldiers, a considerable administrative apparatus. This then is also a period of the rapid growth of the machinery of government, of which the English kingdom provided no mean example.

England at this time had come through a period of political upheaval and civil war. Historians differ in their interpretation of the politics of this period, but there is general agreement that the great lay and ecclesiastical landowners of the kingdom were very wealthy, powerful in relation to all other social classes and sufficiently self-conscious as a class to hold in check a king of strong will, considerable ambitions and great material resources. This baronial class had become divided during the so-called Barons' Wars, and there continued, as a matter of course, to be divisions of interest within it after the wars were over. Nevertheless, there was no European aristocracy which, as a class, had the same power in the state as the English barons. We should remember this when we consider the local people over whom they ruled.

But if, when considering the problems of regional society, we remember the wider social and political pressures of the period, we must also bear in mind other general conditioning factors. In a

2

peasant society which relied for its livelihood on grain crops, the weather, or rather the effect of the weather on the crops, was of primary importance. In 1315 and 1316 there was a famine of European dimensions, so severe that some historians have thought it a more important factor than the bubonic plagues of mid-century in causing the prolonged economic crisis which they suppose to have dominated the fourteenth and fifteenth centuries.[1] During this famine, the price of wheat on occasions reached a price of more than 20s a quarter. Conditions were never as bad as this during the period which interests us. However, continual fluctuations in the price of various grains must have brought an atmosphere of great uncertainty to the majority of the population. Low agricultural prices were not mourned by the agricultural population as they are now, since the first charge on the harvest was the subsistence of the peasant family. Low prices resulted from abundance, high prices from dearth and these meant high mortality. The great pioneer of agricultural history, J. E. Thorold Rogers, thought that at the end of the thirteenth century, a price per quarter of wheat in excess of 6s was high, though recent expert writing has suggested that only when the price of wheat rose above 7s a quarter did the poorer peasants experience more than ordinary privation.[2] Peasants did not of course depend on wheat alone for their own subsistence. They grew wheat primarily to sell, relying much more on rye, barley and oats for their own food. In the west midlands it was barley and oats or a mixture of the two called 'drage' or 'dredge' which was the principal alternative to wheat. Barley prices followed the fluctuations of wheat prices fairly closely, so the conditions of production as well as of supply and demand must have been similar. Oats, however, were less harmed by wet weather than the other two grains, and tended to be an alternative to wheat and barley. Fluctuations in oat prices were therefore less violent.

Grain prices fluctuated not only from year to year, but within the year. After the harvest they tended to be low and then to rise progressively until the eve of the following harvest. This favoured those who were well enough off to keep a supply in reserve, but most peasants had to sell their surplus quickly in order to raise cash. When, therefore, we write about the average grain price of a particular year, it must be understood that this average is based on wide variations within the year. Between 1265, the year in which Simon de Montfort's army was defeated at Evesham, and the great famine years of 1315 and 1316, the average price of wheat exceeded 6s a quarter in seventeen years. It was fairly high in the early 1270s and early 1280s and reached famine levels in 1294 and 1295. There was another bad period, the end of the first decade of the fourteenth century. On the other hand, the late 1260s, the late 1270s and the early 1300s were years of reasonably low prices, while the late 1280s was a period of abundance. Within these broader trends however, there were more or less considerable year by year fluctuations, which, it seems clear, resulted almost entirely from the effects of the weather on the harvest. For we can take it that prices during the period were not affected by any alterations to the currency.

The years between the end of the Barons' Wars and the great famine of 1315–6 did not therefore know any abnormal natural, political or social catastrophe. Conflicts between peasants, and landowners, townsmen and countrymen, laymen and clerics, kings and barons occurred as normal incidents of medieval society at this particular stage of its development. The well-known legislative and military activity of Edward I seems rather less significant at the level of the village, hundred and county than it appears to be in the writings of national chroniclers, or in the records of the central government. Perhaps the fiscal and administrative pressures resulting from the king's constant wars against his neighbours made more acute existing tensions in regional society by the turn of the century but such changes are difficult to measure. It is not suggested that in medieval England the political antagonisms and combinations of king and aristocracy had nothing to do with the problems of the rest of society. It is possible, however, that by looking from the bottom upwards we might get a more accurate picture of the whole of society, and of the state, than if we look at society from on high, assuming that king, council, Parliament, chancery, exchequer and household were as important and effective as they would have wished to be.

A note on medieval monetary values

It is very risky to attempt to give modern equivalents of medieval monetary values. The increase in the prices of different common commodities since the middle ages has not been at the same rate. It is not right, therefore, to draw conclusions about the general rate of increase from a few examples. Some prices (the price per quarter of grain for example) are mentioned in the introduction and in other chapters. But perhaps the best way to appreciate the enormous difference in monetary values is to consider the payment of labour. At the end of the thirteenth century, the daily wage, in cash, without food provided, of a skilled worker such as a carpenter could be 3d. With food provided it would be 1½d or 2d. An unskilled labourer, man as well as woman, would get 1d or 1½d without food. Permanent farm servants got varying rates. Ploughmen and carters usually got about 5s a year in cash with an issue of a quarter of mixed grains every ten to thirteen weeks. The value of other perquisites is not calculable. There are, of course, further variations in daily and annual wage rates, as between occupations and districts. This note does not aim to discuss these, but simply to give one or two typical figures to help the reader to get prices quoted in the book in perspective.

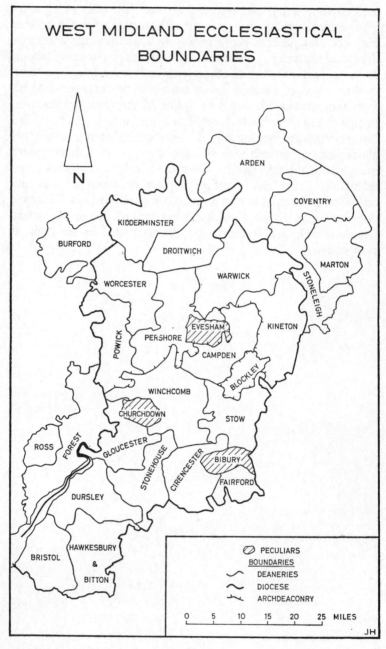

WEST MIDLAND ECCLESIASTICAL BOUNDARIES

ARDEN

COVENTRY

KIDDERMINSTER

BURFORD

DROITWICH

MARTON

WORCESTER

WARWICK

STONELEIGH

POWICK

PERSHORE

EVESHAM

KINETON

CAMPDEN

BLOCKLEY

WINCHCOMB

CHURCHDOWN

STOW

ROSS

FOREST

GLOUCESTER

STONEHOUSE

CIRENCESTER

BIBURY

FAIRFORD

DURSLEY

BRISTOL

HAWKESBURY
&
BITTON

PECULIARS
BOUNDARIES
DEANERIES
DIOCESE
ARCHDEACONRY

0   5   10   15   20   25 MILES

JH

CHAPTER 1

THE REGION

There were few countries of medieval Europe which were as unified as the English kingdom at the end of the thirteenth century. One reason was that it was small, both as regards population to be controlled and distances to be travelled. It is true that the Marches of Wales, the north-western counties from Cheshire to the north, and the country north of the Vale of York were somewhat remote from the centre of government, and apt to be ruled by the local baronage with little help from the king and his officials. But these were very sparsely settled areas. The weight of England was in the lowland zone, south of York and Chester, east of Hereford and Shrewsbury. It was there that the bulk of the population of town and village, city and seaport, was to be found, with its attention already focused in the direction of London and Westminster, an urban concentration overwhelmingly big compared even with Bristol, the next largest town, and with York, the second capital.

Even so, the regional differences of medieval England were by no means insignificant. The English kingdom had only known three centuries of political unification under the Wessex, Norman and Angevin dynasties. In spite of the commercial growth of London and the south-east, there was nothing like a national market for agricultural or industrial products. The ruling class still spoke a language foreign to the majority of the population, and the regional dialects of English were still strongly marked. While there were important factors making for intercommunication, such as the journeys of merchants, government officials, barons and their servants visiting their scattered estates, judges on circuit, and ecclesiastics, most people lived their whole lives within a twenty- or thirty-mile radius of their place of birth. It should be said, however, that

7

within these circumscribed limits there was a great deal of mobility. Middle and lower class Englishmen (and women) may not normally have travelled long distances, but they moved about over shorter distances a great deal. Consequently, regions in which communications were relatively easy developed something of a regional identity, and can be studied by the social historian in greater depth than is possible even for so small a state as the English kingdom. But such regions were by no means hermetically sealed from their neighbours. Naturally, they overlapped at the edges, and for reasons already given, their more influential inhabitants were in the habit of travelling considerable distances for business or pleasure.

The medieval west midlands is a region with extremely vague frontiers when considered from the standpoint of economic and social structure. Some would include within the region the counties of Shropshire and Herefordshire. But those really belong to the Marches of Wales, a regional society well worth studying in its own right. Others would include Staffordshire. But that county rather looks north and east to Derbyshire and the Trent Valley.* There was, however, an ancient nucleus to the west midlands which persisted as a unit of economic, social and cultural life throughout the middle ages, as well as being a unit of ecclesiastical administration. I refer to the diocese of Worcester. As has been convincingly demonstrated, this diocese had the same boundaries as the ancient Anglo-Saxon kingdom of the Hwicce, which was absorbed into the larger midland kingdom of Mercia in the eighth century.[1] The Hwiccan kingdom was occupied in the early days of the Anglo-Saxon conquest by Saxons from Wessex and the Thames Valley as well as by Anglians moving across midland England from the Wash. But these invaders found an already ancient and strongly rooted native culture with its focus in the Cotswold Hills and the Avon and Severn valleys. The small frontier kingdom, in the manner of the times, also became, after the conversion of the English, a diocese of the church, served by priests from their minster in the capital of the kingdom at Worcester.

---

* The west midlands of modern times which includes the counties which I exclude is determined partly by the existence of the great Birmingham–Black Country conurbation. The centre of gravity has moved north as a result of post-medieval industrialization. Cf. *Birmingham and its regional setting: a scientific survey* (British Association, 1950).

The diocese of Worcester, in the apparently illogical fashion of ecclesiastical topography, included the counties of Worcester and Gloucester almost entirely (except for the south-west corner of Gloucestershire and the north-west corner of Worcestershire, in Hereford diocese) but the eastern boundary of the diocese runs down the centre of Warwickshire, including Stratford-on-Avon, but excluding Coventry. This is because the counties were created after the Hwiccan kingdom had disappeared as a political entity. Coventry was in fact the seat of one of the two electoral chapters of the diocese which adjoins that of Worcester. This diocese was known during most of the middle ages and early modern times as that of Coventry and Lichfield, though in the twelfth century it was still called by its old name, the Bishopric of Chester. However, we shall include the whole of Warwickshire in our west midland region. Firstly, because even though county boundaries sometimes cut across natural regions their original creation as administrative units was not purely artificial, and their continuous history as units of taxation, government and jurisdiction added to their individuality. Secondly, Coventry itself, already by 1300 a large industrial and trading town, completed the commercial and therefore the social and economic unity of the west midland region whilst at the same time linking up this region with others and with the capital.

Like many regions of midland and southern England, the west midlands contained within it much variety as well as features which gave it unity. We must first describe their unifying features, for those provide our justification for studying the region as an entity. Foremost are the two major river valleys, those of the Severn and Avon. The Severn was, in the middle ages, navigable as far as Shrewsbury; merchants and shipmen argued that it should be free for navigation as far as the sea, and that the weirs put up by riparian landowners to catch fish were illegal.[2] Below Bridgnorth in Shropshire there were only two bridges, one at Worcester, and one at Gloucester. This of course enhanced the importance of both towns for it concentrated upon them many of the routes from England to Wales. The fact that Bristol, the second biggest town of thirteenth-century England, was close to the estuary of the Severn meant much both for the Severn river traffic itself and for the life of those districts through which the river flowed. Bristol was a contact with the world at large, from Iceland to the Mediterranean. It imported and redistributed commodities from those foreign parts, often of course by road, but up the river too. Bristol itself being a market for agricultural commodities, the river was naturally busy with craft taking foodstuffs and raw materials down river to feed the town. This traffic was swelled by other riverside dwellers, for on or near the river's banks were to be found market towns (like Tewkesbury), villages, and landing places both for up and down river boats and for ferries.

The other principal river route of the region was the Avon which flows into the Severn at Tewkesbury. This river was not as navigable as the Severn. Attempts in medieval and early modern times to open it for through traffic from Tewkesbury to Warwick were unsuccessful. Consequently, it was mainly used for local traffic while goods going through to Coventry from the Severn valley had to go overland. River valleys are, however, important as channels of communication not only by boat, but also by foot and pack animal. Air photographs have recently confirmed for prehistoric and early historic times what we already knew from medieval documents, that the valley was a dense and homogeneous area of settlement from the area immediately south of Coventry as far as the confluence with the river Severn.[3]

The road system which bound the different parts of the region together, and with the outside world, is not easy to document, either historically or archaeologically, because of continual modifications and building, and because legal, administrative and similar documents refer to them usually only in passing. We do however know something of the main routes. The Fosse Way, coming from the south-west through Cirencester, ran across the Cotswolds and through Warwickshire to Watling Street, and was the main survivor in the west midlands of the Roman road system. There may have been a riverside road of Roman origin from Bristol to Worcester on the east bank of the Severn, though this is not certain. There was certainly a very important road from Worcester, through Droitwich and Birmingham, to Lichfield and the north. A Roman road, called in the middle ages, and now, Ryknield Street, ran south from Watling Street, passing a few miles west of Birmingham to cross the Avon at Bidford-on-Avon, climb the Cotswold ridge between Saintbury and Weston-sub-Edge and continue across the plateau to Bourton-on-the-Water, where it met the Fosse Way. Ryknield Street was joined at Alcester by another Roman road from Droitwich which then continued and crossed the Avon at Stratford. This

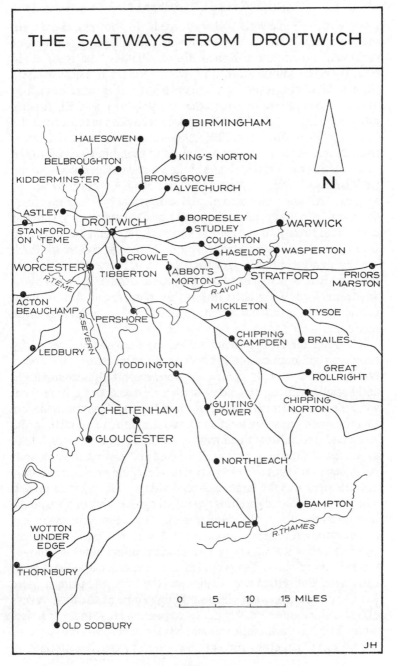

THE SALTWAYS FROM DROITWICH

N

BIRMINGHAM

HALESOWEN

KING'S NORTON

BELBROUGHTON

BROMSGROVE

ALVECHURCH

KIDDERMINSTER

ASTLEY

DROITWICH

BORDESLEY

STUDLEY

WARWICK

STANFORD ON TEME

COUGHTON

HASELOR

WASPERTON

WORCESTER

CROWLE

TIBBERTON

ABBOT'S MORTON

STRATFORD

PRIORS MARSTON

R.TEME

R.AVON

ACTON BEAUCHAMP

MICKLETON

TYSOE

R.SEVERN

PERSHORE

CHIPPING CAMPDEN

BRAILES

LEDBURY

TODDINGTON

GREAT ROLLRIGHT

CHELTENHAM

GUITING POWER

CHIPPING NORTON

GLOUCESTER

NORTHLEACH

BAMPTON

WOTTON UNDER EDGE

LECHLADE

R.THAMES

THORNBURY

0   5   10   15 MILES

OLD SODBURY

JH

11

was the main framework of Roman roads. In addition, there were the innumerable tracks between towns and villages, a function of settlement growth since Roman times. Of these the most easily traced are the saltways radiating from Droitwich, because these leave their traces in local place names.[4] But they were obviously means of communication for other commodities as well. Among other important roads, difficult to trace exactly, is the route from the Severn valley to Coventry. This followed the main road to Lichfield from Worcester as far as Bromsgrove and then branched off to the east, crossing the forested region of the Worcestershire plain and the woodlands of Arden in Warwickshire to reach Coventry by way of Henley. This important road may have been that by which iron from the Forest of Dean reached the smiths of Coventry, not to speak of cattle from Bromyard and central Wales. But Coventry also got iron from Dudley and south Staffordshire. This came by a road which ran through Birmingham, for here was an important crossing over the river Rea, which flooded badly in winter. Cattle from the north and from North Wales also came by this route, so that Birmingham, by the end of the thirteenth century, had already a flourishing cattle market.[5]

The road and river systems unified the west midland region by providing communications between its different parts. These parts however were strongly contrasted, topographically, economically and socially. Among the oldest settled districts, as we have seen, were the main river valleys of Avon and Severn. Apart from the fact that the rivers cut a way for man to pass through the woodlands, the Avon and Severn were lined with five sets of gravel terraces. These produced, for the most part, well drained and easily cultivable soils particularly attractive to early settlers. Here, the predominant type of settlement was the large nucleated village. The agrarian system which was associated with this type of village was that of open fields, intermixed holdings, a husbandry marked by common practices and a concentration on grain production. A similar type of settlement and husbandry was also to be found on the undulating claylands of south Warwickshire, also occupied and cleared of woodland at an early date. But settled even earlier was the Cotswold plateau. Here too there were many big villages, though some of the little valleys also contained quite small hamlet settlements. Husbandry practices were similar to those of the valleys and clay plains, that is to say they were directed largely to grain production and were characterized by open fields, intermixed holdings and common rights. Conditions on the Cotswold plateau were not identical, in spite of the equally early date of settlement, with those of the valleys or of the south Warwickshire claylands. Although many of the lower lying Cotswold river valleys were clay-lined, the uplands had light soils derived from oolitic limestone rocks. These were easily drained and easily ploughed but subject to fast erosion. The traditional method by which erosion was combated was by folding sheep on the arable. As the animals trod the dung into the ploughed land so they made it firm and at the same time restored its fertility. The animals themselves, as well as performing this useful function, also provided fleeces, for local as well as distant cloth-making industries. The open, upland pastures of the wolds were of course of fundamental importance for the maintenance of large sheep flocks but the Cotswold farmer's conception of his husbandry as essentially one of both sheep and corn was strongly held, even when Cotswold wool was at its highest premium.

In other parts of the region, settlement was much later. That is to say that, whereas substantial inroads into the waste had been made even in prehistoric times in the valleys, on parts of the clay plain, and on the Cotswold plateau, elsewhere prehistoric, Roman and even Anglo-Saxon settlement had been scanty and piecemeal. It was not until the eleventh century and afterwards that serious inroads were made into other districts of the west midland region, but these inroads were made under different social conditions from those of the earlier period and resulted in scattered rather than nucleated settlements. They also made less impression on the woodland cover which was natural to the heavy clays of central Worcestershire and Warwickshire. In fact, the woodland cover was deliberately preserved, as far as possible, both by the crown and by such wealthy landowners as had extensive woodlands, in order to give shelter to the beasts of the chase. Consequently, a considerable part of the west midland region in the thirteenth century was wood or forest.

In the middle ages the word forest did not, as it does now, mean a large area of wooded country. It had primarily a juridical meaning. A forest was a region under the law of the forest. This meant that even when private landowners had their estates within the royal forest, the forest law laid down certain rules by which the tree cover and the game were preserved for the king's hunting. And although the nucleus of a royal forest was often a crown estate, by the time the

Norman and Angevin kings had extended their hunting rights most forests contained as much privately owned as crown land within them.

The two chief royal forests in the west midlands in the thirteenth century were those of Dean and Feckenham. The Forest of Dean occupied all that part of Gloucestershire between the rivers Severn and Wye as far north as Newent and Highnam which was due west of Gloucester. As well as being a hunting preserve it was also a source of timber, iron and coal. Its administrative headquarters were at St Briavels, where the constable of the king's castle was usually also the Warden of the Forest. The Forest of Feckenham occupied a very substantial part of eastern Worcestershire and a strip of western Warwickshire. The boundary came on the west to the very walls of Worcester. The river Avon between Pershore and the south of the river Arrow was its southern boundary and in the north it reached the Bell Brook and the Lickey Hills. It had developed to this extent from the royal manor of Feckenham, which was the forest head-quarters, and like the Forest of Dean it contained many manors belonging to private landowners. In the north of Worcestershire there were also small overspills of the Forests of Wyre and Kinver most of which were in Shropshire and Staffordshire. In Gloucester-shire, too, there were one or two smaller forest areas, such as Kings-wood in the south Cotswolds and Alveston in the lower Severn valley.[6]

The royal forests however, were not the only extensively wooded areas in the west midlands. A belt of woodland ran along the western edge of the Cotswold plateau.[7] To the west of the Severn, straddling the boundary between Worcestershire and Gloucestershire, was a timbered area called Corse Wood. Further north and still west of the Severn was Malvern Chase, a private wood much disputed between the earls of Gloucester and the bishops of Hereford. North of Worcester on the east bank of the river was a recently disafforested piece of woodland around the Abbot of Evesham's manor of Ombersley. But these smaller stretches of wood were much nibbled into by settlement. More important was the great stretch of wooded country which was, as it were, the continuation of the Forest of Feckenham into Warwickshire. This was known as Arden. It was not royal forest, or to be more accurate, only that part of Arden between the river Arrow and the Worcestershire county boundary was forest, being part of Feckenham. However, Arden as woodland was older than Feckenham as a legally defined forest, for at the beginning of the thirteenth century it was said that the customs of Arden applied in the Forest of Feckenham.[8] Arden was the name given to one of the deaneries of the archdeaconry of Coventry in the diocese of Coventry and Lichfield.

Arden in fact covered the whole of Warwickshire north of the Avon, thinning out, however, between Coventry and Watling Street. Since it was not a legally defined entity as it would have been had it been a royal forest, its extent is to be traced chiefly by place names. As we have seen, it merged into Feckenham Forest near the Worcestershire boundary. Villages such as Tanworth-in-Arden in west Warwickshire, Henley-in-Arden and Weston-in-Arden (Bulkington) to the north and east show how far it extended. As late as the sixteenth century, topographical writers such as John Leland and Camden contrasted the open, old settled corn-growing land south of the Avon, which they called the Felden, with the wooded, enclosed and much grassed region of Arden to the north.[9]

To the north of Arden was the large private hunting ground of the earls of Warwick, Sutton Chase. This reached into Staffordshire in the north, and contained many villages which have since become part of Birmingham. It was kept as far as possible by the earls as a game preserve, though pressure of population obliged them to allow some clearings. Like Malvern Chase, it was an occasion of quarrels between rival hunting landlords, and the earls had eventually to make mutual arrangements with other magnates such as the Bassets of Drayton near Tamworth.[10]

The contrast between old settled and well-cleared stretches of land devoted primarily to grain production, and quite considerable areas of woodland, whether royal forest or not, must have been the most striking feature of the west midland landscape in the middle ages. It should not however be imagined that this was a contrast between productive agricultural areas and relatively backward woodlands devoted solely to the pleasures of the aristocracy. The woodlands, even the royal forests, were honeycombed with clearings for agriculture. They were also used extensively as pasture. The wastes on the eastern edges of Arden, for example, were stocked with considerable sheep flocks, and merged with the open wold pastures of the villages near Watling Street.[11] Woodlands contained many villages and hamlets as well as isolated farmsteads. As we shall see, their relatively late development had led to early enclosure for both arable and pastoral farming, and in some ways this was more efficient than the earlier open field cultivation. Furthermore, the woodlands themselves had considerable economic resources in supplying timber and feeding grounds for animals. They were of course also the resort of poachers and fugitives of all classes. This is not the least of the important consequences for the social life of the region of the interspersing of woodland with cultivated areas.

In describing the main features of the medieval west midlands we have drawn attention in passing to two contrasting types of settlement and their associated agrarian systems. On the whole, as we have indicated, the areas which were settled earliest were characterized by large nucleated villages and the open field agriculture which is usually (and somewhat misleadingly) called the two- or three-field system. Naturally, these areas were settled earliest because they were easiest to cultivate, or easiest of access, such as the river valleys and the Cotswolds. It does not necessarily follow that these valley and upland soils were the most rewarding. But the adequate drainage and easy tilth they provided naturally predisposed early settlers, with the primitive instruments at their disposal, to choose them in preference to heavy soils. The latter were apt to become waterlogged and tended to have as natural cover the most difficult trees to fell, the oak. Then there may have been an increase of population in the Anglo-Saxon period which necessitated a move to less easily cultivable areas, such as the claylands of south Warwickshire and the vales of Berkeley and Gloucester, where nucleated villages and open field agriculture are also found.

The reasons which can be suggested for the tendency for early settlement to have these characteristic features are speculations rather than established fact, for it may well be that open field agriculture precedes written records. However this may be, it seems certain that in prehistoric and early historic times social organization, however aristocratic, had a much greater element in it of collective activity than in the eleventh or twelfth centuries. The family group, whether consisting simply of blood relations, or of blood relations reinforced by clients and slaves, was much larger than that of later dates. This type of family appears in the written record primarily as a relic of earlier times (as in the system of wergild payments), but it is obvious that for defence purposes and for agricultural production family groups must have been associated closely with each other. It is not difficult to see therefore that the occupation and cultivation of the soil and the allocation of pastures must have been made by a community rather than by individual persons, even though this does not imply any form of communal ownership of the arable land. For this reason (though the details of the process can hardly be recovered) the family holdings were mingled in the open fields; but whether family ownership of the arable parcels was superseded by the common pasture rights of the whole community after the grain was collected in the autumn has been doubted, at any rate in the settlement period. By the end of the thirteenth century, however, the fallows in the open field villages were usually given over to regulated common pasture.[12]

By the time we have adequate written records, the intermixture of parcels was considerable, holdings having become very fragmented. This was the consequence not merely of the buying, selling and exchange of parcels, but also of the earliest inheritance customs. Even as late as 1300, in many English villages, the rule of inheritance was still partibility, in spite of the feudal influences encouraging primogeniture.[13] In the Anglo-Saxon period partible inheritance was much more common. The consequent splitting up of open field holdings made collective regulation even more necessary than when holdings were in larger blocks. In a similar way, the reduction of the amount of rough pasture available on the village waste as a result of the turning of pasture and woodlands into arable as population increased must have made communal regulation more necessary than it had been when woodland waste was abundant. The impression is, in fact, that once an agrarian system with open fields and rights of common pasture had become established its communal features would become strengthened as numbers increased.

It is obvious, but worth insistence, that when villagers' holdings consist of intermixed parcels of arable, with appurtenant rights of common on the waste, their dwellings must necessarily be clustered together. Only with this arrangement could they have more or less equidistant access on all sides to their holdings, scattered as they were at the four points of the compass. Nor could their houses be built in the fields since the arable parcels were commonable after the crops were gathered. Similarly, the jealousy of the commoners would prevent encroachment on the waste for building purposes.

However, it must not be imagined that all old settled villages were large. There were, scattered among the larger townships in the primary settlement areas, many hamlets. Many of these seem to be offshoots from the bigger villages, as if, when land was plentiful, a family group, or perhaps several families, left the main centre to build a few new houses and plough new fields. These secondary settlements are often revealed as such by their place names. Let us take for example the parish of Brailes in south Warwickshire. The centre of settlement was the large village of Brailes itself, now, and probably then, divided into Upper (or Over) and Lower Brailes. Here may have been in 1280 as many as five or six hundred inhabitants. It was a manor of the Earl of Warwick, although at this period it was leased for life to one of the earl's most constant local knights, Sir Richard d'Amundeville. Two hamlets in the parish were held of the earl by military tenure. These were Chelmscote whose lord was Henry Huband, an active knight, with his main estates on the border between Warwickshire and Worcestershire, and Winderton, held by the famous Marcher baron, Roger Clifford. But at an earlier date, probably pre-conquest, Chelmscote was 'Ceolmund's cottage', and Winderton, according to the most likely interpretation of the name, was a winter farm, a settlement used during the winter months. Its position is in a sheltered spot under the ridge of Edgehill. By the end of the thirteenth century, both these places had grown in population, but Chelmscote only had perhaps a hundred inhabitants and Winderton a score or so more. In the 1330s Chelmscote's taxable capacity was only a tenth that of Brailes, and Winderton's one sixth.[14]

In the open field villages the peasant holdings, and very often the demesne, lay very subdivided, as John Smyth of Nibley put it 'all lands in Comon feilds, here one acre or ridge and there another, one mans intermixt with an other'.[15] The peasants' holdings are very often described in some detail in charters describing land transfers. Such a charter is copied in an early thirteenth-century Worcester cartulary and shows to what extent fragmentation and inter-mixture could go.[16] Stephen, the son of Leonard, with his wife's assent (since she might later have a claim) sold seventeen and a half acres of arable and half an acre of meadow to John, the son of Osbert. This was in Charlton, part of the Cathedral priory's manor of Cropthorne. It is in the Avon valley about half way between Evesham and Pershore, and had been in the church of Worcester's possession since the eighth century at the latest. There were two fields, North Field and South Field, and the seventeen and a half acres were distributed about the fields in separate parcels as follows.

In the North Field Stephen's holding consisted of seventeen parcels, fourteen of a half acre each and three of a quarter acre. In the South Field there were also seventeen parcels, sixteen of them being half acres (one of which was a headland), the last parcel being an acre, and three-quarters of 'croftland in Lineworthin'. Both the words 'croft' and 'worthin' imply an enclosure. Such enclosures were often in divided ownership like the furlongs of the open fields, and this is a case in point.

What were these half and quarter acres ? They were almost certainly not measured acres, but rather what are sometimes referred to in a late twelfth-century cartulary of Evesham Abbey as 'feld acras'. 'Field acres' were, in the midlands, composed of ridges, or lands ('londes'), or to use a term derived from the Latin charters, 'selions' (Fr. *sillon*).[17] There were usually assumed to be four ridges of ploughland to a field acre. The approximation of this practical measure to the statute acre may sometimes have been quite close, since the statute acre was derived from the ideal ridge 220 yards long by a perch (16½ feet) wide. But this equation did not always work, as we see in an example of a holding expressed both in acres and ridges from another Worcester Priory charter. Alfred (Elured) of Penhull sold seven acres of his demesne at Lindridge in the Teme Valley to the monks for two and a half marks so that they would pay his debts to the Jews of Worcester. The seven acres consisted of forty ridges (*seliones*) in eight blocks distributed over five furlongs (*culture*), so while there must have been an irregular number of ridges to the acre, the average comes out at more than five. A further item in this charter is worth mentioning as it throws light on typical open fields arrangements: the tenants of this land, it says, are to have such common of pasture 'as reasonably appertains to such a portion of arable land except in meadow and woodland at the time when these are enclosed'. (*Quantum ad tantum portionem prefate terre rationabiliter debuerit pertinere excepto prato et bosco cum jure debuerint esse in defenso*.)[18]

The agrarian system most contrasted with that of nucleated villages and open fields is to be found where individuals had made inroads into wood and waste in the eleventh, twelfth and thirteenth centuries. During this period of rapid population expansion which was also one of increased production for the market, of increased long distance trade and of increased volume of monetary transactions, the coherent groups of family, kindred or clientele seem to have broken up or at any rate to have been reduced in size. Although our knowledge of the earlier family is vague, in this period there is evidence to show that the two generation family was dominant. Clearings were made and enclosed by individuals (or individual families) without any sharing of ploughland such as would result in the intermixture of parcels. It is true that sometimes land assarted in severalty in the fringes of existing open fields might get split up through inheritance or sale, and so come to be assimilated to the pattern of the open field furlongs. But in Arden, Feckenham and other wooded areas a large number of enclosed assarts, mostly made in the twelfth and thirteenth centuries, continued in this form until modern times.

Accurate plans of village streets and fields are not found before the sixteenth century, so our earliest graphic representation of an enclosed west midland field system is a copy of one made of the royal manor of Feckenham in 1591. This shows that beyond a small core of open fields with intermixed strips around the village itself (an old settlement) there is a considerable outer ring of small hedged fields. The court rolls of the Bordesley Abbey manor of Tardebigge, near Redditch, provide written proof of the same phenomenon. From the latter part of the thirteenth century until the middle of the fifteenth century, out of 182 land transactions registered in the rolls, 142 concerned land or building sites that are described in such a way as to indicate that it was held in severalty, and usually enclosed. Only about a dozen holdings contained land described so as to suggest the possibility that they were in intermixed strips. Much of Bordesley Abbey land, besides that at Tardebigge was in the Feckenham or Arden woodland regions, and the early charters (twelfth century) of the abbey indicate a predominance, already, of enclosed assarts. The abbey and local landowners at Oxhill and Stretton in Warwickshire, for instance, were exchanging crofts as enclosed by bank (*sicut fossato clauditur*). Walter of Staines who gave Bordesley the land which was later described as Osmerley Grange, near the abbey itself, gave it *cum omni libertate haiae*, that is with freedom to erect enclosures, implying that no other men's rights of common had to be considered.[19]

If we move east from Bordesley Abbey across Arden, we come to a large parish between the south walls of Coventry and the river Avon, of which the chief settlement was Stoneleigh, in the confluence of Avon and Sowe, sometimes known as Stoneleigh in Arden.

Originally a royal manor, it was given in exchange by Henry II to some Cistercian monks from Radmore in Cannock Chase (Staffordshire) who had been harried in their original home by hostile foresters. Here again we find old settled land by the rivers which had been developed more or less as traditional open common fields. But both north and south of the river were considerable stretches of woodland which the abbey servants and tenants colonized during the twelfth and thirteenth centuries. The monk who completed the abbey's estate book in the fourteenth century, looking back over his records to the middle of the twelfth century, described the expansion from the original settlements in this way: 'In each hamlet in the manor of Stoneleigh there are eight yardlands, and no more. Whatever they have further, they have by the improvement and assarting of the wastes.' (*Et in quolibet hamletto manerii de Stonle sunt octo virgate terre et non amplius. Et si quod amplius habent hoc utique habent de approwacione et assartacione vastorum.*) The yardlands were holdings of traditional layout, intermixed and common. The assarts were held in severalty, often enclosed, varying in size between peasant crofts of one or two acres and those as large as the 192 acres from the waste granted to the Templars of Fletchamstead out of the woodland of Westwood which lay in the north-western part of the parish.* Most of the holdings of the richer tenants were extremely irregular and composite in character, some of the arable belonging to them being in severalty, some in open ridges in fields and furlongs, but without any regular distribution as in the classical two- or three-field system.[20]

Some of the woodland villages had field systems which well before the end of the middle ages were entirely enclosed. Such a place was Packwood in the heart of Arden. This village was owned by the Cathedral Priory of Coventry and according to a rental drawn up in 1411 neither on the demesne, nor on the freeholdings, nor on the customary tenancies was a single element in the quite detailed description of the holdings which would indicate any degree of common husbandry.[21] On the other hand, there was no shortage of villages on the Cotswolds and in the valleys, where the only enclosed part of the area of the township were the tofts and crofts in the village on

---

* The exclusive control implied in the word 'severalty' was slightly modified in the case of the grant, as the Abbot of Stoneleigh and his men were still to have pasture rights for all animals on the three roads going through the waste from Berkswell to Coventry, from Norbrook to Coventry, from Allesley to Kenilworth and from Berkswell to Stoneleigh.

which the house and farm buildings were situated. But these were extremes. Many an old established village or hamlet, where the bulk of the arable lay open and common, had an element of enclosure. Seigneurial demesnes, for example, were often enclosed because the lord of the manor had greater power to rearrange his land than the tenants, more capital at his disposal for extending cultivation into the waste, and legal backing to do so, provided he did not deprive other free tenants of their common rights. If there were extensive areas of waste or woodland available for cultivation without noticeable reduction of common pasture, tenants both free and customary could acquire pieces of assart or other land that was not subject to commonable rights. On the Bishop of Worcester's Severn valley manor of Kempsey, for example, most of the land by 1170 was held in about forty regular open field yardlands (with probably some twenty-five to thirty acres to the yardland). But there were as well seventy-two and a half acres of assart land and thirty or so irregular small holdings which would not be in the common fields. A century later, when the tenant population had increased by at least a half, the number of small holdings outside the land in the open field yardlands was about one hundred.[22]

CHAPTER 2

THE LORDS

Medieval lords were lords of land and of men. These two aspects of their lordship can hardly be separated, for land without men to work it was valueless, and in those days men expected rewards which would keep them faithful, primarily in grants of land. The Norman, Breton and French magnates who had replaced the old English aristocracy still possessed at the time of the Domesday survey enormous estates composed of many men's conquered or forfeited inheritances. In the course of the next century and more, following a universal political and social law of feudal society, these great land-owners bartered land for service, primarily but not exclusively military service. Considerable proportions of their estates were sub-enfeoffed to a second rank in the baronial hierarchy (sometimes known as the honorial barons) and to simple knights. These military tenants owed the lords homage, fealty and suit to the baronial court as well as service in the lord's retinue in the king's host.

The link between lords and men was a most powerful social bond. It was also an ancient bond, in existence before it assumed the special form of feudal tenure. By the thirteenth century, with the fragmentation of fiefs and the increasing reliance on military service paid for in cash, the tenure of land by military service was losing its social significance. However, the bond between the lord and his followers persisted in other forms. The ties of self interest which bound a baron's knights, esquires and clerks to him could arise from grants of land by any sort of tenure. The ties could also include the payment by the lord of cash annuities and fees, and, at certain social levels, family relationships through marriage. A baron with big estates in a district was supported by the lesser landowners for these and other reasons, whether or not they were his military tenants. He in turn supported them in different ways, in the local courts, against royal officials and in advancing their preferment to profitable offices, private and public.

Lords also had various forms of private jurisdiction (to be dealt with in more detail later). These were by no means as extensive as those of their continental opposite numbers. The nearest approach to *haute justice* as enjoyed by French barons, (that is judgement of crimes punishable by death), was normally in England only the baronial privilege of *infangthef*, that is the right to hang thieves caught red-handed within the area of jurisdiction. Other crimes punishable by death were reserved as pleas of the crown for the royal justices. All the same, the private control of hundred courts and the transfer of the petty police jurisdiction of the hundred, known as the view of frankpledge, to their manorial courts, gave landlords considerable control over the daily lives of the inhabitants of the manor. In addition, the jurisdiction they had over their tenants simply by virtue of the fact that they were the landlords gave considerable powers, particularly the discipline involved in the exaction of rents and services, customary dues of a personal character and the admission of new tenants to holdings of land.

Most difficult to estimate are the informal social influences of the landowners. All of them travelled with a numerous retinue. Thomas of Berkeley II (1281–1321) is said to have had a household and a 'standing domestical family' of more than two hundred persons, knights, esquires, serving men and pages,[1] and the first two Beauchamp earls of Warwick, William and Guy, must have had a similar state. The bishops of Worcester were as itinerant as these great barons, with their own reason for absence from the district. But they too, judging by the witnesses to their charters, were surrounded by members of the local gentry as well as by their more intimate household officials. Bishop Godfrey Giffard was said to have a hundred horses in this travelling household.[2] The prior of Worcester Cathedral Priory, like the prior of Canterbury, 'from the social standpoint ... was a baron',[3] and he too had a following, rather different in character, of course, from that of the more mobile lay baronial and episcopal retinues. The cathedral, with its library, was a great centre of native English culture, and it is not difficult to imagine that in addition to the lay nobility and gentry who frequented the Cathedral church and its community of monks, there were writers, poets and musicians. No centre is more likely to have stimulated the west midland school of poets than this, even if it were not the only one. Less is known about the other religious houses as cultural centres but, as we shall see, the Severn and Avon valleys were studded with important Benedictine and Augustinian abbeys which, whatever their level of literary or artistic culture, certainly acted as meeting places for local notabilities. The great lay and ecclesiastical lords must therefore have exercised a social influence additional to that influence which can be traced directly to their ownership of land and private jurisdictions.

The social pattern of the medieval west midlands was a complex hierarchy of old established and new, lay and ecclesiastical, great and small owners and occupiers of land. It was broadly based on a mass of free and servile peasants, some well-to-do, most living on the edge of subsistence. It was diversified by the existence of a number of urban centres, two of them, Coventry and Bristol, among England's biggest towns. It was a society dominated socially and politically, as was the rest of the kingdom, by a comparatively small group of very wealthy landowners whose power and influence was buttressed by a larger class of knights and squires. The special feature of this region was that the ecclesiastical landowners predominated, particularly in Worcestershire and Gloucestershire.

Ecclesiastics

By ecclesiastical landowners, we mean primarily the monastic institutions. Friars, hospitals and chantries, all religious bodies, were important in the general life of the region, but were not outstanding as landowners and lords of tenants. In Warwickshire there were about seventeen landowning monastic institutions, mostly rather small. In Worcestershire there were about ten. Three of these were very wealthy. In Gloucestershire there were about fourteen and at least half a dozen of these were large, wealthy institutions.

Most of the very wealthy landowning abbeys were old Benedictine communities. For the most part, the structure of their landed estates was already established in main outline in the tenth century at the latest. Then there was a number of quite wealthy abbeys of the order of Augustinian canons, founded in the twelfth century. Next in importance, though all small compared with the most important of the Benedictine and Augustinian houses, were a few abbeys of the Cistercian order. In addition there were not a few smaller priories

25

and cells of the three orders already mentioned, as well as of some of the less important religious orders, such as the Premonstratensians.

Records of individual abbeys have survived only sporadically so that we have to turn to general surveys of ecclesiastical incomes from land made either by the crown or by the ecclesiastical authorities for taxation purposes to get some idea of the relative standing of the various houses. The famous *Valor Ecclesiasticus* which was compiled in 1535 for Henry VIII on the eve of the dissolution of the monasteries is the most reliable and detailed of these. It is true that its late date may make it less useful in some respects than earlier surveys such as the Taxation of Pope Nicholas IV, 1291. However the 1291 assessment is itself neither as reliable, nor as detailed as the Valor, and since there were not many additions to monastic land-holdings in the west midlands in the fourteenth and fifteenth centuries, the Valor provides useful comparative figures which are by no means irrelevant in a study of the medieval monastic landowners.[4]

An annual income of more than £500 was enjoyed, according to the Valor, by only a minority of English monastic houses. Still fewer had more than £1,000, and a mere handful more than £2,000. In the west midlands, five houses (all in Gloucestershire and Worcestershire) had more than £1,000 p.a. although there were only twenty-nine such in the whole country; eleven monastic estates in the three counties had incomes of more than £500 (out of eighty in the whole country). Seven of these were Benedictine houses, St Peter's, Gloucester (£1,744), Tewkesbury (£1,478) and Winchcombe (£812) in Gloucestershire; Worcester Cathedral Priory (£1,445), Evesham (£1,313) and Pershore (£726) in Worcestershire; and Coventry Cathedral Priory (£754) in Warwickshire. All were pre-conquest foundations, all except one being fruits of the tenth-century revival. The one exception was the Cathedral Priory at Coventry which was founded by Leofric, Earl of Mercia, in the eleventh century. The other abbeys with incomes of more than £500 p.a. were Augustinian. The most important was that of Cirencester (£1,326), founded by Henry I as an expansion of a college of secular priests which was a Saxon foundation. Many of Cirencester's manors were, however, outside our region. Two of the others were in Gloucestershire. Lanthony (£849) was originally a Welsh house which had moved to the safety of the Gloucester neighbourhood and was known as Lanthony Secunda. St Augustine's, Bristol (£670) was almost a family house of the lords of Berkeley who had considerable interests

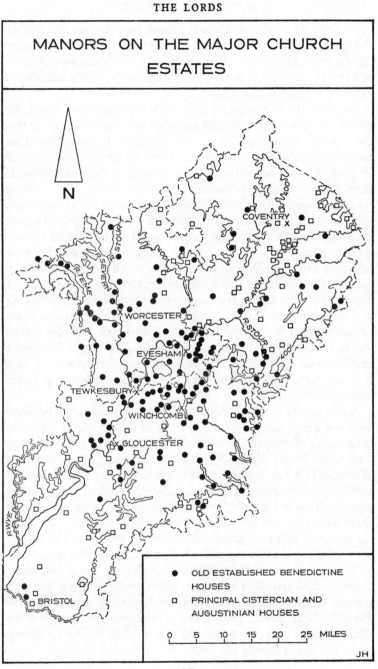

MANORS ON THE MAJOR CHURCH ESTATES

N

COVENTRY

R. STOUR
R. TEME
R. SEVERN
R. STOUR
R. AVON
R. STOUR

WORCESTER

EVESHAM

TEWKESBURY

WINCHCOMB

GLOUCESTER

R. WYE

BRISTOL

- OLD ESTABLISHED BENEDICTINE HOUSES
□ PRINCIPAL CISTERCIAN AND AUGUSTINIAN HOUSES

0   5   10   15   20   25   MILES

JH

in Bristol. The other important Augustinian house was that of Kenilworth (£643), founded by Henry I's powerful minister Geoffrey of Clinton. Since Kenilworth was a royal manor and castle of key strategic importance in the midlands, the house was always closely associated with the royal family.

To these, the wealthiest monastic estates in the region, should be added two other extensive ecclesiastical properties. First there was the bishop's estate which brought him in about £1,000 a year. This estate had once been part of the whole estate of the church of Worcester, but a separation had been made of the bishop's lands from those devoted to the sustenance of the monastic chapter before the compilation of Domesday Book. The structure of the two estates was very similar and in many districts prior and bishop held neighbouring properties. The other important estate was that of a Benedictine house which was situated many miles from the west midlands. This was Westminster Abbey, which, when endowed by Edward the Confessor was given the greater part of the estate of Deerhurst Priory and half of the estate of Pershore Abbey, including half of Pershore itself. The consequence of this was that the abbot of Westminster had a considerable say in west midland ecclesiastical affairs, not simply because of his possession of the former Deerhurst and Pershore estates and their privileges, but also because of such local interests as arose from his claim to the patronage of Great Malvern Priory.

Although these rich Benedictine and Augustinian foundations were not comparable in wealth to some of the wealthiest houses in other parts of England, such as St Albans (£2,102), Canterbury Cathedral Priory (£2,909), Glastonbury (£3,642), Bury St Edmunds (£2,336) and others, they played a great role in the west midlands region, more particularly in Worcestershire and Gloucestershire. This important role was all the more pronounced in that there were only two lay magnates whose local holdings gave them incomes and influence comparable with the religious. The first of these were the Beauchamp earls of Warwick with their main estates in Worcestershire and Warwickshire, and their castles of Worcester, Elmley and Warwick. The other family was that of Berkeley, with manors in the Severn valley and the Cotswolds and a castle at Berkeley. Other potent figures such as the earls of Gloucester of the Clare dynasty were, of course, even more powerful on a national scale, but had relatively few estates in the west midlands.

The existence of the old Benedictine estates had an important influence on the social structure of the region. They were established early in well-settled areas of valley and plain, and in spite of spoliation in war and conquest managed to lead, at any rate from the tenth century onwards, a continuous existence as landowners. They were not subject to the vicissitudes of the lay lords whose estates often became divided among heiresses or confiscated by the crown or other overlords. Such losses as the monasteries suffered at the hands of rapacious lay nobles left the core of the estate untouched. It was possible for them therefore to build a firm administrative system and to establish control over their tenants. This was made the more easy in that, particularly in the west midlands, the bigger old Benedictine foundations, and some other religious institutions, had (for England) relatively important rights of private jurisdiction. Apart from their private jurisdictions in the manor courts these consisted mainly of private control of hundred courts. These will be considered in greater detail later. For the moment, however, it is worth emphasizing that three out of the five Worcestershire hundreds and twelve out of twenty-eight of the Gloucestershire hundreds were in religious hands. As in other respects, Warwickshire was a contrast to the ecclesiastically dominated counties of Worcestershire and Gloucestershire. The only private hundred in the county was the small liberty of Pathlow whose lord was the Bishop of Worcester.

The grip of the ecclesiastical magnates did not stop short at their manors, lordships and private jurisdictions. Much of their income and their influence was due also to the control which they exercised over parish churches, their incumbents and the parish revenues. By the thirteenth century they were the only landowners to have this control, although laymen had enjoyed such control up to the end of the twelfth century, and were to resume it in the sixteenth century. A word on how this came about would not be amiss.

Very little is known about how the church was organized locally in Christianized Roman Britain. When the Anglo-Saxon kings and nobles accepted Christianity during the course of the seventh century it must be remembered that the country contained a number of independent kingdoms, with sub-kingdoms under their hegemony. Christian organization at first was based on a central church in a tribal capital, at Lichfield for example in Mercia, or Canterbury in Kent. As we have seen, Worcester was the capital of the Hwicce. The bishop and his priests served the kingdom and diocese from the cathedral church, and it was only gradually that local churches were built to supplement their work. It was necessarily the great men of the localities who built these churches, supplied a priest and supported him by a levy on their own lands and on the lands of their subjects. This was the origin of tithes and of the parish system. Even when the system was regulated by canon law, the lords of manors still retained the right to nominate priests and to consider the parish revenue as their own. Founders of monasteries, it might be added, had the same attitude with regard to the nomination of abbots and the disposal of the monasteries' revenues. It was not until the strengthening of the international church, in the eleventh and twelfth centuries, and the formulation of its demands for emancipation from lay control, that the rights of manorial lords were whittled away. In some European countries they vanished altogether. In England, they survived in the shape of the right of manorial lords to present a priest to the bishop for approval. This right of presentation, known as advowson, has lasted until the present day.

It was not, however, even after the reforming and systematizing Fourth Lateran Council of 1215, considered improper for monastic houses to have control of parish revenues. Many of them had earlier been given parish churches by lay benefactors and continued to nominate the priest and dispose of the tithes. In some cases they only had the same rights of presentation as other landowners. But since there was nothing in canon law to prevent them from advancing beyond the right of advowson to complete appropriation (*in proprios usus*) of the parish revenues, they frequently got papal and episcopal permission to do this, appointing a vicar, that is, a substitute, to the cure of souls, with a mere fraction of the tithes to reward him.

The old Benedictine foundations were well endowed with straightforward landlords' revenues from the products of their demesnes and the rents from their tenants. Towards the end of the twelfth century however began a rapid rise in prices, an increase in taxation demands at the same time as a general expansion of upper-class demand for expensive items of consumption. At first this hit the smaller landowners hardest, but by the second half of the thirteenth century many rich abbeys were in financial difficulties. A good way out was to appropriate a parish, for this brought a permanent increase in annual income for an initial investment, in the form of fees and *douceurs* to help the petition for appropriation through the correct episcopal and papal channels. Even short of complete appropriation the monasteries often enjoyed a fair income from parish revenues, known officially as 'portions'. The enjoyment of a 'portion' of a parish was an aspect of the same sort of landowner control over ecclesiastical revenues which was implied when a religious house had the whole parish *in proprios usus*. It could result from the division of a parish when the manor with which it was coincident was divided. And there were other reasons, too, for this diversion of the tithe income from the incumbent. Many monasteries, for instance, got the right to retain for themselves the tithes from their own lands in a parish; or had been given tithes from a benefactor's lands in the days before the courts of canon law prevented such deals.

Much of the diversion of parish revenues from the incumbents responsible for the cure of souls to others (primarily to monasteries) took place after the end of the thirteenth century. The proportions of 'spiritual' income given on the eve of the dissolution of the monasteries cannot therefore be taken as accurate for the thirteenth century, however justified we might be in using the *Valor Ecclesiasticus* figures for quick overall comparisons of the relative total wealth of the medieval monasteries. For the thirteenth century it is necessary to look at the assessment of values made on the instructions of Pope Nicholas IV in 1291. As we have said, these are not altogether reliable figures. There was certainly a general underestimation of the annual incomes from ecclesiastical property. We can however use the figures in order to arrive at some idea of the relative proportion of spiritual and temporal income. In the diocese of Worcester as a whole, including not only Worcestershire and Gloucestershire but also most of west and south Warwickshire, the total assessed value, for taxation purposes, of the parish churches and their revenues was about £5,355. Of this figure well over a fifth (c. £1,155) was diverted from the parishes in the form of portions of the revenue (mainly tithes) payable to various persons and bodies, mostly monastic, as well as in the form of complete appropriation. The proportion varied from district to district, largely because of the accident of endowment. The diocese was subdivided into two archdeaconries, Worcester and Gloucester, and further into nineteen deaneries. In some deaneries such as Dursley or Winchcombe in Gloucestershire, the ratio of revenue going to an outside landowner was as high as one to two, whereas in Bristol it was only one to about thirteen. But however unevenly distributed were monastic claims on parish revenue, the total, as early as 1291, represented a considerable reduction in the income of the incumbents whilst at the same time giving wealth and influence to the owners of these claims.

Some idea of the possible scale of these appropriated parish revenues may be given in order to show the reason why the religious houses so eagerly sought after them. Many small payments known as pensions, in recognition, for example, of vague claims in the past, might only amount to a few shillings a year, but the total revenues of an appropriated parish could be as lucrative as those of many a manor, and a good deal easier to administer and collect. A striking case is that of the parish of Bromsgrove and Kings Norton in Worcestershire, appropriated by Worcester Cathedral Priory. Its annual revenue as assessed for ecclesiastical taxation in 1291, at £33 6s 8d was much greater than the assessed revenue of any of the priory manors, the nearest being £29 8s 0d from a group of properties in the eastern Cotswolds at Blackwell, Shipston-on-Stour and Tredington. Even after the payment of £8 to the vicar who held the cure of souls, the Bromsgrove revenue was higher than that of most manors. Nor is this surprising when one considers that in mixed farming country, well populated, the parish revenues regularly included not merely the tithes of grain, of hay, of all other crops, and of all animals but also the various parishioners' payments for burials and other services, for altar offerings and such like. Berkeley parish in Gloucestershire had a total assessed revenue from tithes and other ecclesiastical dues of £54 13s 4d, and this not only supported the appropriator (£24 6s 8d) and the vicar (£12 13s 4d) but provided portions for the abbot of Reading (£13 6s 8d), the bishop of Worcester (£3 6s 8d) and the abbot of Stanley (£1).[5] When the underassessment of the real values is taken into account, these are very substantial sums. Conversion of medieval to modern monetary values is an impossible task, but it may be borne in mind that at the end of the thirteenth century, the crown considered that those landowners with an income of £20 a year were rich enough to undertake the very expensive honour of knighthood.

Important as was this distortion of the economic arrangements of the parishes, the claims to tithes and to the presentation of priests to benefices was only a supplement to the main form of income enjoyed by the big Benedictine abbeys. They were primarily lords of manors and regarded themselves as such, even to the exclusion of the original cloistered devotional purpose of their existence. For although their libraries were full of books of devotion or matters of ecclesiastical moment written by the fathers of the church, theologians, canon lawyers, universal historians and philosophers, their own most characteristic literary productions were annals,' whose main subject matter was the acquisition and disposal of property and privilege. In the case of the chronicle of Evesham Abbey, the annals in some few places almost achieve the dignity of true historical writing. But those of Worcester Cathedral, St Peter's Abbey, Gloucester and Tewkesbury remain dry-as-dust monuments to the monks' preoccupation with material things.[6]

It would be pointless to describe each of the big Benedictine estates, but a brief outline of some of the main components of the biggest of them will give some idea of the scope of their enterprise as landowners. The Benedictine Cathedral Chapter at Worcester, with a monk prior as its effective head and the bishop as purely titular abbot, was among the greatest. Its property, furthermore, was entirely localized in the diocese. It possessed twenty-six manors distributed over the Avon and Severn valleys and the Cotswolds with some important properties in less developed areas, in particular up the Teme valley towards Herefordshire and to the east of Worcester in Feckenham Forest. It possessed a considerable amount of urban real property in Worcester both within and without a considerable area round the cathedral which was exempt from the jurisdiction of the burgesses. It had ten appropriated parishes and portions and pensions derived from the revenues of some sixty other parish churches. This estate had its twin in the property of the bishop, as we have already shown. He had some sixteen manors in Worcestershire, five in Gloucestershire and three in Warwickshire. He too had considerable town property in Worcester, including most of the northern suburb of Northwick. At the end of the thirteenth century his income from his landed estates was larger than that of the priory, and indeed greater than that of most other church landowners, but his total income was less than that of the priory because, more like his lay counterparts than like the monasteries, he had established relatively few claims to parish revenues.[7]

St Peter's Abbey at Gloucester, traditionally an ancient Mercian foundation, but virtually refounded afresh after 1066, soon became one of the most influential Benedictine houses of the region.

Although, like Worcester, it was placed in the middle of an ancient and active urban community and possessed much urban property, its estates consisted of some thirty manors. Like those of other Benedictine houses of the neighbourhood, they straddled valley, wold and forest. It had huge and highly organized manors in the central Cotswolds, important properties in the Gloucester region and much land in the Forest of Dean. It soon became much richer than the older royal foundation at Winchcombe. This too was a town-based institution, for Winchcombe was a royal borough and had been the administrative centre of a shire older than Gloucestershire. Many of its seventeen manors were intermingled on the Cotswold plateau with those of St Peter's Gloucester, and although it had some properties in the Avon valley and at Enstone in the Oxfordshire Cotswolds its main interests were in a cluster of manors around the market town of Northleach (a St Peter's possession) and Winchcombe itself.[8]

The estates of the other big Benedictine houses of Evesham and Pershore had a similar geographical distribution to those of the cathedral priory and the two Gloucestershire houses we have mentioned in that the rich manors on the valley gravels were complemented by properties on the wolds with their special land use features. Evesham's valley property was remarkably concentrated in a group of about a dozen manors around the town, a group which had not only an economic but an ancient ecclesiastical unity, for their parishes comprised the Deanery of Evesham, the rural dean was an obedientiary of the abbey and the churches (including the two town churches) were regarded as chapels of the abbey. In the Cotswolds, Evesham Abbey had an equally remarkable set of properties centred on the very old market town of Stow-on-the-Wold.

Pershore and Westminster Abbey properties lay side by side, but Westminster's presence was naturally less pronounced than that of the local institution. Its estates followed the pattern we have already noticed. It had a group of manors in the Cotswolds centred on Todenham; it had an experimental market town at Moreton-in-Marsh; it had valley manors, one at Pershore itself, and several others on the banks of both the Severn and the Avon; it even had property in the Arden woodland, at Knowle (Warwickshire). Pershore too does not seem to have impressed itself locally to anything like the degree to which Evesham made itself felt. Its estates have an interest for us, however, in that like the other old Benedictine houses we have already mentioned, its estates straddled vale and wold. A large and important manor, an early centre of the rural textile industry, was situated in the southern Cotswolds at Hawkesbury, just north of the market town of Chipping Sodbury. Linking the valley and the wolds was the manor and incipient (but never to prosper) borough of Broadway.[9] This estate, like the others we have briefly described, typifies an important feature of the regional economy and culture which is also expressed in the administrative divisions. In spite of apparently contrasting soils and other topographical features, there was clearly a considerable complementarity between the Cotswolds and the valleys, based fundamentally on the transport of Cotswold barley to consuming centres in the vales (whether or not this was a market operation), and by transhumance of sheep flocks between summer pastures in the wolds and a winter retreat in the valleys.

The other major Benedictine establishments in the region were those of Tewkesbury, Great Malvern and Coventry. Tewkesbury was under the patronage of the earls of Gloucester who were lords of the town of Tewkesbury. For those earls, Tewkesbury Abbey church provided their family vault, and their patronage gave them a right at least of consultation when a new abbot was to be elected. In spite, however, of its great local wealth and its central position, Tewkesbury Abbey's local influence was less than that of Worcester or Evesham, for much of its territorial wealth lay south of the Thames. Tewkesbury was the second home of an abbey at Cranborne (Dorset). The move was made at the end of the eleventh century and Cranborne remained as a dependent cell. Great Malvern was a dependency of Westminster Abbey, of some purely local, rather than regional importance and at the end of the thirteenth century, undergoing considerable internal difficulties.[10] Coventry Cathedral Priory on the other hand, although smaller than the major Worcestershire and Gloucestershire abbeys, with its fifteen or so manors in Warwickshire and Leicestershire, was the largest Benedictine house in Warwickshire. Like the other important religious, landowning institutions, it was situated in an urban environment and a good deal of its property was in Coventry city and suburbs. The abbot was lord of half the town as well as being a property owner and the burgesses did not get the better of him until the middle of the fourteenth century.[11]

In addition to the bigger Benedictine abbeys, there were, scattered through the region, a number of smaller houses for Benedictine monks and nuns, some of them mere cells of bigger establishments. The priory of Wootton Wawen for example, was a cell of the Norman abbey of Conches. These small priories and nunneries were not of much importance in landowning society in the thirteenth century, but there were religious houses belonging to the new orders, founded mostly in the twelfth century, which played a noteworthy role in the economic, social and political life of the times. These new orders were the Cistercian monks, who followed an ascetic version of the Benedictine rule, the Augustinian and Premonstratensian canons, whose rule was in fact very similar to the Benedictine, except that the canons were not necessarily cloistered; and the military orders of which, in the west midlands, the only important one, until its dissolution in 1309, was that of the Knights Templar.

The new orders, to a greater or lesser degree, shared an important characteristic. As far as landed society was concerned, they arrived somewhat late on the scene, when the social structure and pattern of land tenure, at any rate of the old settled areas, was firmly established. Consequently, their endowments tended to be of uncultivated land; of tenanted land which did not, however, necessarily constitute a manor in the sense of an organized group of tenants subject to manorial jurisdiction and labouring on an established demesne; of appropriated churches, and other piecemeal gifts or purchases. The Cistercians deliberately aimed to settle in uninhabited places as part of the policy outlined in the *Carta Caritatis* drawn up by Stephen Harding, an Englishman who was one of the earliest abbots of Cîteaux.[12] The canons envisaged some participation in pastoral work, so there were no obstacles to the acceptance of parish churches as endowments. Hence the policies of the new orders were, deliberately or not, suited to the conditions of their period of growth.

The Cistercian abbeys were mostly situated in forest or in woodland areas. The earliest foundation was that of Bordesley (Worcestershire) (1138), with its endowments distributed principally in the Forest of Feckenham. Next was Kingswood (1139), situated on the wooded western scarp of the Gloucestershire Cotswolds. Stoneleigh Abbey (Warwickshire), affiliated to Bordesley, had been originally a community of hermits in Cannock Chase (Staffordshire). Converted in 1140 to the Cistercian rule, they moved to the

royal manor of Stoneleigh in 1153–4 where they found old established agricultural communities but where, to the north, there was
the hitherto unexploited Westwood, part of the woodland of Arden.
Merevale (1140) and Combe (1150) were also situated in Arden, but
Combe, perhaps unjustly, has, like Stoneleigh, become notorious,
not for having settled in a desert, but for having made a desert to
conform to their rule by expelling existing tenants from the places
where they had decided to settle.[13] The Combe Abbey title deeds or
charters which are enrolled in its cartulary, when studied as a whole
give a remarkable picture of how this small foundation expanded
its estate economy. It was situated in the Arden woodland and
many of its acquisitions consisted of wood which the monks could
clear and enclose, or of land which the donor had already enclosed.
They also expanded eastward acquiring arable land, and, even more
important, pasture rights on the low wolds of the townships between
Coventry and Watling Street. The total effect of these piecemeal
acquisitions during the course of the late twelfth and early thirteenth
centuries was that the abbey had become, by the beginning of the
fourteenth century, one of the region's most important producers
of wool for export.* Flaxley Abbey, founded in 1151, was situated
in the Forest of Dean. The other important Gloucestershire Cistercian abbey, Hailes near Winchcombe, came much later, being
founded at great expense in 1251 by King Henry III's brother,
Richard, Earl of Cornwall. This was hardly a typical pioneering
Cistercian establishment, for the Avon valley and north Cotswolds,
where most of its property lay, were very old settled parts of the
region.[14]

The Cistercian estates were not big, and were composed of
granges from which (as contrasted with the Benedictine manors)
there was relatively little domination of the local peasants. But the
Cistercians had considerable prestige, greater of course in the mid-
twelfth century than a century later when the ascetic life which had
originally distinguished them from the contemporary Benedictines
had disappeared. Their religious prestige was buttressed by the
social prestige derived from the elevated status of their founders.
Three of them, Bordesley, Stoneleigh and Hailes, were royal found-

* See the table below, p. 82. The high figure of available wool in the same table
from Merevale, Combe's near neighbour, is because of lands it possessed in
Leicestershire and the Peak district. The Merevale cartulary is lost, as is that of
Kingswood.

ations. Flaxley was founded by Roger, Earl of Hereford, and Merevale by Robert, Earl of Ferrers. Combe's founder, Richard of Camville, and Kingswood's founder, William Berkeley of Dursley, were the only founders not of the highest social rank.

The orders of regular canons were much more strongly represented in the west midlands than were the Cistercians. The richest of them, as we have seen, were concentrated in Gloucestershire, and of these that of Cirencester was outstanding. It well illustrates the importance of appropriated parishes in the estate structure of these late foundations. A mid-thirteenth century survey shows that its 'spiritual' income, derived from its appropriated parishes in eight counties amounted to about £370. From this the vicars had to be paid just over £80. In addition, the value of the nine parishes to which they had the right of presenting the rectors, amounted to some £90. Although this sum could not be added directly to the annual income of the estate, it must be remembered that patronage of all sorts was considered, rightly, to be a real asset for a medieval lord. As compared with this spiritual income, the income from manors (possibly incompletely listed in the survey) only amounted to £182.[15]

Lanthony Priory, the Augustinian community which had been moved to Gloucester from its original exposed position in the Black Mountains north of Abergavenny, had one of the most valuable estates in the region. Like other foundations of the same order, it had a considerable 'spiritual' income. Its cartulary also illustrates the process of growth by piecemeal acquisition which is characteristic of the twelfth century orders. For example, one of Lanthony's richest manors at the end of the thirteenth century was Brockworth, a village at the foot of the Cotswolds to the east of Gloucester. The priory holdings had grown from small beginnings, a couple of assarts given before 1142 by the steward of the then lord of Brockworth manor, Roger de Chaundos. The various Chaundos lords added to this original donation, by gift and exchange, a whole range of properties including the parish church, woodland, meadow and arable. The last Chaundos who was lord of Brockworth abandoned, with his family's permission, the last vestiges of their Brockworth property to the priory and in 1264 entered the priory as a pensioner or corrodian. The deeds recording the final sales of land hint at financial difficulties of which the priory was able to take advantage. After buying up the Chaundos lands, the priory continued to buy up local freeholders. The date of the last Brockworth deed in the cartulary is 1361; it is the three hundred and thirty-first charter concerning Brockworth and the immediate environs. This in itself is a striking testimony to the patient persistence of the religious in rounding off their estates.[16]

There was another, less important, Augustinian house in Gloucester town, that of St Oswald of which no more need be said, but the Augustinian foundation of St Augustine's, Bristol, merits an extra word. Like so many of the bigger foundations of this order, and of the Benedictine order, it was an urban monastery, with town property and interests. Like Cirencester and other Augustinian houses, it had important sources of spiritual income. Its manorial property reflected on a smaller scale the location and type of property to be found on the estate of the founding family, the Berkeleys of Berkeley Castle.[17]

The regular canons were less well represented in Warwickshire and Worcestershire, although the Augustinian Priory of Kenilworth, founded by Geoffrey of Clinton, Henry I's Chamberlain, was only a little less wealthy than the cathedral priory of Coventry. It was well endowed with lands in Warwickshire and other counties, but especially with parish churches, so that by the end of the middle ages its spiritual income was well over one third of the total. There was one other Augustinian house in Warwickshire before 1300, at Studley in the centre of the county. It was less important than Kenilworth, though it had quite widespread interests, especially in appropriated churches.

There was too, on the borders of Worcestershire and Staffordshire an interesting Premonstratensian house of canons regular at Halesowen. Halesowen itself was a market town with nascent urban features, but the lordship was established in an agrarian setting, which contrasted sharply with that in the valleys and on the Cotswolds. It consisted of a number of small hamlets in broken hilly country, probably imperfectly manoralized, so that the problem of the abbey was to establish its domination over a local population which was unwilling to accept the serfdom which was the lot of the tenants of the old Benedictine estates. It was not until the fourteenth century that the abbot was able to reduce his recalcitrant peasants to submission.[18] Not all the new orders had these problems. The Knights Templar (who followed the Augustinian rule) had a group of estates in the Cotswolds with their centre at Temple Guiting and here the rents and services of the tenants, according to the great survey of 1185, were almost identical with those on the long-settled manors of the abbey of St Peter at Gloucester.[19]

The Barons

The greater abbots had few peers as landowners in the west midlands. As persons of general social and political influence they were, however, outdistanced by lay magnates who, in some cases, had much smaller local concentrations of territorial power than the abbots. One of the interesting features of the region is that certain powerful earls and barons whose territorial interests were, at the best, peripheral, nevertheless intervened personally or through agents with considerable effect in local affairs.

The most striking group whose main territorial holdings were outside the west midlands were the lords of the Marches. These families had great lordships either in Wales or on the Welsh borders which, although held of the crown, were outside the jurisdiction of the regular machinery of government. They were almost independent principalities and formed the basis of the power of their owners. Even though they might yield less revenue than English holdings, the freedom that was enjoyed from royal officials and the consequent control which the lord had over the population easily made up for the shortage of income. These Marcher lords were all deeply interested in politics at Westminster and some of them had English estates. Hence it was useful for them to maintain a few manors in the west midlands as staging posts on their way to Wales.

The most important of the Marchers from the west midlands point of view were the earls of Gloucester of the Clare family. The chief blocks of Clare estates were in East Anglia and Glamorgan (their Marcher lordship), but their manor and abbey of Tewkesbury in Gloucestershire and their castle at Hanley in Worcestershire were clearly of pivotal significance. In addition they had seven other wealthy manors in Gloucestershire and the lordship of the private hundreds of Tewkesbury and Thornbury. The famous potentate of the central Marches, Mortimer of Wigmore, had a couple of Worcestershire manors, private woods in the Forest of Wyre (attached to his Shropshire manor of Cleobury Mortimer), and two manors in Gloucestershire.[20] There was another Marcher family, the Mortimers of Richards Castle, no relations however of their greater namesakes, who had three or four manors in Worcestershire. Of similar status were the Shropshire Corbets and Burnells, both of whom too had interests in Worcestershire and Gloucestershire.

Other influential families with only peripheral interests in our region were the Somerys, lords of the castles of Dudley and Weoley. Their interests were mainly in Staffordshire. A description of the John de Somery who died in 1322 is worth quoting here, because there were others like him in our region. He was said to have such mastery in the county of Staffordshire that none could get justice there; that he had made himself more than king; that no one could dwell there without buying protection from him in money or by helping to build his castles; and that he attacked people in their houses, threatening to kill them unless they paid money to get his protection.[21] The ancient family of Stafford, later to be reinforced territorially by inheritance from the properties of Bohun and Clare, had estates in south Warwickshire, and the east midland family of Hastings also had some Warwickshire properties as the westernmost outlier of their holdings.

All of the lay magnates we have mentioned were powerful men with strong midland influence, but this influence was not of major social and political importance in our region, except possibly for that of the Clare earls of Gloucester. None of them had anything approaching the number of manors which the big Severn and Avon valley and Cotswold religious houses enjoyed. None of them, of course, by the end of the thirteenth century possessed appropriated parish revenues, though some of them had rights of advowson. It was left to the Beauchamps and the Berkeleys alone to rival the local concentrations of territorial wealth and influence possessed by the religious, and to these two families we must now turn.

The Beauchamp family originally climbed to fame and power as a result of the fortunate marriage between Walter de Beauchamp and a daughter of William the Conqueror's notorious sheriff of Worcester, Urse of Abetot. Urse's male heir forfeited, his brother Robert Dispenser died heirless, and half of their estates came to Beauchamp, the other half going to Roger Marmion of Tamworth who had married the other daughter. Part of the estate had been taken by force by Urse and Robert in the conquest period from the church of Worcester, including Elmley, which became the chief Worcestershire possession of the Beauchamps. This village lies at the northern foot of Bredon Hill, half a mile from a spur of the hill on which Robert Dispenser is supposed to have built his castle. This is not an adequately documented dating, however, and it is not until 1216 that there is an uncontrovertible documentary reference to the castle. It may, however, have been a very ancient site, for it has been suggested that the huge outer bailey may well once have been an iron-age hill fort.[22]

At the beginning of the twelfth century, the Beauchamp properties were scattered over some fifty Worcestershire villages, but they subenfeoffed much of this land to military tenants during the course of the century, keeping relatively few manors 'in demesne', that is under their direct control. In this they acted as did other beneficiaries of the Conqueror's redistribution of the lands of the old English aristocracy. For landed property was, in the middle ages, always worth letting out in order to acquire supporters. By the second half of the thirteenth century, the original Beauchamp land had become stabilized as between manors held in demesne and those held by sub-tenants, and their main features are to be seen in the inquisitions post mortem. These inquisitions were made by royal officials, known as escheators, whenever a tenant-in-chief of the crown died. The principal reason was that, as feudal overlord, the king had the right to the custody of the lands if the heir was a minor, to the guardianship of the heir himself, to the disposal of her marriage in the case of a female heir and to the payment of a 'relief' by the heir for the succession to the estate. The officials of the Exchequer needed to know precisely how much revenue to expect during the period of vacancy, for the escheator had to account to them for this revenue, his accounts being checked against the estimate in the inquisition. An escheator would, of course, be tempted to minimize the revenue in his inquisition so as to make a profit. If he was (as he might well be) under the thumb of powerful relatives of the dead man, he might also underestimate the revenues for their benefit. Inquisitions post mortem, therefore, can be expected to give the main items of revenue of an estate. They may even have been based on existing estate surveys, though they were supposed to be a record of returns made by a local jury of knowledgeable men. But we must normally assume that they would be under- rather than overvaluations.

The earliest detailed Beauchamp inquisition is that of William who died in 1298.[23] His inquisition gives us details not only of the original Worcester estates of the Beauchamps, but also of the estates which he acquired when he became Earl of Warwick. This event, of great importance in west midland history, resulted from the marriage of his father, always known as William de Beauchamp of Elmley, with Isabel, the sister and heiress of William Mauduit, Earl of Warwick (d. 1268). William of Elmley, who died in 1269, was never given the title of earl, and was never a person of national importance. It was his son, a friend of King Edward I, who was given the title in his father's lifetime and who brought the Beauchamps into the front rank, not merely of the midlands, but of the English baronage.

Like most great lords, the Beauchamps' lands were distributed over many counties, in his case, eight. But the manors in the west midland counties, nine in Worcestershire, ten in Warwickshire and three in Gloucestershire, formed the core of the estate. This was the political as well as the economic centre of gravity of their power. We have already spoken of the village and castle at Elmley, surveying the lower reaches of the Avon from the Vale of Evesham to Tewkesbury. The castle itself was, judging by its remains, an immense structure, and was kept inhabitable and in repair until the end of the fifteenth century. But the Beauchamps were also castellans of the king's castle at Worcester, having been granted by Henry I the hereditary shrievalty of the county, thus dominating the city and the Severn crossing. Next, on acquiring the earldom of Warwick, they also obtained the ancient castle – the site pre-conquest no doubt – at Warwick, which from the fourteenth century onwards became their principal seat.

However, it is clear that their sympathies remained long with their county of origin. The will of William Beauchamp of Elmley, as one would expect, shows this very strongly. He left instructions that he should be buried in the church of the Franciscan Friars at Worcester, and his legacies, which were many, were almost entirely confined to Worcestershire religious houses and local personalities, such as to the Worcester and Gloucester Franciscans; to the Gloucester Dominicans; to the Gloucester Carmelites; to a hospital in Worcester and another in Gloucester; to two houses of nuns in Worcestershire; and to a number of monasteries including Worcester Cathedral Priory, Evesham, Pershore, Bordesley, Hailes, Great Malvern, Winchcombe, Tewkesbury and Alcester. His son's will does not show the same indiscriminate piety, but still manifests an attachment to Worcestershire, for he too wished to be buried in the church of the Worcester Franciscans. Even Guy, the second

Beauchamp earl who died at Warwick Castle in 1315, and whose interests were moving northwards, as is shown by his purchase of Barnard Castle from the crown in 1307, wished to be buried in a Worcestershire monastic church. This was the church of the Cistercians at Bordesley, of which he was a benefactor. He was also the founder of a college of priests at Elmley.[24]

The Beauchamps were like other medieval landed families in that the consolidation of their family fortunes depended on the production of enough sons to ensure that there would always be a male heir who would keep the estates intact. In this, the Beauchamps, like the Berkeleys, were more fortunate than most. In addition, they had enough sons to send some into the church and to endow others who founded important collateral branches of the family and thus extended the family influence. In the west midlands, the two best-known Beauchamp collaterals were those whose principal seats were at Holt, on the Severn north of Worcester, and Alcester in south-west Warwickshire. These branches were founded by John and Walter, sons of William of Elmley and younger brothers of Earl William. Each of these branches lasted in the male line until the fifteenth century.

The Berkeleys at Berkeley Castle, though rich and powerful beyond most of the locally based Gloucestershire families, did not achieve the wealth and eminence of the Beauchamps.[25] It was not until the end of the middle ages that they were raised beyond the simple status of baron. They were, however, the only lay family beside the Beauchamps to rival the landed wealth of the Benedictines in the west midlands. Their origins are somewhat obscured by legend but it seems likely that the man who laid the family fortunes, Robert Fitz Harding, was a moneyed man from Bristol who helped the Empress Mathilda and her son Henry II financially in the civil war with King Stephen. As a reward, he was given the town of Berkeley, Berkeley Castle and various appurtenant manors in the Hundred of Berkeley, together with the jurisdiction of the hundred. These were taken away from Roger of Berkeley, lord of Dursley, who had been on the losing side. At the end of the thirteenth century, the Berkeleys had more than a dozen manors in Gloucestershire, mostly in the fertile vale of Berkeley, some on the Cotswold Edge overlooking the vale. In addition to their ownership of manors in Wiltshire and Oxfordshire, they were lords of the Somerset bank of the Bristol Avon, having the private hundreds of Portbury,

Bedminster, and Hartcliffe. Above all, this Somerset property included Redcliffe which in truth was completely urbanized and really part of Bristol. This caused much bitterness between the Berkeleys and the Bristol burgesses, who objected to the feudal jurisdiction of these powerful barons over their fellow merchants and tradesmen, across the river.

The Berkeley influence spread widely, for these lords seemed prolific in the generation of males. Thomas I (d. 1243) for instance, had five sons, the eldest, Maurice II succeeding him, the others, Thomas, Henry, William and Richard all living to assume knighthood. Some of the younger males founded more or less long lasting collateral branches. Sir Robert Berkeley, for example, son of Maurice II (d. 1281), founded a dynasty in the family manor of Arlingham which was still flourishing in the sixteenth century. The family also, wisely perhaps, allied itself by marriage to the other Berkeleys that it had supplanted. Helen, the eldest daughter of Robert Fitz Harding married Robert Fitz Roger Berkeley of Dursley, and Maurice I of the main branch (d. 1189), her brother, married Robert's sister Alice. Like the Beauchamps, their territorial and religious interests met in the endowment and patronage of religious houses, hospitals and chantries, of which the most important was the family abbey of St Augustine's, Bristol. Thomas II (d. 1321), whom we have already quoted as a typical employer of an immense retinue of dependants, was, besides being a great dispenser of hospitality in his own castle, a frequenter of the abbeys with which he maintained close relations of patronage, such as St Peter's, Gloucester, St Augustine's, Bristol. and Kingswood and was in addition a familiar of the abbots of Cirencester, Lanthony and Flaxley. It should be added, however, that these close relations did not exclude quarrels and litigation about lands and rights with these ecclesiastical lords. This was a familiar feature of medieval landowning society.[26]

In spite of the peripheral interests of other magnates in our region, the Beauchamps were unchallenged on their own ground in Worcestershire and Warwickshire, as were the Berkeleys in Gloucestershire. There were, however, a few families of intermediate status between the two outstanding baronial families just mentioned and the mere county gentry. Such was the family of Giffard of Brimpsfield.[27] Brimpsfield is a Cotswold village a couple of miles from the western edge of the plateau and a mile west of the Roman road from Cirencester to Gloucester. The Giffards were already established there at the time of Domesday Book and lived next to the parish church where they built a powerful castle whose ruins are still to be seen. During the twelfth and thirteenth centuries they made a number of important marriages with members of such families as the Berkeleys, the Cliffords (originally a Marcher family before the transfer of their interests to the north), and the Longe-spees (family of earls of Salisbury). John Giffard, who died in 1299, was a figure of more than purely local importance for he played an important part in the Barons' Wars. He was not, however, at the top of the social hierarchy. He was a follower of the earl of Gloucester, and abandoned the party of Simon de Montfort at the same time as the earl.[28]

This family also illustrates that element in the upper ranks of the church hierarchy whose promotion was probably mostly due to its aristocratic connections. Contemporary with John Giffard were his two cousins, clerical Giffards of considerable importance. One was Walter, archbishop of York, who died in 1279. The other, of greater interest for the west midlands, was Godfrey Giffard, Bishop of Worcester between 1266 and his death in 1302. The archbishopric of York, since pre-conquest times, had always had a close link with the diocese of Worcester, and in his official capacity the archbishop was lord of the barony of Churchdown which included several Cotswold manors. In his personal capacity he also held the manors of Norton and Weston-sub-Edge at the foot of the northern edge of the Cotswold scarp, between Broadway and Stratford-on-Avon, together with eight properties scattered in other (mostly west country) counties. Godfrey, who became Bishop of Worcester in order to help to clean up the subversion left in the diocese of Worcester by the Montfortian bishop, Walter Cantilupe, was his heir.[29] When he died, this collateral Giffard dynasty continued at Weston-sub-Edge through the descendants of William, a brother of the two bishops. This branch of the Giffards also provided abbesses to the two most fashionable nunneries in the country, Shaftesbury and Wilton.

If we return to the main branch, that is to those of Brimpsfield, we find that their religious connections locally were also of great significance in the social texture of the region. The Brimpsfield Giffards were, like many Cotswold landowners, closely associated with St Peter's Abbey, Gloucester, as well as with the Gloucester-shire establishment of the Knights of the Temple. The John Giffard who had become a royalist at the same time as Gilbert de Clare during the Barons' Wars even founded that cell of St Peter's at Oxford which became Gloucester Hall or College, the principal scholastic establishment of the English Benedictines.[30] A royal grant to Giffard in 1281 of the right of free warren in his manors, that is exclusive hunting rights over the smaller game, shows how considerable at that time were his possessions.[31] Apart from Brimpsfield itself there were five manors in Gloucestershire, five in Wiltshire and as many again in the Marches of Wales. No wonder his son John, who ended his life, and his dynasty, in 1322 as a rebel in support of Thomas, Earl of Lancaster was known as 'John the Rich'. This John's inquisition post mortem values his estate at £231, certainly an underestimate.[32] Even so, this is an income, for its era, of handsome proportions, fully justifying the baronial status which the Giffards enjoyed, and to which they were entitled by tenure. For the castle and manor of Brimpsfield together with the Gloucestershire and Wiltshire lands was held of the king in chief by barony.

An example of a Warwickshire family of the same type is de Montfort of Beaudesert. The family was already established in the county at the beginning of the twelfth century, and during or before the civil war between Stephen and Mathilda had built their castle of Beaudesert which was to remain the centre of their power in mid-Warwickshire until the extinction of the family in the middle of the fourteenth century. The most famous member of the family was Peter de Montfort, an important supporter of Simon de Montfort (to whom he was no relation), with whom he was killed at Evesham in 1265. Apart from a couple of properties in other counties, the family had, beside the castle and a few tenants at Beaudesert, three big rural manors at Ilmington, Whitchurch and Wellesbourne Mountford, the small borough of Henley-in-Arden and rents in a couple of other Warwickshire villages. The valuation of the Warwickshire estate in the inquisition post mortem of Peter's grandson, John, in 1296, was £108 a year.[33] Peter's friendship with Simon may have arisen from his association with the Cantilupe family, and consequently with Simon's warm supporter Walter Cantilupe, Bishop of Worcester. His importance is also representative, perhaps, of the political importance of the knightly or lesser baronial class in Simon's party, members of which remained with him until the defeat at Evesham when many of the earls and barons who had once been with Montfort had joined the king.

Another similar family in our region, whose holdings too entitled them to baronial rank, was Verdon. They held the great castle of Brandon in eastern Warwickshire, with which was associated the neighbouring rural borough of Bretford. However, important though the Verdon family was, it had only one other property in Warwickshire (Flecknoe) and a small manor in Gloucestershire at Bisley. Otherwise its estate was scattered over six other counties, mostly in Leicestershire and Staffordshire.[34] More like the Montforts, with the core of their interests in the region, were the families of Hastang, Trimenel, Bereford and Pecche mainly in Warwickshire; Abetot, Saltmarsh and Ombersley in Worcestershire; de la Mare and Cardiff in Gloucestershire. Other families, such as Sudeley and Langley, had interests in all three counties. Their estates varied in size between four and eight manors.

But the lesser baronial families of this type, though prominent, are not typical. Those with half a dozen or so manors, and incomes of perhaps £100 a year or more, are clearly a minority of the families whose members witness local charters, or sit on grand assize juries, or perform the many tasks of local administration laid upon them by the sheriffs or the central government. Most had only half the income and landed holdings, or less, of these more prominent persons. It is this mass of the county gentry, rather than its more prominent members, which, as a social class, is the most difficult to grasp.

The Knights

There were, inevitably, landowning families whose wealth and social position shaded off from that of such baronial families as the Giffards, in a downwards direction. Even in the most hierarchical societies with little social mobility there are not clear cut divisions between one class and another. English society was by no means one of the most rigidly stratified of European feudal societies, in particular in its upper ranks. This is shown by the fact that at the end of the thirteenth century, there was not, as there was beginning to be in France and Germany, a noble caste with legal privileges separating them from the rest of the people. The English aristocracy was certainly very self-conscious politically and socially, but its younger sons, formally at any rate, enjoyed only the same privileges as other free men. The rigid dividing line in English society came lower down in the scale, separating free men from serfs. But about this more will be said later.

We must not suppose, of course, that the real lines of social division could be defined in purely legal terms. An English free man could be an impoverished, landless labourer, a master craftsman, a rich merchant, or a wealthy franklin endowed with as much landed property as many a knight. There was however in every county a group of families who may be called 'knightly families', analogous to that class which in the sixteenth and seventeenth centuries is called the gentry. Not all, perhaps at any particular time not any, of the male members of such families would be dubbed knights, but it was from these families that those who became knights were normally drawn. The wealthiest of these families, as we have seen, may have had estates which gave them the status of barons. The lesser men are more obscure and unfortunately their real landed incomes are difficult to estimate. On the whole, the knightly families of the thirteenth century have left few archives behind them, even their fourteenth- and fifteenth-century descendants are only exceptionally documented. Consequently most of our information has to come from references to them in the estate records of the lay and ecclesiastical magnates or in the records of the central government.

What did the honour, or burden, of knighthood imply at the end of the thirteenth century? We must bear in mind that knighthood as an important social distinction had only existed for about a century. At the beginning of the twelfth century the Latin term *miles* or French *chevalier* had had a technical implication, that is, a warrior mounted on a horse armed with helmet, hauberk, shield and lance. He might or might not have been given land in return for a promise of military service (a knight's fee) and he would certainly have sworn homage and fealty to his lord. This sort of oath was one of the most important social bonds, and the military vassal who swore it would be expected to serve his lord. But at first this did not give him any particular social distinction.[35]

It seems that it was not until the middle of the twelfth century that knighthood was becoming a social in addition to a military distinction.[36] This was partly because of the social and religious prestige now firmly attached to the part played by knights in crusading activities. It was also due to an increase in the actual social standing of the upper crust of free landowners. This increase in social standing, as is so often the case, accompanied a severe social and economic

49

crisis for the class as a whole. The records of many wealthy religious houses show that from the middle of the twelfth century, many free landowners were having great difficulty in maintaining the increasingly expensive standard of living of aristocrats or would-be aristocrats. All prices were going up, particularly the prices of war horses and military equipment. Taxation, which was in effect war taxation, was increasing similarly. What the monastic cartularies show is that these lesser or middling landowners, in order to raise money to pay their debts, were obliged to mortgage their lands, or sell them outright to wealthy ecclesiastical institutions. In this way the big landowners (lay as well as ecclesiastical) got richer, and the financially embarrassed disappeared. What was left of the free landowners was a considerable number of families, some perhaps hardly removed from the mass of the peasants, who either abandoned or made no attempt to keep up knightly social habits and expenditure. At the other end of the scale were those who became the 'knightly families'. The ones who disappeared were the ones whose incomes did not match their social pretensions, and of them the thirteenth-century records provide many examples.[37]

The early thirteenth-century cartulary of Worcester Cathedral Priory is full of examples of sales by local landowners to the priory under the pressure of urgent need. Simon de Mauns, lord of the manor of Doddenham (Worcestershire) in the last quarter of the twelfth century began to divest himself of his patrimony, beginning with the advowson of Doddenham and Knightwick chapels which he gave to the priory. Some of the deeds which follow this grant show him alienating his lands in his lifetime to his sons, Walter and William, Walter (the heir) then giving his lands to William. But by the early years of the thirteenth century, William is selling all to the priory, including the reversion to his widow's dowry. The last of his estate, a meadow, was sold to the priory *ad maximum et urgens negotium meum*, 'for my greatest and urgent business'. Another landowner at Knighton-on-Teme, Stephen de la Law, sold some of his land to the priory under apparently normal circumstances, but another part of his land was sold in return for the prior redeeming him when he was *in gravibus vinculis detentus et per exquisita tormenta ad redemptionem fuisset compulsus*, that is 'when he was detained in heavy chains and compelled to redeem his land by exquisite torments'. Another landowner, Alfred of Penhull, gave all his lands to the priory in the middle 1230s. These lands were already pledged to the Jews, so the prior must simply have paid his debts and got all his land. The prior also gave him a house and a croft to live on (part of his mother's dowry) and a life pension in grain and cash for himself, his wife and his mother. With the transfer of all this man's land to the priory, in exchange for a life pension, the family as a landowning group simply ceases to exist.[38]

A similar situation occurred some years later on the estate of the abbey of Winchcombe. From about 1245 John, the son of John le Knyth of Sherborne (a village between Burford and Northleach), began to sell portions of his estate, including what must have been his family home, Burimilde Hall, to the abbot and convent and to another free tenant Elias of Foxcote, the abbey steward. The transactions, testified in eighteen charters, and usually made because of 'urgent' need, culminated in an act, probably in the 1270s, by which John finally quitclaimed his right to any lands and rights in Sherborne to the abbey in return for a life pension, or corrody, in food, clothing and shelter. However, a slightly different light is thrown on the pension system by another charter, immediately following that which establishes John le Knyth's pension. It is in favour of Elias of Foxcote, is dated 1278 and establishes a rather more lavish corrody for him. Elias makes over all his Sherborne land to the abbey and in addition makes a cash payment of a hundred marks (£66 13s 4d). This is an investment for a comfortable old age whereas the pensions of John le Knyth, and of Alfred of Penhull before him look more like acts of charity to men who could not stand the pace of the thirteenth-century inflation.[39]

This granting of pensions was not confined to religious landlords who felt obligations to those whose patrimony they had bought up. William Beauchamp of Elmley, father of the first Beauchamp earl of Warwick, endowed another son, James, with his manor of Acton Beauchamp. James then began to round off his Acton estate by buying up all the local freeholders. One of these, John, the son of Robert of Abetot, gave James all his land in Acton. In return James paid off his debts to Isaac, Jew of Worcester, and assigned a life pension to his (John's) mother, Mathilda. The pension consisted of as much grain as James issued to his servants, and a tunic or cloak every year. This transaction probably took place sometime in the 1260s. The deeds are not dated.[40]

Now it was precisely at the period of the social polarization of this class that its more successful members became conscious of the social prestige of the title of 'knight'. It is not until the beginning of the thirteenth century in this region that charter witnesses begin to call themselves *miles*, if entitled to do so, and not until the thirties or forties that the custom became so regular that we can be fairly sure that those not so designated had not in fact assumed the honour of knighthood. Since the cost of being dubbed a knight could exceed the new knight's annual income, it is not surprising that they should insist on the use of their title.[41]

It had become an honour in many different ways. Firstly it had the religious and social prestige of association with crusading activity. Secondly, it had been taken up by the aristocracy – for it must be emphasized that the old English and continental nobility had not at first regarded knighthood as bringing them any social status additional to that which they already possessed. Thirdly, the knights had become a sort of minor service nobility, used not merely for military but also for legal, administrative and political purposes by the crown. The innovations in legal procedure associated with the reign of Henry II led to the frequent empanelling of county knights as jurors of the grand assize in cases about the ownership of land. Even though the grand assize soon fell into disuse, sworn enquiries by knights on a variety of subjects were asked for, knights or members of knightly families were placed on innumerable local *ad hoc* committees, and as early as the reign of King John, they were consulted as representatives of the county communities of landowners about fiscal and political matters.[42]

Many historians have attempted to calculate the number of knights at the end of the thirteenth century, mainly in order to understand the apparent shortage which provoked the king to order the distraint of knighthood, that is, to make knighthood obligatory for persons with incomes of £20 a year or more, or to amerce those of full age in possession of a full knight's fee who had not yet become knights. It has even been found that in some counties not enough knights were available for empanelling a jury of twelve.[43] This situation occasionally arose in our region. However the numerical strength of the knights is much more difficult to estimate than that, for instance, of the ecclesiastical landowners. Some sort of quantitative estimate is essential for our analysis of social structure, so we must attempt to combine all possible sources in order to get a list of the knightly families, and to see what part these families played in rural society.

The sources for the west midland knights include all contemporary documents in which persons are named, with their social status and place of origin. An obvious source for the names of knights are the rolls of arms which name those who were on military expeditions. The one which is of most use for our purposes is a roll which was reprinted in *Parliamentary Writs*[44] and is thought to have been compiled in about 1312 for the Scottish campaign. Its advantage is that apart from knights in the royal household the rest are classified by counties. But rolls of arms only include that small proportion of the knights who were 'strenuous', that is militarily active. Tax lists, which in general are very valuable for personal names, are less useful for the period before 1300 as far as counting the number of knights is concerned, because the personal designation *miles* does not appear to be used in tax returns until well into the fourteenth century. The Warwickshire tax return of 1332 gives men's titles apparently in all cases, whereas the Gloucestershire return for 1327 does so only in a few cases, and the Worcestershire return for 1275 not at all.[45] The records of the itinerant justices are of more use, in that knights, named as such, not only occur in pleadings but are named as grand assize jurors. The most abundant source of information is however the most difficult to use. It is the deeds of one sort or another which are copied into monastic and other cartularies. The difficulty lies in the fact that a majority are not edited or even printed, and that the dating of charters is often uncertain. Even so, charter witness lists, giving the status of witnesses, provide the largest number of names of west midland knights. Finally, the instructions and letters sent out from Chancery to the localities often give indication of the status of addressees and others.

Taking the various sources in combination we find that in the second half of the thirteenth century, and primarily during the three decades of Edward I's reign, there were at least two hundred families from which knights were dubbed, the majority coming from Gloucestershire, Warwickshire providing more than sixty and Worcestershire about fifty. There was some overlapping of course, for some families had land in more than one county.

These figures hardly bear out the suggestion that there was such a great shortage of knights that administration could hardly be carried on. It is not, of course, that at any one time each of these two hundred and more families contained a member of the knightly order. It would be impossible to make such a calculation. But even allowing for those who had not yet taken up knighthood, or for families none of whose members intended to do so, there should have been at least enough knights to carry on the county administration. We must not, of course, imagine that, even including the bishop, the earls and the barons, there would be a member of the landed aristocracy living in every village in the region. It would be impossible to say exactly how many separate hamlets and villages there were at the end of the thirteenth century, but since taxes tended to be assessed on the unit of settlement, with occasional groupings of more than one unit under one name, we can at any rate give a minimum figure. In the three counties there were about 1,040 taxation units, representing at least 1,100 real villages and hamlets. In numbers, therefore, the aristocracy was spread fairly thinly on the ground.

A feature of the social and political life of the time which may have given the impression of a smaller number of available knights than there actually were, is that it would seem that the places in the limelight, the jury service, the membership of government commissions, the membership of great lords' retinues, were shared among a relatively small number of important families. In Worcestershire, we find such names as Ombersley, Saltmarsh, Bracy, Cokesey, le Poer, Cardiff; in Warwickshire, Murdak of Compton, Braundeston, Charneles, Endesover, de Chastel, Ladbroke, Pecche, Arden of Haseley, Arden of Ratley, Wolverton; in Gloucestershire, de la Mare, Berkeley (collaterals), Sudeley, Poyntz, Maunsell, Muscegros and Musard. It must not be assumed, however, that this willingness to accept official responsibility is only to be attributed to the public spirit of those concerned. Public office was also a means by which private advantage could be obtained. It was natural that the wealthiest of the knights, who were themselves (after the barons) the wealthiest of the free landowners, should dominate the county and hundred courts, be well known to the sheriffs, to the visiting itinerant justices, and so to the officials of the central government. And because this was a society where violence, bribery and corruption were normal means of settling the issues which arose between men, the knights themselves were violent, corrupt and being the stronger, were usually the successful ones, either for themselves or for those who served them.

These knights as we have seen, were led by a very small group of families of baronial, or almost baronial status, with estates containing perhaps half a dozen manors. The majority of knightly families had less land, as did those other lords of manors who never aspired to knightly status. The most suitable illustration of this point is to be found in the Worcestershire tax return of 1275.[46] The advantage of this return over those of later date is that it includes taxation on the movable goods of the clergy as well as the laity, with one or two exceptions, such as the Cistercians. By this time taxation on movable goods was becoming standardized, the assessment of property values being in practice confined, in the countryside, to animals, grain and other agricultural produce, and in the towns to household goods, merchandise, artisans' tools and animals. Those with goods under 6s 8d in value were not taxed, and there were certain goods which were statutorily exempt from taxation. It is impossible to know how many were too poor to pay any tax, but all peasants who had the minimum number of animals and grain to carry on at all must have been included. The main point, however, is not that we can rely on the absolute figures of the assessment, but that the assessments indicate the relative values of the movables of the population. The assessments of well-stocked manorial establishments, in particular, stand out in contrast with peasant household assessments. Since we are given the names of the tax payers we have an excellent indication of the distribution of the property of the different classes. There is this important defect however: if a person had no manorial establishment in a village, but only a title to rents from tenants, this would not appear in an assessment of movables. Other types of evidence are needed to reveal this sort of income.

The results of an analysis on these lines are quite startling. Once we have accounted for the establishments of the wealthy ecclesiastics, the earls and the barons, we find the merest handful of families of knightly status with establishments in more than one or two villages. The assessments show that the bishop and priory of Worcester between them have establishments, on which tax was levied, in twenty-nine Worcestershire villages or hamlets, the abbot of Evesham in twelve, of Pershore in four, the prior of Great Malvern in three, and of Little Malvern in five. The Beauchamp family (main branch) have eight establishments, and other barons, such as Mortimer of Wigmore, Mortimer of Richards Castle, William of Valence and Gilbert de Clare have a few peripheral manors of which we have already written. The wealthiest, apparently, of the local knights, was Richard of Ombersley with establishments of very moderate value in four villages. Geoffrey d'Abetot and Peter of Saltmarsh also had establishments of similarly modest size in four villages each. The difference in scale between the rich ecclesiastical establishments and those of the wealthiest knights can be seen in the fact that the average tax paid by the bishop for each of his establishments was 48s, by the abbot of Evesham 55s, and by Richard of Ombersley and Peter of Saltmarsh 16s.

To illustrate the scale of the estates of the knightly families, we will list those whose heads were put forward in 1275 as jurors of the grand assize.

Put forward for grand assize	Number of Worcestershire taxation assessments 1275	1275 average amount per assessment	Land elsewhere (possibly under-estimated)
Richard of Ombersley	4	16s	
William of Saltmarsh	3	24s 10d	
John of Botley	1	20s	
Adam of Elmbridge	2	10s 6d	Property in Salop
William de Bovey	2	14s	
William le Blund	2	16s 8d	
Walter of Cokesey	1	46s 1d	Property in Salop
William de Furches	1	20s	
William le Poer	3	13s	
Henry of Ribbesford	1	25s	Property in Salop
Grimbald Pauncefot	1	26s 8d	Property in Gloucestershire
William of Houndsacre	1	30s	
Paulinus of Cardiff	1	13s 4d	Property in Gloucestershire
John of Wotton	—	—	Property in right of wife in Kidderminster, in Wiltshire and Hampshire
John Esturmi	2	10s	
Roger Pickard	1	6s 8d	
Henry Huband	1	26s 8d	Property in Warwickshire
Giles of Berkeley	1	10s	Property in Gloucester
Robert of Chenny	1	6s 8d	
Peter of Saltmarsh	4	16s	
John of Brompton	—	—	
William de la Mare	1	8s	
Richard Syward	2	9s 5d	

Some of these knights, it will be seen from the table, had land outside Worcestershire, and it is not certain that the tax collectors netted all their Worcestershire goods. But even taking these things into consideration, the class of gentry of which these were the leading members must have been as individually meagre in resources as they were collectively important politically and socially. In Gloucestershire and in Warwickshire, as well as in Worcestershire, the majority had only one or two manors. The aristocratic hierarchy was no pyramid. It could better be likened to a collection of skyscrapers towering above the plain where dwelt the great mass of petty lords of hamlet and village.

Our knowledge of the aristocracy, great and small, is largely dominated by the details of their land transactions, their landed holdings, the assessments on their movable property, the routine tasks of government which they undertook. Their social and personal relationships, their political aspirations, their cultural activities and experiences can be grasped only transiently and unsystematically.

An aspect of their lives which seems very different for the great as against the lesser landowners is the geographical area of their normal activities. The great men had estates widely scattered over the country and political interests at the king's court. In war time, they were the generals of campaigns and were to be found in every sphere of military activity, France, Wales or Scotland. During times of political crisis they hurried backwards and forwards making sure of allies, organizing demonstrations in force against the court or against rival factions. The abbots naturally moved around less, but even they were to be found as often as not away from their house, either visiting the estate, the castles and houses of other landowners, or the king's court. The exchange of hospitality between the lords of Berkeley and the great abbots of the Severn valley will be remembered.

Did the knights and the lesser lords move around in the same way? We know that some of them were frequently to be found in the retinues of the great men, and we have already cited Thomas II of Berkeley whose retinue contained two hundred persons. But this included the lesser and permanent servants of the household as well as the knights and esquires. When the great Roger Mortimer of Wigmore attended the famous Kenilworth tournament of 1279 known as the 'round game' (*lusus rotunda*) he was said by the chronicler of Hailes Abbey to have brought with him a hundred knights and as many ladies.[47] But chroniclers' numbers are notoriously unrelated to reality, round figures simply being employed to imply 'very many'.

Undoubtedly, some of the lesser men led their lives on a wider stage than that provided merely by their own locality, and there were times when they were prepared to go far, not so much for the king's wars, but in the civil wars which engaged their political enthusiasm. There were, for example, getting on for a hundred of the lesser landowners of the region who were involved in rebellion with Simon de Montfort, and whose lands were temporarily confiscated. Many of them fought at Evesham, some were killed.[48] Many of them must have been with baronial forces outside the west midlands, though one supposes that their main sphere of activity must have been in their own region. Sir John Giffard and Sir William Mautravers, for instance, were at the Battle of Lewes, where Giffard captured three prisoners whose release at de Montfort's behest eventually contributed to Giffard's abandonment of the baronial cause.[49] But Giffard's most striking exploits were in Gloucestershire.

In war and in political disturbance, knights and other lords no doubt moved in the armed retinues of the magnates. But a study of their appearances as charter witnesses suggests that many of them were extraordinarily localized in their movements. It is often supposed that witnesses to charters originated by important persons were probably associates or dependants. It might further be supposed that they might be part of a great lord's retinue. This does not, however, seem necessarily the case. The impression one gains from the witness lists is of local communities of knights and gentry who gathered together as visitors on the arrival at his castle or manor house of the baron, bishop or abbot. It must not be supposed, of course, that these local witnesses were all present when the land transaction which was the subject of the charter took place, nor that they were gathered there for purely social reasons. Their testimony was needed because they knew about local circumstances, including land boundaries.

Charters of the Beauchamps (1268–1316) concerning property in Sutton Coldfield, Erdington, Great Barr and North Warwickshire are witnessed by such local personalities as Arden of Hanwell, Clinton of Coleshill, Clinton of Maxstoke, Erdington of Erdington, Whitacre of Whitacre, Basset of Drayton, Oddingseles of Solihull, and other personalities with such local names as Sheldon, Pipe, Pirye, Hamstead, Handsworth, Aldridge. When one moves over to the old centre of the Beauchamp estates, at Elmley Castle in Worcestershire, the charter signatories during the same period are quite different, Saltmarsh, Poer, Bracy, Pypard, Ombersley, Abetot, Muscegros, Cardiff, all names of Worcestershire knightly families. Again in South Warwickshire, near to the Oxfordshire border, we have Arden of Ratley, Upton, Lucy of Charlecote, Ladbroke, and Winderton.

The bishop of Worcester's estates were almost as widely distributed through the region as those of the Beauchamp family, so that geographical coverage of the late thirteenth-century bishopric cartulary, known as the *Liber Albus*, is of equal interest. As one would expect, witness lists to charters contain a high proportion of clerical persons, that is, diocesan officials, rectors, vicars, monks, all of whom would be in attendance on the bishop during his travels. But he was also a great lord, and many of the gentry attended him at his various manor houses. Hence, in southern Worcestershire, the persons present as witnesses to deeds of interest to the bishop or issued by him include Saltmarsh, Poer, Cardiff, Abetot, names also found testifying Beauchamp Elmley charters. The witness lists in the bishop's cartulary are sometimes even more localized than those of Beauchamp, as this example shows.[50] At no great distance from the southern Worcestershire manors of the bishop we find a group of properties, in which the bishop was interested, at Coughton and Sambourne, on the Warwickshire–Worcestershire border. A charter of the early years of Edward I's reign by which the last of the old manorial family of Coughton near Alcester handed over its holdings to the new lords, the Spineys, contains a typically local witness list: Peter de Montfort of Beaudesert, Walter de Beauchamp of Alcester, Henry Huband of Ipsley (near Redditch), Thomas Camvill of Arrow, all knights; Philip Durvassal of Spernall, Robert of Burley in Coughton, Robert de Bois of Alne, Richard Clinchamp of 'Herlesale', Robert of Roudiche and others: a natural local grouping.

There were, of course, occasional names in witness lists that appear with frequency in charters concerning property in widely separated districts. Some of the charters issued by magnates were issued at their main castle, at Warwick for instance by the Beauchamps, and consequently even charters concerning far off properties would be witnessed by persons temporarily or permanently in the central household. The Beauchamp charters of the late thirteenth and early fourteenth centuries, whilst revealing the local groupings referred to, also suggest that such men as the Warwickshire knight Sir Richard d'Amundeville, Sir Walter of Cokesey from Worcestershire, Sir Bartholomew of Sudeley near Winchcombe, and others were more often with the earl than most local signatories. But in so far as charter witness lists can be taken to reflect the location of the persons appearing in them, the overwhelming impression from the two cartularies cited, as well as from others, such as those of Pershore, Gloucester or Cirencester is of communities of gentry and freeholders with very local interests.

The Clerks

The ecclesiastical magnates, such as the bishops, the abbots and the monks, clearly fit into the social hierarchy alongside the secular lords of manors and jurisdictions. Can the whole clerical order be regarded as part of the ruling class of society? In medieval documents, not only the incumbents of benefices but unbeneficed chaplains are called 'dominus', that is 'lord', the same prefix which distinguished the knights even from undubbed members of the same family. On the other hand, the clerical order was by no means socially coherent. In the first place, it was drawn from many different social strata. Godfrey Giffard, bishop of Worcester from 1268 to 1301 was, as we have seen, a member of an important though not top rank baronial family. What of his episcopal neighbours? St Thomas de Cantilupe, bishop of Hereford from 1272 to 1282, nephew of Giffard's predecessor at Worcester, came from a baronial family. Roger Longespee, Henry III's cousin, and bishop of Coventry and Lichfield during most of Giffard's pontificate, was of the family of the earls of Salisbury. Robert Burnell, bishop of Bath and Wells and Edward I's chancellor, had a baronial estate in the west midlands and Marches to which we will refer again. Other bishops came from lower social groups. Thomas Cobham, bishop of Worcester between 1317 and 1327, was a member of a Kentish knightly family which later throve to baronial status. John Stratford, who became bishop of Winchester in 1323 and archbishop of Canterbury in 1333, came from a Stratford-on-Avon burgess family. He was a typical prelate whose rise was the reward for official service to the crown. On the whole, while a fair number of high ranking aristocrats and very few persons of peasant origin achieved high rank in the church, the vast majority of those who did well came from the knightly families.

But not all persons in clerical orders did well. Below the higher positions in the hierarchy, there was a vast mass of clerics who did not achieve higher preferment than a rectory or a vicarage. A greater number did not even reach this level. In the diocese of Worcester in the thirteenth century, there were four hundred and forty-five parishes, and about thirty chantries, that is, benefices of less value than a parish, whose duties were not cure of souls, but saying masses for the dead. In the last twenty years of Giffard's pontificate there were some 5,000 ordinations of secular clergy in the diocese.[51] A large number of clerks appeared twice or three times as ordinands for the orders of sub-deacon, deacon and priest, so there must have been available in the diocese 2,000 or more men in one of these three orders. In addition to them, there was a clerical or semi-clerical underworld at whose numbers we cannot even guess. Ordination by the bishop was the only official way into the clerical order, but proof of literacy still remained a proof of clergy, so many men who could read or write a little may have claimed clerical privilege.

What was the social position of these 2,000 and more clerics of the diocese? The ordination lists normally give no details apart from the candidates' names. One of the lists (that of 1291) confirms by a note to each candidate's name, that if he had not a benefice to go to already, he had private means or a patron, so that the bishop was not bound to support him. He was ordained that is, *ad titulum patrimonii sui*, or *ad titulum x* (a patron).[52] The overwhelming majority of candidates' surnames indicate that their origin was within the diocese, Adam of Cirencester for example, and on the whole they are not aristocratic names. Since the difficulties facing the son of a villein becoming a cleric were, if not insuperable, very great, the only class left from which the ordinands could come is that of the free tenants and gentry. When these men were ordained, then, and, more important, when they were beneficed, did they then step into a different, perhaps a higher social class?

When a cleric from this social group becomes a bishop or a high ranking diocesan official, he certainly assumed the social role of a magnate. But what was the social role of the parish clergy? It varied, not only from parish to parish according to the amount of parish revenue, but from person to person. In some cases younger sons of gentry families were presented to livings by their relatives or friends, and no doubt continued to live the lives of gentlemen. The incumbents of the parish of Pillerton Hersy during the whole of Giffard's episcopate were all members of the Hersy family, lords of the manor. The rector of the Berkeley manor of Slimbridge in 1270 was Simon de Berkeley (a minor), and he was followed in 1290 by Anselm, a thirteen year old member of the gentry family of Gyse. Roger de Somery, a great baron, presented Simon de Somery to the parish church of Clent, and Osbert d'Abetot, lord of Croome d'Abetot, presented Alexander d'Abetot to the family living. Altogether there are forty-three well-known names of this sort among those holding benefices during Giffard's tenure of office.[53]

This is not a great number and only affected a minority of benefices. There were also a few outsiders. For example, when Peter Escot, rector of Blockley, died in Rome in 1296, Pope Boniface VIII, as was his right, gave it to an Italian, Bartolommeo di Ferentino. In 1301, the ambitious politician, Adam of Orleton, future bishop of Hereford, Worcester and Winchester, was presented to the church of Wotton-under-Edge by the abbot of St Augustine's, Bristol. There is no evidence of probability that either of these two took up residence in their parish. The majority of names, like those of the ordinands were, however, local, that is from within the diocese.

Whatever his social origin, just as the new bishop stepped into magnate society, so the new rector or vicar stepped into a lordship analogous to that of a manor, and judging by investigations made of medieval rectors' and vicars' houses in other parts of the west country, lived in solid comfort and style.[54] The incumbent was, in the first place, the father of his flock. He distributed the sacraments which were essential to salvation, and had the duty of admonition and the imposition of penance. He was also a landowner, the possessor of glebeland which was usually equivalent in area to the rich peasant holding of one or two yardlands. He often had tenants. The rectors of Bishops Cleeve and Pucklechurch in Gloucestershire in 1327 had so many that they were assessed separately in the tax returns from the rest of the villagers.[55] But the fact that he only had glebeland equivalent to a large peasant holding must not persuade us that he shared the social position of the upper stratum of the peasants. He did not work it himself, but let it to farm or hired men to work it for him. In addition he had an income from the tithe of all growing things. This tenth of the grain, hay, and other crops and of the young of all animals represented a good deal more than a tenth of the peasant's surplus, since it was the tithepayer, not the tithe owner, who bore the expenses of producing it. It has been suggested that it was really equivalent to a twenty per cent levy on agricultural production.[56]

The incumbent with a full claim to the parish revenues must have appeared as much in the role of an exploiter as of a father, especially when we add fees and altar offerings to the tithes. But many incumbents did not get the full income from the parish. When a church was appropriated by a religious corporation, that corporation became rector and was entitled to the revenues. Since the corporation, especially if it was one of cloistered monks, could not perform the duties of the cure of souls, it instituted a vicar who was only given a fraction of the total revenue. His entitlement almost always excluded the corn and hay tithes, and though vicars' incomes were fixed at a minimum of five marks a year by ecclesiastical authority, the overall proportion of rectorial and vicarial incomes was usually established on favourable terms to the authority appropriating the rectory.

Owing to absenteeism by rectors and even by vicars, the cure of souls in a parish was often given to a poorly paid stipendiary priest who had no title to any part of the parish revenue. His social position was probably nearer to that of the majority of the parishioners than was that of the well-to-do rectors. It was from this group that priests who were mixed up in social rebellions probably came.

It must not be imagined that many clerks of local origin, once appointed to a benefice, were content to remain there. Apart from frequent leave of absence in order to go abroad or study, it seems to have been the aim of most incumbents to move quickly from one benefice to another. This was sometimes done with the natural aim of increasing the annual income. Yet changes were not always made to an obviously more lucrative benefice. The object may have been convenience for some other purpose in the clerk's life which had little to do with cure of souls. The consequence of all this licensed (or unlicensed) absence, chopping and changing, was, as we have seen, the absorption into paid work of part of the surplus of ordained men. Another form of paid employment which must have absorbed many, full or part time, was in the service of secular or ecclesiastical administration, where literacy was essential. Although thirteenth-century English society was in many ways very primitive, it had a considerable number of administrators at all levels. The amount of parchment that must have been written on to make records of the proceedings of ecclesiastical, manorial, hundred, county and assize courts, to make and duplicate manorial and estate accounts, to draw up deeds of gift, indentures, charters, registers, surveys, rentals, letters and so on, would have made mountains if all gathered together. Only a fraction has survived in our national and local archives, but even this is impressive in volume. Almost all the writing that was done on this parchment was done by members of the secular clergy, from the humble reeve's account to the elaborate folios of the bishop's register. Only the more elaborate literary productions were the work of monks in the scriptoria.

The clerks ranged socially, then, from the well-to-do rector, enjoying revenues which, as we have seen, could exceed the revenue of many a manor, to the poor stipendiaries doing the routine work of the parish or the intermittently employed men working as scribes. The wealthiest were the familiars of the nobility and gentry, the poorest, of peasants and artisans. Some of them were active in their calling. But there is little doubt that the clerical life could leave a man with considerable leisure. Some used it to gain education and preferment. Many others were idlers, and idleness could easily turn into anti-social channels. The clergy were among the commonest disturbers of the peace in the thirteenth century because they had little else to do. Poaching, for instance, was a favourite occupation. At the Feckenham Forest assizes of 1270 and 1280 a tenth of those accused of stealing deer were clerics, including some monks. Eleven of them were incumbents of local parishes including a particularly persistent offender, Ralph Bagot, the parson of Morton Bagot.[57] If, as has been calculated, the clergy were two per cent of the whole population, the fact that five times that proportion were caught stealing deer is of some interest, not because this form of law breaking was regarded as particularly reprehensible, but because it is so clearly the distraction of an idle life.

CHAPTER 3

THE ESTATES

Now that we have given in outline a picture of the aristocratic land-owning class of the west midlands, there remain many aspects of their life to be described in more detail. Nothing is more important for understanding them than an estimate of their incomes and of the sources of that income.

England is unique among European countries of the middle ages in the abundance of documentary evidence about the estates of the landowning class. These (apart from documents emanating from the public authority, such as the inquisitions post mortem) can be divided into three main classes: surveys, accounts and court records.[1]

The surveys, usually referred to in thirteenth-century documents as extents (*extenta*), were descriptions and valuations of each manor of which the estate was composed, to which might be added descriptions of any extra-manorial elements in the estate or its income. This type of document has a long history, the polyptichs of estates in Carolingian Gaul in the ninth century being the earliest extant examples, but no doubt being preceded by other examples which have disappeared in earlier centuries. The purpose of the document was simply to inform the landowner and his officials what were the component parts of the estate and what income could be expected from them. The manorial surveys were already becoming stereotyped in the twelfth century although they did not reach their final form until the latter part of the thirteenth century. Their almost invariable pattern was as follows. First, there was a description, more or less detailed, of the demesne, or home farm, consisting of the manor house or castle, the gardens and orchards, the arable, meadow and pasture land, and the lord's rights in the common lands of the village. Next there was a list of

65

all the tenants, often going into great detail, giving their names, the acreage of their holdings, the nature of their common rights, and the money rents, labour services and customary dues which each of them owed. The tenants were usually divided into three categories: free tenants, customary or villein tenants, and cottagers. Finally there would be miscellaneous information about the lord's income from markets and fairs, from private jurisdictions within, or attached to, the manor, and so on.

The west midlands estates can produce a number of good, detailed twelfth- and thirteenth-century surveys. The earliest are those of the manors of Minchinhampton and Avening, owned by the nuns of Holy Trinity, Caen, in Normandy. There is a succession of three, of uncertain date (save that they are certainly to be placed between about 1130 and 1180). Two of them are in the Holy Trinity Cartulary in the Bibliothèque Nationale, Paris, and one (a fragment) was recently found in the Worcester County Record Office. This is now published. Minchinhampton itself is on a plateau in the west Cotswolds, near the Stroud valley, but many of the tenants of the manor lived in the valleys which enclosed the plateau on the north and on the south. These manorial surveys are part of an unusually rich documentation of this estate which carry its story through to the fifteenth century. Slightly later than the Minchinhampton surveys is one of the whole of the bishop of Worcester's estate, usually attributed to the year 1182; and at about the same date, contained in an unpublished cartulary of Evesham Abbey are descriptions of the manors of Evesham Abbey. A few years later than these (c. 1185) is the survey of all the English estates of the Knights of the Temple which include their properties in the Cotswolds and in Warwickshire. In contrast to the thirteenth-century surveys, these of the twelfth century do not contain descriptions of demesne as well as of tenant land; they do, however, give the names and obligations of the tenants.[2]

The next detailed survey is that of the estate of the cathedral priory of Worcester, contained in a finely written book, dated 1240, now kept at Worcester Cathedral, and published over a century ago by the Camden Society. This estate, as we have seen, is the counterpart of that of the bishop, so that this survey forms a useful link with the very elaborate survey of the bishop's estate which was drawn up in 1299, just before the death of Bishop Godfrey Giffard. The originals of the two bishops' surveys (1182 and 1299) and of a shorter valuation of 1288 have not survived, but a copy was made in the eighteenth century by Dr William Thomas, and has recently been published. The great cartulary of St Peter's Abbey, Gloucester, which was published in the Rolls Series 1863–7 in three volumes, contains, in addition to a large number of charters, a series of manorial extents, of uncertain date, but probably mostly drawn up in the 1260s. Apart from the descriptions of two Wiltshire manors, these unfortunately do not contain a description of the demesnes, but the names of all the tenants with their rents, labour services and customary dues are set out in detail.[3]

None of the other great west midland estates have systematically compiled extents on the scale of those mentioned above. A series of extents of the bishopric of Hereford includes those of two Gloucestershire manors, Prestbury and Sevenhampton, drawn up in the 1280s. There is a sketchy outline summary of the values of Cirencester Abbey, again of uncertain date, to which we have already referred. But there is no comprehensive series of Cirencester manorial extents. Nor have we any such from Tewkesbury, Winchcombe, Pershore, Lanthony, St Augustine's, Bristol or Coventry, at any rate for this peak period in the development of the economy of the great estate. The rentals of the west midlands manors of Westminster Abbey are also too late for our purpose. There are, however, some very detailed surveys of the estates of the rebel Maurice of Berkeley. These are among the public records, and it seems likely that they were drawn up in 1322 when Maurice was in royal custody. They could be classed along with the thirteenth-century surveys already mentioned since they were drawn up before the mid-century demographic crisis. A brief summary of the contents of one of these extents may serve to illustrate the nature of this type of evidence as well as to throw some light on the manor which is described.[4]

The manor is that of Cam which is under the edge of the Cotswolds, overlooking the Vale of Berkeley and about equidistant from Berkeley and the Stroud valley. It was in the hundred of Berkeley and had been part of the Berkeley estates since Robert Fitz Harding was endowed at the expense of the Berkeleys of Dursley. The demesne is described first, consisting of the manor house with its gardens and closes, a dovecot and two water mills. One was for grinding corn, the other for fulling cloth, for this is an area on the way to industrialization. The arable land in demesne was 147 acres. About sixty acres were already in enclosures, valued at twice as much a year as the land in the open fields, because of the latter being subject to common rights and fallow every third year. There were twenty-six acres of unenclosed meadow, and there were fifteen acres of pasture held separately from the commonable pastures. There was an unusually high proportion of free tenants. These were divided into two categories, those holding in fee, that is with hereditary right, and those holding for life. There were twenty-one free tenants in fee, one of them being an important lord, Sir John Botetourt, whose estate included the neighbouring hamlet of Woodmancote. There were forty-one free tenants holding for life. Almost all of them had substantial holdings, some with more than sixty acres of arable. All of them paid a money rent only. It seems almost certain that many of these free life tenures were customary holdings with labour services recently commuted, for there were only four customary tenants of the traditional type rendering labour and other customary services. Finally, there were sixteen cottagers, only one of whom owed a few reaping services in addition to money rent. The rest paid a rent in money only. The total value of the manor was £79, which is high. It is worth emphasizing that it was the tenants who were the valuable assets on the manor. The home farm was only valued at a little over £5, whereas free tenants' rents came to £61 and customary tenants' rents to a little over £5.

The manorial surveys were the corner stone of the manorial administration, for, so long as they were kept up to date, the estate auditors could always check the annual accounts of the various manorial and estate officials against the sums listed in the surveys. The accounts themselves are the chief evidence that we have for the dynamics of the manorial economy. On a large estate there was a considerable number of accounting officials, so many in some cases that the administration tended to become over-bureaucratized and consequently inefficient.

The beginnings of the accounting system cannot be traced owing to the lack of documentary evidence. The earliest estate accounts are those of the bishopric of Winchester and begin at the end of the first decade of the thirteenth century.[5] But in principle the method of accounting resembled that employed by the sheriffs who accounted at Easter and at Michaelmas for the receipts of their counties at the royal exchequer. The earliest of their enrolled accounts extant, known as the Pipe Roll, is for 1130, and clearly this was not the first. The principles of accounting were simple but did not resemble modern methods. Each accountant was 'charged' with the expected annual receipts and it was his duty to acquit himself of the sums charged against him so that he was not in debt at the end of the financial year (usually Michaelmas, 29 September, that is, after the harvest). Consequently although the first part of the account was usually called the Receipts (*recepta*), it was sometimes called the Charge (*onus*). The second half of the account was usually called the Expenses (*expensa*). If the items on the expense side of the account equalled the receipts the accountant was discharged, quit, or as the invariable phrase was, *et quietus est*. If the expenses fell short of the expected receipts, or charge, then the accountant was in debt. He either had to find the money, or more frequently carried the debt over as arrears to be added to the next year's charge. If the expenses exceeded the receipts (the less usual case), the estate owed the difference to the accountant, who could add it as a *superplusagium* to the next year's expenses.[6]

The most interesting accounts are those of the manorial reeve or bailiff because these deal with the day-to-day profits and expenses of agriculture. 'Bailiff' (or sometimes 'Serjeant') is the name given to a professional farm manager, a free man who was often put over a group of manors, or over one very large and complex manor. An example of this form of organization is the Westminster Abbey bailiwick of Todenham (Gloucestershire), administered by a serjeant (*serviens*), and containing the manors of Todenham, Sutton-under-Brailes (Warwickshire) and Bourton-on-the-Hill (Gloucestershire) each with its own reeve.[7] The reeve was an official who performed the same function as the bailiff in a single manor, but who was chosen from among the wealthier customary tenants, and was therefore usually unfree. He was not paid a wage (as the bailiff was) but was let off his rent, and no doubt could enrich himself during his period of office. The reeve (or bailiff) was mainly concerned with the management of the home farm, so that while tenants' rents might bulk large on the receipt side of the account, the sale of produce could often produce a greater gross annual income than rents. However, the productivity of medieval agriculture was low and the net profits of agriculture on the home farm were not great. This, however, is by the way: the point is that, since net profits were so low, the estate auditors paid great attention to expenses which had to be entered in great detail, very satisfying to the historian.

The details contained on the expense side of the accounts range from the cost of pieces of cord used by the carters to the smallest metal parts of the plough; from the money spent buying tar to cure the sores on sheep to the tips given to manorial servants at harvest time. A fairly complete picture of the agricultural year can be built up from them. Finally, a special feature of the medieval manorial account, which completes the detailed picture derivable from the items on the expenses side, is the grange and stock account. This was invariably written on the outside, or back, of the parchment roll, the cash account being on the inside, or front. The grange account gives the amount of each type of grain received from the previous year's production, or by purchase, and the manner in which it was expended. The detail here often goes down to the amount of seed sown on each named piece of demesne land. The stock account shows what livestock of all sorts was taken over by the reeve at the beginning of the year, what was acquired and what was disposed of. In sheep rearing country this also included an account of fleeces and skins. After the stock account the bailiff or reeve sometimes accounted for the way in which the labour services had been used during the year.

Manorial accounts for single years in isolation are, of course, of some interest, but for understanding the manorial or the estate economy properly, it is essential to have a series of accounts over a number of consecutive, or near consecutive years. Although there are a few isolated accounts from manors in the region in the period before the Black Death, satisfactory series are unhappily only found for one or two estates. The best series for the late thirteenth and early fourteenth centuries are those from half a dozen manors in Gloucestershire, Worcestershire and Warwickshire of the Westminster Abbey estate, the earliest (Todenham, Gloucestershire and Sutton-under-Brailes, Warwickshire) being that of 1252–3.[8] Other important series are for the manors of the Worcester Cathedral Priory estate, although even here the best material is later. There are also some short series for Forest of Dean manors of the Earl Marshal and a broken series for Minchinhampton. The other useful series are from the second half of the fourteenth century and the early part of the fifteenth century. They are only useful in so far as they reflect the situation before the lords ceased to cultivate their demesnes, for those manorial accounts which only deal with the collection of rents are not of great interest. When a manorial demesne was leased out to a tenant, it was, of course, taken out of the hands of the reeve, and no agricultural details are entered. The most abundant and informative of these later accounts (additional to the continuing series from the Worcester Cathedral and Westminster Abbey manors), are from the manors of the bishop of Worcester's estate. Pershore and Winchcombe Abbey estates have useful, if short, series of accounts, and so does the archbishop of York's Gloucestershire barony of Churchdown. There are also a few series from manors of the Beauchamp earls of Warwick.[9]

Manorial accounts were not, however, the only documents of this type which were by-products of estate administration. There were other accounting officials in addition to manorial reeves and bailiffs, officials who (as we have mentioned) tended to proliferate into a bureaucracy. This type of bureaucratic proliferation was most marked on the monastic estates. There were good reasons for this within the terms of reference of the monastic life. Each monastic community had to appoint officials to look after its material needs as well as the requirements of the cult. A typical group of officials is to be found at Evesham Abbey, listed in a disposition of 1214. This confirmation of the customs of the abbey lays down that the abbot was to choose his obedientiaries with the agreement of the greater or wiser element in the chapter of monks. They were to be, first, the prior, the sub-prior and the third prior, that is to say deputies to the abbot, whose duty was to help the abbot to ensure that the rule was kept. The precentor looked after the sacred books and the order of the services. The dean of Christianity (monastic official peculiar to Evesham) acted as rural dean to the churches of the Vale of Evesham. The sacristan was in charge of the sacred vessels and vestments. The chamberlain provided the monks' clothing. The kitchener is self-explanatory. The interior cellarer looked after the general victualling inside the walls. The infirmarer was in charge of the establishment for sick monks. The almoner provided for and controlled the giving of alms to the poor, one of the bounden duties of the monks. The office of warden of the garden and vineyard explains itself, as does that of the master of the fabric of the church and of the master of the guest chamber. The most important official, however, is not in this list, though he is provided for by name in the original Rule of St Benedict. This was the cellarer (or general cellarer). He was in effect the overall supervisor of the material endowment of the monastery.[10]

Each of the obedientiaries was allotted one manor or more or a group of rents to administer and from which to derive the income needed for his office. Consequently, they and the cellarer, for the bulk of the monastic property, had to account four times a year before a committee of auditors consisting of the abbot or his appointed deputy, the prior and six cloister monks who were not themselves obedientiaries, three appointed by the abbot and three by the monks. The kitchener, however, had to account every week. The arrangements about accounting varied from house to house. There was a tendency in the twelfth and thirteenth centuries, because of the incompetence or corruption of many obedientiaries, to take away from them their separately administered incomes and to put all money through a central treasurer who simply allotted money as needed. Worcester Cathedral Priory had a cellarer-bursar who controlled the bulk of the revenue. Cirencester adopted a system of financial centralization about 1200–5 by which a committee of three treasurers received all income and allotted it to obedientiaries to be spent in their offices. They were to receive accounts and to render them four times a year. This system, however, was slightly modified by 1250 by giving back their financial autonomy to some of the obedientiaries. St Peter's Abbey, Gloucester, in the middle of the thirteenth century had a similar system by which all receipts and issue of money had to go through the hands of bursars or receivers in a central exchequer.[11]

In the lay estates, there are no accounting officials corresponding to the monasteries' obedientiaries. There were bailiffs of fees who collected feudal revenues from military tenants, but the most important financial officials were the receivers who collected the cash surplus from the manors. On a big estate, such as that of the Beauchamps, there would be local receivers for geographically separated groups of estates, who would turn their moneys in to a receiver-general. He would account to the auditors of the whole estate. The treasurers or cellarers of monastic estates would, it is clear, be the nearest equivalents of the lay receivers-general, and it is from the accounts of either type of official, lay or monastic, that one gets a bird's-eye view, so to speak, of the finances of the estate as a whole. This usefully complements the fuller and more detailed accounts of the manorial bailiffs. Unfortunately, the

only available central accounts before the middle of the fourteenth
century are those of the Worcester Cathedral Priory bursar-
cellarers and of one or two minor obedientiaries. The earliest of the
Beauchamp receiver-generals' accounts is not until 1395.[12]

The overwhelming majority of records from courts of private
jurisdiction are those of manorial courts, a most important source,
comparable with the manorial accounts. But whereas the manorial
accounts present almost exclusively the agricultural management
of the lord's demesne, the manorial court records tell us about the
relationship between lord and tenant. Naturally, court records tend
to survive as part of the survival of estate records as a whole. When
estate records survive in this way they tend to be the records of the
estates of barons, bishops or large religious houses. Consequently,
most of our surviving manorial court records are those where the
maximum possible private jurisdiction was enjoyed by the lord of
the court. This means that in addition to enforcing suit to his court
by his tenants, by virtue of that tenure, the lord could also enforce
suit to special sessions of the court known as the 'view of frankpledge'. This was, in effect, the public jurisdiction of the hundred
court transferred to the private court. It did not give lords the right
to deal with pleas of the crown, but it did give them petty police
jurisdiction as well as the coercive sanctions inherent in land-
lordship. In addition the lords, lay and (especially) ecclesiastical
who claimed baronial privileges, symbolized these in the possession
of a private gallows, on which they were entitled to hang thieves
caught with the stolen goods still on them.*

Manorial court records contain minor forms of litigation between
suitors about such matters as debt, trespass, breach of contract.
They also functioned as land registers. When a tenant died, fled
the manor, or surrendered his holding through poverty, the incident was reported by a local jury, or by the chief man of the
tenant's tithing, or mutual security group, at the next court session.
The holding was regarded as having fallen into the lord's hand,
even if the customarily recognized heir was there to take over as a
matter of course. His entry on to the holding, or that of any taker,
was also recorded, together with the rent and other terms of tenure.
These records are the best mirrors of village life that we have, and
it is because the actions of the peasants appear with most vivid
actuality here that we prize them so much. They are also, however,

---

* These matters will be dealt with in greater detail in Chapter 6.

an important monument to the social and jurisdictional power of the lords.

Fortunately, they survive in relative abundance from the west midland estates. There are better series of them than there are of manorial accounts. The reason probably is that owing to the persistence, almost unchanged, of customary terms of tenure into the sixteenth and seventeenth centuries, lords of manors or their stewards were still interested at that late date in medieval precedents. They frequently needed to look back at the medieval court records, and sometimes made abstracts of important cases which survive. As one would expect, therefore, those estates which have the greatest number of surviving manorial records of other types have good court records as well. These include series for many manors on the bishopric and cathedral estates; on the estates of Westminster and Pershore Abbeys, and of the earls of Warwick; even some fourteenth-century fragmentary extracts for Evesham Abbey manors. There are also, among other surviving rolls, records of the big Feckenham Forest property at Tardebigge, near Redditch, of the Cistercian abbey of Bordesley; of the Premonstratensian abbey of Halesowen; of the crown manors of Bromsgrove and Feckenham and of many others. On the whole, Gloucestershire survivals are disappointingly few in view of the number of large estates, though the Mortimer manor of Bisley should be mentioned; the same is true of Warwickshire, though this, in a county of smaller estates, is less surprising. Much of this court roll evidence is, however, late for the purposes of this study. The earliest Westminster court roll, for instance, is one for Pershore in 1338. There are, however, some earlier series from individual estates, of which that of Halesowen is the most remarkable.[13]

The main thing to be said about the estates which provided the material basis for aristocratic life in the thirteenth century, is that money revenues were higher then than at any time before or afterwards. This must have seemed at any rate on the surface, a positively euphoric era for that class, comparable to the prosperity of the financiers and industrialists of Victorian England. It was the consequence of a number of factors quite outside their control. The most important factor was the growth in population which had (judging by estimates for England and Europe as a whole) been continuous during the twelfth and thirteenth centuries, and can certainly be shown in the west midlands to have been considerable in the thirteenth century. A comparison of the Worcester bishopric lists of tenants in 1182 with those of 1299 suggests a sixty-five per cent increase at least in the tenant population during the period and a corresponding increase in the amount of land under cultivation. These figures, however, almost certainly underestimate the population increase. The number of registered tenants in any survey is not the same as the number of families in the manor or village, for the court records indicate that there was a considerable amount of subletting by the main tenants to families who might make no direct payment to the lord and so not appear in his records.

This scale of population increase meant a substantial increase in rent-paying tenants. And since there was demonstrably a growth during the period of towns of all sizes, not to speak of all sorts of non-producers of agricultural foods – clerics, merchants, craftsmen – the demand for foodstuffs also increased. This is shown by the threefold increase in agricultural prices during the period.[14] The response of the estate owners to the increase in food prices was to produce as much grain, wool and livestock for sale as possible. Their response to the increase in the number of would-be tenants was to increase rents. Although in appearance (that is, in the detailed manorial surveys) the increase in peasants' rents seemed to be mainly in the amount of unpaid labour services which they owed for their holdings, these increases in labour services were all valued in money and in practice a high (though varying) proportion of them was commuted from year to year into money. Cash, in fact, was the overwhelming need of the thirteenth-century English aristocratic landowners, barons, bishops and abbots alike. The same economic conditions which made cash available, that is an increasing market demand for the products of agriculture from the estates, also made more cash essential if the landowners were to maintain their status and their power. This century was one of an increasing volume of international trade as a result of which more and more luxury goods, many of Mediterranean provenance, became available. As standards of living went up, so did costs. Furthermore the military activities of the king of England became increasingly expensive as he defended his position in Gascony and embarked on the conquest of Wales and Scotland. These expenses had to be paid for by taxes, and much as they tried, the landowners could not pass all the taxes which they granted to the king in

Parliament on to their tenants. We must try to illustrate the way in which these circumstances influenced, and were faced by the west midland landowners, from their accounts. Unfortunately, the late thirteenth-century evidence, as we have seen, is fragmentary. We can only hope that it is representative.

Let us first consider some overall income figures. We are told that, in the 1260s, an average earl would have a net income of £1,600 a year, though such a person is rather a fictional creation since some, like Clare, Earl of Gloucester or Bigod, Earl of Norfolk, were in the £3,000 to £4,000 class.[15] Furthermore such incomes would certainly fluctuate from year to year according, for instance, to a policy decision such as large scale sales of stock or wool, or over a longer period according to the fortunes of the family in the marriage market. The only figures of the lay nobility that we can quotè here are unfortunately mostly derived from inquisitions post mortem, and as already stated, are likely to be underestimated. Guy de Beauchamp's Warwickshire and Worcestershire estates were valued at about £700 at his death, so taking into account undervaluation, and his holdings outside the west midlands, he probably comes near to the average as far as net income is concerned. The Berkeley receivers' accounts, according to the family historian John Smyth of Nibley, show that Thomas III had a clear income in 1328 of £425, £659 in 1335, £977 in 1345 and £1,150 in 1347. The royal custodian of the vacant bishopric of Worcester in 1303, having held the estate for about a year accounted to the exchequer showing that the net revenue from the estate was something in the region of £900.[16]

These totals, while giving some idea of the scale of opulence enjoyed by the magnates concerned, are not over-useful. More interesting is the way in which these totals are made up, because this gives us an idea as to the active participation in the economic life of the region of the landowner. What does this mean? The landowner's income came partly from the rents paid to him by his tenants. If he wished he could let all his land to tenants on various terms of tenure. In so far as the terms embodied provisions for good husbandry and the tenants were supervised the landlord (or his expert agents) could affect the agricultural economy significantly. But this type of guidance, through terms of tenure, is not characteristic of the middle ages. It is not found until there was a new interest in husbandry manifested by landlords in the seventeenth and eighteenth centuries. It was when the medieval land-lord kept his demesnes, or home farms, in hand, to be supervised by his reeves and bailiffs, with the object of producing for the market or for the victualling of the household (or monastery) that he made his impact on agricultural practice. We can see at a glance the extent to which this was done by comparing income figures from rent with that from sales of demesne produce, even though this might give a distorted impression should much of the demesne produce go to the household without passing through the market.

The annual accounts of the Worcester Cathedral Priory bursar-cellarer, who received the bulk of the estate income, illustrate the point.[17] The following percentages show the proportionate rela-tionship of rents and sales in the receipts. Other items which appear in the receipt, such as manorial bailiffs' arrears and irregu-lar outside payments have not been included. The regular *auxilium* or aid from the tenants of about £27 has been included, except for the 1313–4 account. By this year aid may have been embodied into the general rent total. A very large sum collected from the tenants for the 1294 tax on clerical income has also been excluded as not being part of normal income.

	1291–2	1293–4	1294–5	1313–4
Rent	30	33	35	25
Aid	15	17	17	—
Grain sales	38	35	41	41
Wool sales	11	14	—	19
Other sales	—	—	6	15

These are not unusual figures for this period. The treasurer of Leicester Abbey, for instance, received income in 1297–8 in the following percentage proportions: rents thirty-two; grain sales twenty-seven; wool thirty-five. On the English lands (mostly in Wiltshire) of the Norman abbey of Bec income percentages in 1288–9 were as follows: rents, court fees and aid forty-three; grain sales forty-three; wool sales fourteen.[18] All these figures, being those of central accountants, ignore internal consumption and cash expenditure within the manors. It is clear that on these highly organized ecclesiastical estates, manorial officials had not much autonomy and that sales of produce surplus to local requirements were conducted centrally. Grain surpluses on the Worcester estates, for instance, were sent to the sub-cellarers. Even at the manorial level the importance of sales of produce as an element in cash income appears from the following broad percentages from some selected years on Westminster Abbey manors and on the large property of the nuns of Caen at Minchinhampton.*[19]

	Rent, etc.	Stock, etc., sales	Grain sales
Westminster Manors			
Hardwick 1306–7	48	7	45
Hardwick 1322–3	52	8	48
Knowle 1293–4	36	63*	1
Knowle 1301–2	64	22*	14
Todenham 1281–2	69	25	6
Todenham 1293–4	42	45	13
Minchinhampton Manor			
1306–7	36	61	3
1310–1	34	50	16
1315–6	32	52	16
1320–1	23	66	11

* Fifty-two per cent in 1293 and eleven per cent in 1302 were timber sales.

It is true that the Worcester cellarer-bursar receipts may exaggerate the proportion of sales from the demesnes in relation to other items of income, for the smaller obedientiaries tended to have a high proportion of rent in their total income. Nevertheless, during the course of the thirteenth century, the priory had been increasing the number of its demesnes kept in hand and exploited directly through the manorial reeves. The writer of the priory annals, interested mainly in the affairs of the estate, mentions under appropriate years the lapsing or renewal of demesne leases. The information he gives makes it clear that something like two-thirds of the priory demesnes at the end of the twelfth and the beginning of the thirteenth centuries, were in the hands of 'farmers' to use a word which then had the technical meaning of

* Rent is not only direct payment from holdings, but includes other tenant payments.

lessee. Some of these farmers were individuals, such as Sir Thomas of Erdington who took Alveston and Shipston-on-Stour on lease in 1201 for sixteen years. In many cases the villagers took a collective lease of the demesne. This happened at 'West', 'Offacomba', Henwick, Harvington, Phepson and Cleeve Prior at various times in the first decades of the century. However, demesnes whose leases lapsed began to be kept in hand, so that by the date of the compilation of the register (1240–2) most of the demesnes were being dírectly cultivated by the priory's servants.[20]

Whether demesnes were kept in hand or let out, the main requirement of the estate owners was a cash income. The experience of a constantly rising level of agricultural prices naturally made estate owners reluctant to lease out demesnes for long periods of years, twelve, fifteen or sixteen, as they had been doing at the beginning of the century, for if the rent was fixed on the basis of prices at the beginning of the lease (£30 a year for instance paid by Erdington for Alveston and Shipston) towards the end of the lease the farmer would be picking up the increment in prices. The demesne produce was not thought of primarily as a means of sustaining the monastic or lay household, but as an asset realizable in cash. This is vividly illustrated in the case of Worcester Priory. In 1293–4, the cellarer, Hugh of Inkberrow, accounted for grain sold from demesne and from customary rents in grain amounting to £56 10s 8d in value. During the same year of account, he spent £173 on grain of various types. In 1294–5, £62 worth of grain was sold and £320 worth bought. In 1313–4, £123 worth was sold and £106 worth bought. Only in 1292–3, from the cellarer's accounts which survive can we see the sort of excess of grain sales over purchases (£69 to £48) which might seem more normal in the financial dealings of a big agricultural producer.

The point was, as we have seen, that grain prices varied considerably from place to place and from month to month during the course of the accounting year. This is well illustrated for the late thirteenth century by a series of figures from Bristol. The figures come from the annual accounts tendered by the constable of Bristol Castle. He had to account for all the king's income from various properties and rights in Bristol, including sales of corn from the king's mills below Bristol Castle. This was grain which was paid as multure by those grinding their own corn there, the multure then being sold by the king's official in the market. In

1293–4 there were seven sales of wheat and six of mistil (*mixtillum*, a mixture of wheat and rye). Beginning in the autumn at 6s a quarter, the price of wheat rose steadily to 9s 4d, until the last sale, probably just before Michaelmas, when there was a slight drop to 9s. The price per quarter of mistil began at 4s 8d, rose to 7s then dropped in the last sale to 5s. In 1294–5, wheat started at 5s a quarter, went up to 9s 6d, then dropped to 7s 6d for the last sale (six sales). In 1298–9 it began at 4s a quarter, went steadily up to 10s over ten sales, dropped to 4s 8d for the next sale, and up again to 6s 9d for the twelfth sale of the year.[21]

Prices recorded in manorial accounts show similar fluctuations during the year to these we find at Bristol. We do not usually know where the sales actually took place, so we do not have here a contrast between town and country prices. At Todenham, between Shipston-on-Stour and Moreton-in-Marsh, the wheat prices recorded in the account of 1276 vary between 2s 8d and 5s, rye between 4s and 5s and oats between 1s 7d and 3s. At Knowle in the Arden woodland in north Warwickshire in 1294, purchase prices of wheat were between 6s 8d and 8s 2d. At Hardwick, in the Severn valley, north-west of Cheltenham, wheat prices in 1307 varied between 2s 10d and 4s a quarter, barley prices between 2s 1d and 2s 10d and oats between 1s 10d and 2s.[22]

If we had a series of figures from Worcester town market similar to those of Bristol at the same period, it would undoubtedly show the same fluctuations, or rather general trend from low prices during the period of abundance after the harvest, to high prices when grain was getting scarce in spring and summer. The fact that Worcester Cathedral Priory was buying and selling the same commodity is ample demonstration that the main aim of its administrators was cash. This was certainly true of the king's lands attached to Bristol Castle. The constable's accounts contain an ordinary manorial account for King's Barton, including a grange account. This shows that, apart from seed, every ounce of grain was sold on the Bristol market. The overwhelming need to convert this produce into cash is shown by the fact that, quite against normal manorial practice, the agricultural labourers on the king's manors received no part of their wages in kind. It was all needed for sale.

It will have been noticed that the other large item of demesne produce sold besides grain, was wool. Wool was more of a cash crop than grain because (Worcester Priory's experience notwithstanding) most lords, lay or ecclesiastical, did consume a substantial part of their grain production. Few landowners (if any), however, organized the manufacture of woollen cloth. The wool clip from English estates at the end of the thirteenth century either went for export – 30,000 sacks from some eight million sheep by 1290 – or to the native manufacturer, an unknown quantity. Our shortage of estate accounts to show how the west midland landowners were taking part in this trade is partly compensated by recent investigations which have revealed the activities of a small group of London exporters,* and by an early fourteenth-century list, made by F. B. Pegolotti, agent in England of the Florentine Bardi Company. This list shows the rough quantity of wool which could be bought up for export from certain monastic landowners. The Italian merchants had much earlier established commercial relations with the religious houses, in the first place as collectors of ecclesiastical taxation for the Papacy. But since Florence itself had a very large wool cloth manufacturing industry, and since, in addition, the Florentines had firm commercial connections with Flanders, another important woollen cloth manufacturing area, they soon began, in effect to take payment of the taxes in wool, remitting the cash value to the Papacy. From this it was a natural step to establish normal commercial relations.[23]

An analysis of the figures in Pegolotti's list for the wool-exporting monasteries of the west midlands brings out some rather surprising results. The Cistercian abbeys were all producing moderate to good quality wool, properly sorted for export, and even the small Warwickshire and Worcestershire houses were expected to find a good quantity of wool each year for the exporter. This was undoubtedly because of the abundant woodland pastures of Arden and Feckenham. The Benedictines, on the other hand, seemed to be taking, as yet, very little interest in the export market. None of them was expected to produce properly sorted wool but only fleeces straight off the sheep's back (or straight from the fold, *come viene della falda*, as Pegolotti put it). Consequently, it was rather low priced compared with the sorted Cistercian wool. The only exception among the Benedictine houses was Winchcombe which produced a large quantity annually of middle priced wool which had been cleaned, but not apparently sorted. It cannot be concluded from these figures, of course, that the Benedictine

* See below, Chapter 5, pp. 178-9.

WEST MIDLANDS ABBEYS IN PEGOLOTTI'S LIST

House	Price of 1st quality sorted wool (marks per sack)	Price of 2nd quality sorted wool (marks per sack)	Price of 3rd quality sorted wool (marks per sack)	Price cleaned but not sorted	Price of fleeces from the fold (sack)	No. of sacks p.a.
CISTERCIANS						
Kingswood (Gloucestershire)	26	15				25
Hailes (Gloucestershire)	19	10	7			20
Flaxley (Gloucestershire)	15	10	8½			6
Combe (Warwickshire)	19	12	10			18
Merevale (Warwickshire)	17	10				30
Stoneleigh (Warwickshire)	18	11	10			10
Bordesley (Worcestershire)	19	11	11			10
BENEDICTINES						
Winchcombe				13		40
Evesham					12	10
Pershore					12	10
Tewkesbury					12	8
Gloucester					13	5

houses other than Winchcombe were not grazing sheep on a large scale, for there are other indications that they were. There were sheep flocks on most of the west midland manors of the abbey of Westminster, especially on the Todenham bailiwick, which included Sutton-under-Brailes and Bourton-on-the-Hill. These do not always appear in the stock accounts of the manors, since like most big graziers, the monks moved their flocks from manor to manor. But they could leave their traces in other ways, as on the combined account for Todenham and Sutton-under-Brailes (Warwickshire) for 1253. In this year the reeve accounted for 311 fleeces sold. In 1277 the only sign of sheep in the Todenham account is a payment for making a sheep fold at Sutton. But in 1293 the reeve started the year at Todenham with a flock of 297 wethers, 357 ewes, 140 yearlings and 101 new lambs. At Bourton-on-the-Hill in 1280 there was a flock of some three hundred sheep and wool sales brought in £15. At Knowle in 1293, 250 sheep passed through the reeve's hands, some ending up in the abbey larder, but the bulk were kept during summer and autumn.* Hardwick, which in some years harboured no sheep, in 1307 had about 360, more than half of them wintering there from the Cotswold manors of Todenham and Bourton-on-the-Hill. Moreton-in-Marsh was also a manor where the abbey wintered its upland sheep. At Pershore, in the following year, when stock was being sold off in considerable quantities, the reeve accounted for the price of 220 sheep, 90 lambs and 200 fleeces.[24] The Worcester Priory cellarer's accounts of this period show that a large proportion of the income from this estate came from wool sales, though the priory does not figure at all in Pegolotti's list. The answer must be that some abbeys had geared themselves to the export trade, whereas others were selling on the home market. For example, although Pegolotti only counted on getting five sacks a year for export from Gloucester Abbey, the abbey chronicler tells us that by the beginning of the fourteenth century there were 10,000 sheep on the estate producing for sale forty-six sacks a year.[24a] In view of evidence, which we will discuss later, of the growth of the woollen cloth industry in both villages and towns of the west midlands in the thirteenth century, it seems clear that there was no shortage of local outlets for monastic wool.

The central accounts, whether of monastic cellarers, bursars or treasurers, or of lay receivers, demonstrate not only the attempts by the estate owners to realize the highest possible cash income, but the cash demands upon them which spurred on those attempts. Estate, that is current agricultural, expenses were largely met on the spot from the income of each manor, with perhaps some occasional subventions from central funds. The central expenses which were the heaviest burden were not connected with estate management, for there was very little investment for improvement even on the best run estates. On the contrary it was the expenses involved in keeping up hospitality and status, sweetening friends, litigating against opponents and paying taxes which caused the most con-

* These details appear in the cash expenses, not in the stock account.

siderable drain on cash resources. Let us turn again to the Worcester Cathedral Priory cellarer-bursary accounts to see where the money went.

In 1313–4, the cellarer spent about £250 on hospitality, bribes, tips, retaining fees and expenses of litigation. The persons entertained varied immensely in social status. The most eminent were probably Edward Burnel, great-nephew of Robert Burnel, Bishop of Bath – the Burnels had an estate of baronial proportions in more than a dozen counties but the centre of gravity was in the west midlands and the Marches; John Hastings of Allesley; Robert Mortimer, probably a member of the Richards Castle family; various local knights such as John de Sapy; the constable of Elmley Castle and other members of the Earl of Warwick's household; local officials such as the steward of the forest and other foresters; royal servants such as the king's cook; and clerics such as the Abbot of Peterborough, the Bishop of Bangor and of course the Bishop of Worcester himself. All of these persons were entertained with wine or game. But others were given presents in cash, the sheriff, the regarders of Feckenham and Kinver Forests, officials of the bishop and of the Earl of Warwick among them. A barrel of wine was bought for £3 6s 8d (no small sum) and sent to the Queen.

Business and legal expenses are separately listed, and amount to £44. Priory agents in pursuit of priory affairs had to go to London, Canterbury, Ludlow and York. Pensions (amounting to £25) were paid to some nine or ten clerics with the title of Master, that is with university degrees, who were probably qualified canon lawyers or important cogs in royal or ecclesiastical administration. Finally there was a miscellany of payments, under the title of 'Forinsec', that is 'outside' payments amounting to £151 in all. These included £11, part of the payment of an ecclesiastical tenth to the pope; £10 to the king for Scottish military expenses; pensions to important persons; and some money gifts on a grand scale which look much like bribes, such as £20 to the Archbishop of Canterbury; £26 13s 4d to the Bishop of Worcester; and £10 to the insatiable Hugh Despenser. Money penetrated to the very pores of landowner society, and this when the peasant economy on which these landowners entirely depended was still largely one of subsistence, much affected by the market certainly, but by no means, as yet, completely dominated by it.

For the landlords, therefore, the strict husbanding of their financial resources was more essential than ever during this period of rising costs and increasing financial demands. This is why, all over England, we have evidence of lords and their estate managers reading treatises on estate management, such as Walter of Henley's famous and much re-copied *Husbandry*, and using accounting manuals and pro-formas to attempt to stop the leakage of cash through the peculation of petty officials. No estate owner laid down a more meticulous or stringent set of rules than the Abbot of St Peter's, Gloucester, and his advisers, for these were not simply general precepts, as in Walter of Henley, or in Bishop Robert Grosseteste's rules for the household of the countess of Lincoln. They were specific instructions for concrete situations.

There are two sets of rules, both being included in the main Gloucester Abbey cartulary. They are not dated, but their position in the cartulary suggests that they were compiled some time in the second half of the thirteenth century. The first, the *Constitutio Quaedam*, is principally concerned with the central organization, the second, the *Scriptum Quoddam* with the organization of the manor. It is the *Constitutio Quaedam* which begins with the instructions already mentioned about the payment and issue of all cash *spectans ad communam* through the bursars or receivers in the abbey exchequer. It goes on to lay down the means by which payments are only to be made when the existence of a transaction is proved by the production of a tally, a notched stick which could be split in order to give each of the two parties to a transaction an identical record. It is stated for instance, that the receivers will not pay money to creditors of such obedientiaries as the cellarer, the sub-cellarer or the kitchener, even on the production by the tradesman of a tally, unless the corresponding counter-tally is produced by the obedientiary. Again, it was laid down that buyers on the abbey's behalf, on returning from Bristol or other places where they might have been buying animals, poultry or fish, were to report to the exchequer immediately on return and account for their receipts and expenses. Any buyers who were involved in big purchases such as oxen had to be accompanied by a prudent monk or lay brother as a witness. The system of checking transactions by means of tallies was insisted on from top to bottom of the administrative system, but additionally a further personal check at manorial level was laid down. The cellarer, whenever he visited the manors, was to check on the efficiency of management and to see whether the bailiff was able to exercise discipline over the lower officials. He was to make a close examination of receipts and expenses and to draw up a written *status manerii*, or summary of the current economic position of the whole manor.

The estate economy is looked at from the centre in the *Constitutio Quaedam*. In the *Scriptum Quoddam* there are seventy-five paragraphs, each containing an instruction to the manorial officials, the first instruction being that the reeve was to see that all these instructions were to be read out in his and the hayward's presence, both being presumed illiterate. Twenty-two of the articles were considered to be more important than the rest, because they had to be sworn to by the reeve; the remainder were simply enjoined on him, without oath. There is the same insistence on strict accounting as in the *Constitutio Quaedam*. The reeve was only allowed to use parchment rolls provided by the steward, with the heading already written by the steward or by another clerk whose handwriting was known. There were careful instructions about the choice of permanent farm labourers and concerning labour discipline as applied to all tasks and agricultural operations. Laid down times of work were to be observed; servants who had completed tasks were to be given other work; dairymaids, when their farm work was finished, were not to be allowed to do any of their own work. Other regulations show a keen eye on the way economies could be made. In order to control the amount of hay given to the animals, cords of fixed length to measure the fodder were to be put in the cowshed. The dovecots were to be swept out twice a year and the dung used for the gardens; and these gardens were to be so managed that there was adequate seed for garden vegetables and leeks the following year.

A few of the articles attempted some guidance in technical matters. Enclosure by wall or live hedge was encouraged; manure was to be dug in quickly so as not to be washed away by rain; dung and chaff was to be collected for rotting down in a place in the fields lest harmful grasses should grow in it. But the main emphasis of the articles is preventive. Most of them aim at stopping cheating of one sort or another. In this way, and by the careful use of existing resources, the thirteenth-century landlord aimed to solve his financial problems. Two possible solutions which might have contributed more to the solution of these problems were quite outside current social thinking. The scale of expenditure on hospitality and the maintenance of a following would not be cut down, because this was inseparable from the aristocratic life. Nor would estate profits (even if spared from this other type of expenditure) be re-invested so as to raise the level of production, because neither mental attitudes nor the existing level of technique made it possible to think in these terms.[25]

Just as it would be mistaken to assume a modern attitude to productive investment by medieval estate owners, even when they show a theoretical concern for economy and careful management, it would also be wrong to assume from their attempts to establish an accounting system for their huge cash incomes and expenditures that they always managed to avoid financial difficulties. Increasing royal and papal taxation, and unpredictable fluctuations in the amount of grain, stock and wool available for sale resulted in the indebtedness of all the Worcester Cathedral Priory obedientiaries at the end of the thirteenth and the beginning of the fourteenth centuries. This is partly the explanation for the priory's search for rich parsonages to appropriate and the sale of corrodies for big cash down payments. Bishop Walter Reynolds, whose problems as an estate owner must have been similar to those of the priory, even proposed a general policy overhaul in 1312. Writing from his manor of Alvechurch, to Robert of Clitheroe, his steward, he proposed a policy for an overall increase in rent income.[26] This was to be achieved by the following measures: the improvement and letting out of the wastes, the leasing of outlying or infertile portions of demesne, and a systematic commutation of week works outside the haymaking and harvest seasons. The priory's problems and the bishop's solution were certainly not unique. Their experience shows the other side of the landlords' story: the times of trouble in mid-fourteenth century were not unheralded.

CHAPTER 4

THE PEASANTS AND
THEIR HOLDINGS

The vast majority of the rural population were peasants, that is, members of families who lived by cultivating a holding composed of arable, meadow and pasture land, the bulk of whose product they consumed. This peasant holding was essentially a family concern, however poor or rich the family might be. In other words, although wealthier peasant families might employ one or two hired hands, the essential labour force was derived from within the family. Poorer peasant families, whose land was neither adequate for subsistence nor extensive enough to absorb their labour, worked part-time (or in the case of younger sons full-time) either for their richer neighbours or on the manorial demesne.

The best documents illustrating the day-to-day details of rural life are manorial documents, so we are liable to place the manor and the lord of the manor too much in the centre of the picture. In fact, important though the manorial lord was in the peasant's life, the village and the parish were its real focus. Sometimes manor, village and parish coincided, to the strengthening of all three institutions. More often they did not. Sometimes the lord of the manor was the only great man in the village, and lived there in his manor house. But quite often there was no resident squire even when a lord living elsewhere had manorial rights over tenants. In such case the only class distinctions in the village were among the tenants. Important differences in income certainly distinguished the well-to-do peasant from the almost landless cottager, though the difference in their style of life was less than that which distinguished the peasant class as a whole from the gentry.

In Worcestershire in the 1270s, judging by the subsidy return, more than a third of the villages were without gentry or even without particularly well off residents (and this includes ecclesiastical establishments). According to the 1332 subsidy return for the Kineton Hundred of Warwickshire, in at least a quarter of the villages there were no lay manorial establishments indicating the presence of a resident squire. And, of course, even where the subsidy returns indicate the presence of a manor house and home farm buildings, it would not follow that anybody more important than the lord's bailiff would be living there. The subsidy returns for Gloucestershire of 1327 suggest that perhaps two-thirds of the settlements treated as units for taxation purposes had no resident lay lord. These figures from tax returns are very rough and cannot be assumed to give precise proportions, since the village or hamlet was not always the taxation unit. But they indicate none the less that the presence of the lord was by no means invariable, and perhaps not even a dominating aspect of life in many rural settlements.

The Village and Its Houses

What sort of a setting did the village or hamlet provide for the peasant population? There are no census returns to show us how big the villages were. As we have already stressed, the subsidy returns are very useful in that we have an estimate of the taxpaying population of all the villages in a county in one year, and we can use them to compare one with another. They will give us a rough idea as to which were the big villages and which were the hamlets. But the assessments which were made excluded the exempt poor, and this was a proportion of the total village population which we cannot estimate. Nor can we be certain that the proportion was constant from village to village. The other source which gives the names of the inhabitants of the villages and hamlets are the manorial rentals, but these have defects too. They are only of use in throwing light on the number and character of the village population if the manor and the village coincided, or if in the case of a village with more than one manor we have all of the manorial rentals at the same date, a rare occurrence. Furthermore, while tax returns omit the exempt poor, the rentals omit the sub-tenants.

There is however a document which, while describing only the actual tenants of land, and therefore omitting the entirely landless, does include, as far as we can see, a substantial number of sub-tenants. This is the royal survey of 1279–80 which is usually referred to as the Hundred Rolls. The king had already five years before sent out commissions to enquire throughout the country, hundred by hundred, about usurpations of royal rights and about oppression by royal and private officials. The results of this enquiry are also known as the Hundred Rolls of 1274. The object of the 1279–80 enquiry seems to have been to enquire not only into every lord's holdings and privileges, but also into the holdings and obligations of every tenant down to the smallest cottager. This immense enquiry, if carried out for the whole country, would have utterly dwarfed the Domesday survey of 1086. Unfortunately the returns only survive for a few south-east midland counties. These surveys have all been in print for a century and a half. The enquiry also touched on the west midlands at one point, the central and southern part of Warwickshire, Stoneleigh* and Kineton Hundreds. This part of the survey is still in manuscript.[1]

The information in the Warwickshire Hundred Rolls can be treated with some confidence, if also with some caution. It clearly contains the names of many more country dwellers than the tax returns. Let us, for example, compare the information in it with that which is in the tax returns of 1332. It is unlikely, from what we know in general about population trends, that between 1280 and 1332 the population of Kineton Hundred had dropped much, if at all. For although we suspect a long term proportional decline in the south Warwickshire population as compared with the wooded region around Coventry and further north, the general population increase of the period probably meant that in absolute terms the population in the south was still increasing slightly at the end of the thirteenth century. It is very revealing then that the number of tenants in the Kineton Hundred villages in 1279–80 is very often as much as twice the number of taxpayers in 1332. In other words the Hundred Rolls, as a source, net many more human beings than the tax returns, and this is what we want.

Having satisfied ourselves about the number of tenants, we next have to ask how we can estimate the total population of a village from this figure. The strict scientific answer is that we cannot, because we do not know the number of inhabitants who were not tenants, and we do not know the average number of persons to the household. We must, however, make an attempt, even unsatisfactorily, since for the readers as well as for the writer of this book an

* A subdivision of Knightlow Hundred.

imaginative understanding of the medieval village depends very greatly on a quantitative appreciation. This is bound to have a modern point of reference, such as the contemporary statement that a village is 'a compact grouping of anywhere between a hundred and fifteen hundred people'.[2]

We cannot supply the number of the labourers to supplement our information about tenant households, though many of the village labourers (younger sons perhaps), should be counted in with the tenant households. But we can suggest a figure for the average number of inhabitants of a peasant household. The pioneers of English medieval social history, such as F. W. Maitland, took the figure five. This has been attacked on the basis of elaborate statistics by J. C. Russell who would reduce the multiplier to three and a half. He, however, is not without convincing critics, who in recent investigations are bringing the multiplier up to four and beyond. The complexities of the argument cannot be repeated here, but we shall accept Maitland's multiplier of five, dubious though we may be about the possibility of arriving at a figure for the average number of persons to the household.[3]

If we use this multiplier, then, on the data from the Hundred Rolls for the south Warwickshire hundreds of Stoneleigh and Kineton, we find, as we might expect, that there is a considerable range of village and hamlet sizes. Finham, a hamlet in Stoneleigh parish a few miles south of Coventry, probably had about fifty inhabitants. At Milburn, where there was an abbey grange, there was only one tenant household. Stoneleigh itself, an old established valley settlement, had a population of some four hundred to four hundred and fifty people. Brailes, in the far south of the county not far from the Oxfordshire border, as we have seen, had about five to six hundred inhabitants. Compton Scorpion, a hamlet about seven miles west of Brailes on the way to Chipping Camden only had about thirty to forty people in it, and has since disappeared. Over the whole area covered by the Hundred Rolls, that is from the Oxfordshire boundary up to the suburban manors of Coventry, about forty-five per cent of the villages had populations of roughly 150 to 300 people. Only about ten per cent of places had larger populations, the rest were smaller. But the hundred of Stoneleigh, much of which was covered by the Arden woodland and which was still in the process of settlement, had a higher proportion of small villages and hamlets than there were in the old settled south.

The shape of the village of course varied enormously. Some were clustered around a village green. The Gloucestershire village of Hinton-on-the-Green which once belonged to St Peter's Abbey, Gloucester, preserves this village form not only in its present shape but in its name, in which the element 'Green' can be traced back to the early sixteenth century.[4] Greens form the nucleus of many present-day villages, and may have done so in the middle ages. We must however be wary about assuming that the apparently venerable village with timber framed or old brick houses had, in the middle ages, the street plan which we now see. There was an enormous rebuilding boom between about 1570 and 1640 which involved the replacement of many medieval structures, and which did not necessarily result in a street plan identical to that of the previous period.[5] Furthermore, excavation of medieval villages has shown that there was often a reorientation of houses during the frequent rebuilding that happened in the thirteenth and fourteenth centuries.[6] In other words we cannot expect any visible remains to tell us with any certainty about the nature or location of any structure lying beneath. We can only believe contemporary evidence, whether written or archaeological, and this is rather scarce. Village archaeology is still only in its infancy, and detailed surveys of holdings usually ignore topography, classifying tenants according to status rather than by their position in the village.

Some village forms are indirectly reflected in the documents. Sherborne, a manor and village of the Abbey of Winchcombe, lying a mile to the north of the main road from Oxford to Gloucester which runs across the Cotswolds, is described in a rental of 1362.[7] The tenements are located in the document, some in the 'East End', others in the 'West End' of the village. As it happens he division between east and west ends survives today, the church and the manor house being in between the two ends. But topographical indications in rentals, like this, are rare. There are no west midland rentals comparable with those of the Peterborough Abbey manors (c. 1400) which describe the tenants' houses as they lay along the village streets.[8] In fact, the only topographical indications in the documentary evidence which is at all reliable are not of nucleated village or hamlet settlements, but of the dispersed farm-houses in the woodland regions. A charter of about 1312 for example describes a Feckenham Forest holding in Bentley in the following terms 'a messuage, two thirds of a garden and a croft lying between the Abbot of Bordesley's wood and the lane leading to Hemlokgate, between Henry the Shepherd's land and that of William Attelyze'.[9] This sort of isolated homestead is referred to frequently in the Tardebigge court rolls, and is found in the Arden country as well. But these individual descriptions add up to an impression rather than to a precise picture of settlement patterns.

The only reliable evidence about the physical shape of the villages is archaeological, not documentary. The desertion of villages in the west midlands between the middle of the fourteenth century and the middle of the sixteenth century, without subsequent rebuilding, has left the skeletal remains, sometimes visible without excavation, as they were at the time of desertion. Not many of these have been accurately surveyed, but a number have been photographed from the air. Some of the earthworks are in the low-lying plain and valley clays and gravels where the main building materials were timber, wattle and daub; some are in the Cotswolds where, by the thirteenth and fourteenth centuries, the main material was oolitic limestone. But whether timber villages in the plain or stone villages on the wolds, they have very much the same shape, or perhaps it would be more accurate to say, shapelessness.

The normal village or hamlet does not have the regularity of plan of a place laid out, as a colonizing venture, at one particular moment, like Stratford-on-Avon. Nor does it often give the impression of being built along an existing road. There were village streets, of course. But for the most part they give the appearance of having come into existence after the enclosed crofts and the messuage places had been established and the farm buildings put up, as ways between the crofts. These ways would soon get worn and sunken as people, animals and carts passed along them. Those that were used most to get to the fields and to adjacent villages would be worn the deepest. But whether we examine the plan of Middle Ditchford, a typical clay and timber site just off the Fosse Way near Moreton-in-Marsh, or of Upton near Blockley in the Cotswolds, a typical stone-built settlement, it is impossible to find any element of coherence other than the contiguity of crofts and house sites, more determined as to position by proximity to water than by the convenience of the road system.

If we may picture most of our west midland villages as being composed of houses linked by paths rather than streets, we must not think of the houses as in any way resembling the terraced or detached houses of modern English villages. In the villages of the valleys and plains each peasant family occupied a complex of structures consisting of the dwelling house, the buildings for various animals, the barn and miscellaneous outhouses, but, as we shall see, in the Cotswolds the tendency was for all to be under one single roof. In both cases, the buildings were situated on the plot of land called the messuage which was regarded as the keystone of the whole holding.[10] The messuage was not of course completely covered with buildings, and included the yard where the poultry would wander and where such stacks of hay or grain as were not under cover in the barn would be situated. Beyond, or even surrounding the farm buildings was the croft, an enclosed piece of land, which might in whole or in part be cultivated, by the spade (or by foot as the medieval people said) rather than by the plough.[11]

There were two contrasting types of construction. Over the greater part of the area, timber was the most easily accessible material. The wood most commonly used was oak because of its durability, though elm is occasionally found. The timber was used to provide a framework on which a roof could rest and in whose vertical spaces walls of daub supported by oak or willow rods could be built. The framework was erected according to two different methods, the historical primacy of which is still undecided. The first, common in the west midlands, and considered by some to be the older method, involves the use of crucks. A cruck is the trunk and main branch of a tree trimmed to make a single bent or curved support for both roof and walls. The cruck when shaped and placed on the footings or on the ground cill of the building, branch end downwards, made one half of an arch, the other half of the arch being another trimmed tree and branch. The crucks were used as gable ends, and as intermediate supports for the rest of the framework. As can be imagined, suitable oak trees for making crucks were not all that common, so another means of making gable ends was used which did not involve the use of crucks but of posts, principal rafters and a tie beam. This is known as a truss. Buildings were composed of one or more bays, that is the space between the two gable ends in the case of a one bay house, or in the case of a house with two or more bays the space between gable end and intermediate crucks (or trusses) or between two internal crucks (or trusses). The gable ends and intermediate crucks or trusses were joined together by horizontal members, that is the

94

ground cills, the wall plates and (for the roof) the purlins and the ridge pole, if there was one. The framework was strengthened by timber studs, that is uprights between the ground cill and the wall plate. It was in the panels made by the conjunction of the studs and the horizontal members that the wattle and daub walls were filled.[12]

This timber-frame construction (described here in the most simplified outline) is not found in the Cotswold Hills. Instead we find a different type of building, resulting from the relative scarcity of timber as compared with easily split, easily worked stone. This was the situation already by the thirteenth century, although it is possible that up to the eleventh or twelfth centuries the availability of timber even in the Cotswolds resulted in timber being preferred for house construction. The evidence for this is archaeological and too scanty for certainty. It is certain however that by 1300, the Cotswold peasant house was mainly a stone construction. The evidence for these houses comes mainly from excavation, and from this we can tell that the stone used was the local oolitic limestone which is fissile. The construction of the walls resembles in appearance those of the carefully constructed dry-stone field walls which can be seen in the Cotswolds today. The medieval Cotswolds building walls were however packed with clay for extra firmness and in order to keep out the wind and rain. The walls were only about four or five feet high and there was a steep pitched timber roof, which was thatched, like the roofs of the timber-framed houses. It is true that already in the fourteenth century the manufacture of the famous Snowshill limestone roof slates had begun, but they were costly and used on manorial rather than on peasant buildings.[13]

There is a good deal of evidence about the size of peasant houses in the court rolls of the late fourteenth and fifteenth centuries when the custom had developed, particularly in Worcestershire, of making the construction of a house of determined size a condition for the granting of a holding. This practice is not recorded in the late thirteenth-century court rolls, so we have to take some risks in reading back to that period from evidence taken after the great population decline. It seems that in the timber construction areas in the later middle ages the most common type of peasant dwelling house was one which contained three bays. These make up sixty-six per cent of all cases extant from Worcestershire court rolls. The next most frequent were the two bay houses (twenty-one per cent); then four bay (ten per cent) and finally, at the two ends of the scale, one bay and five bay (one and a half per cent each). There were also court instructions about making barns, the vast majority of which were three bay (twenty-eight out of thirty-five), the rest being four or five bay buildings.[14]

The bay, it will be remembered, is the space between crucks or trusses. The size of the bay varied a good deal, but not many were as long as twenty feet, and not many were as short as eight feet. They were usually about fifteen feet wide. The fact that the manorial courts could give instructions in terms of numbers of bays implies that there must have been from district to district a customarily accepted size, determined partly by habit, partly by the availability of timber, partly by structural possibilities. The key men, of course, in the building of these houses in the timber areas were the carpenters, whose importance in creating the capital resources of society can hardly be overestimated, but is very much neglected.

Very little is known about the country carpenters, especially as early as the thirteenth century. The excellence of the construction of timber-framed buildings, at any rate of those which have survived, better finished in fact than those of the sixteenth century, suggests a professional level of skill of a high order. In other words, these were not amateur jobs. We do not, of course, have any building accounts of peasant houses, only details about the hiring of carpenters for the timber parts of the mainly stone structures of the upper classes. The wording of the accounts suggests that skilled men were sought out by the employers and given a contract for a job, the price including the wages of the labourer as well as of the master. In 1307 for example, the Abbot of Westminster's steward made a contract with a carpenter for seven marks ($£4$ 13s 4d) to build anew a mill called Middle Mill in Pershore. This price did not include the sawing of the 2,325 feet of timber, nor the making of the necessary earthworks. There was no mention of a mate, so the carpenter probably brought and paid his own. When we eventually get sufficient detail about plebeian buildings, in fifteenth-century Stratford-on-Avon, we get the impression that the carpenters who worked in the timber-framed building industry were operating on a regional scale in town and country alike.[15] This would be inevitable since they would not find continuous employment in one place except perhaps in a large town. We have no evidence to show that the fifteenth-century pattern was much different from that of the thirteenth century, but it is unlikely.

The structure of one, two, three, or more bays was repeated in the Cotswolds where the individual rooms of houses, divided off from each other by stone walls, correspond roughly in size to the bays of the timber areas. But in the timber-framed building there was no barrier between bays. This type of timber-framed house is known as the hall-house and in its peasant form is basically the same as the lord's hall. In the middle of the hall there was usually an open fire, but no chimney. These, for peasant houses, were much later innovations. At one end there might have been a platform and a ladder making an open upper room, or solar. At the opposite end there were usually two opposite doors, the cross route between them sometimes being referred to as the screens passage because of the light wooden screens which acted as a protection from draughts for the rest of the hall. The kitchen was usually a lean-to outside the hall, and there seem generally to have been separate buildings for oxen and pigs.

It can be assumed that the number of bays in a house, by which its size was determined, reflected the peasant's economic and even social standing. The family which occupied a three bay house tended to be tenants also of the fifteen to twenty-five acre holding of the middling stratum of village society. It would be the cottagers, poor artisans and hired labourers who would have one and two bay houses. There are few authentic descriptions of such houses, of which we can give two examples. An artisan house at Hunningham in Warwickshire is vaguely sketched in a case which was tried before the itinerant justices in 1306. It was a murder charge against Richard the Wright (some sort of carpenter) who was one day returning home to supper to a 'certain small cottage where he lived' when he was followed by William, the son of Christiana atte Grene, who entered the cottage with a drawn knife with the intention of killing Richard. Richard (so the jury said) wanted to get out, but as there was only one door, and William stood in the way, he had to defend himself. He did this, effectively, by taking a stick, hitting William on the head and killing him. This small cottage with one door was undoubtedly a one bay house. Another such, rather better equipped, is described in the Halesowen court rolls for 1281. On taking over his widowed mother's holding, Thomas Brid, apart from providing her keep, promised to build her an adequate dwelling house (*mansum competentem ad inhabitandum*), the inside measurements to be thirty feet long and fourteen feet wide including the posts. There were to be three new and adequate doors and two windows.[16]

There are very few easily recognizable houses of thirteenth-century date in the west midlands, or elsewhere. This is partly due to the fact that many old houses are disguised by later accretions. There are, however, one or two still standing which give some idea of the peasant's dwelling, which, as we have seen, in late medieval Worcestershire, were mostly of three bays. Noake's Court at Defford near Pershore is a three bay house of cruck construction, of about thirty-seven feet overall length without the added outhouse or 'outshut' at the upper end. The upper and lower bays are about twelve feet and the central bay about fourteen feet long. The width is about eighteen feet. The lower and middle bays were probably open to the roof in the middle ages, only the upper bay having a floored upper room, making a miniature hall structurally comparable with the great halls of the nobility and gentry. The internal height to the apex of the rafters is about eighteen feet.[17] If this was the normal sized dwelling of the yardlander or half-yardlander it can be imagined in what cramped quarters the cottagers lived.

The stone-built Cotswold houses often presented an appearance rather different from those of the villages of the valley and plain. It is true that in many villages, the artisans and smallholders lived in one-room structures comparable with the one or two bay timber-framed houses. But there were special conditions of climate, land use and possibly construction, which led to the presence in the Cotswolds of the 'long houses' which were occupied by the richer peasant families. This type of building is characterized by the presence, under one roof, of both human beings and animals, and has been found since prehistoric times in many upland regions where there was an important stock-raising element in the economy. The Cotswold region, as is well known, was famous in the middle ages for its sheep, and there is evidence, from documents illustrating the manorial home farm, that sheep were kept under cover.[18] Whether the peasants were able to keep their sheep under cover as well is not known, but houses up to one hundred feet long, of which the dwelling portion was rather more than a third of that length, must have been able to accommodate the plough oxen at least, and possibly some sheep as well.

A peasant house of this type has recently been excavated at Upton, a hamlet in the Bishop of Worcester's manor of Blockley which was abandoned in the second half of the fourteenth century and left undisturbed until today. The pottery and other finds in the house suggest a life span of roughly a century from the middle of the thirteenth century. Although it began as a dwelling house about thirty-eight feet long and just over twenty feet wide (outside dimensions), extensions for beasts and storage were added until it was a tripartite structure under one roof about ninety-eight feet long. Before it was abandoned, however, a middle room twenty-eight feet long (inside dimensions) was turned into a courtyard separating the living end from the byre. There are indications that the house was built on an earlier, possibly timber structure. The house may not be entirely of the classic long-house type, since the rooms do not seem to have been intercommunicating. Another. house with which it is roughly in line and which is of similar dimensions is of earlier date and had intercommunicating rooms. Earthworks suggest that many of the other houses in the hamlet were also long houses of this type.

Peasant Chattels

We are naturally in the deepest ignorance about the furnishings of the peasant house. It is not until we have probate inventories in the sixteenth century that there are complete lists in writing of the contents of houses. For earlier periods we have to rely on different sorts of incomplete records which we hope will converge sufficiently to give a complete picture. But as in the case of the house, much of the documentary evidence is of the late fourteenth or fifteenth centuries. Some of it comes from the manorial court rolls and consists of the *principalia* or household chattels which were provided by the lord for the tenant and which had to be returned when the holding lapsed at death. Occasionally other glimpses are given of peasant household goods when we get lists of the confiscated chattels of condemned felons. This written evidence is however incomplete and must be combined with the archaeological evidence from excavations from medieval sites.

An enquiry was made at Broadway, Worcestershire, in 1393, as

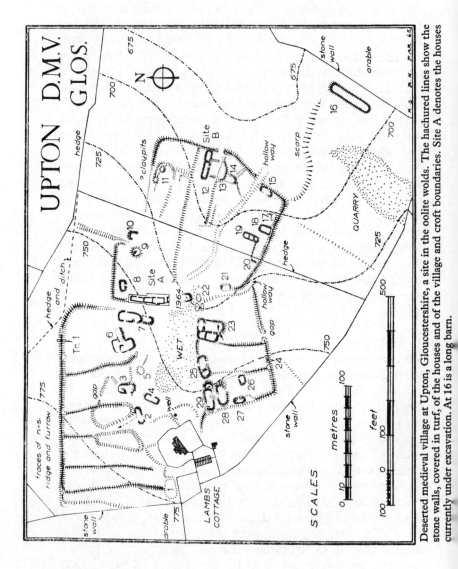

Deserted medieval village at Upton, Gloucestershire, a site in the oolite wolds. The hachured lines show the stone walls, covered in turf, of the houses and of the village and croft boundaries. Site A denotes the houses currently under excavation. At 16 is a long barn.

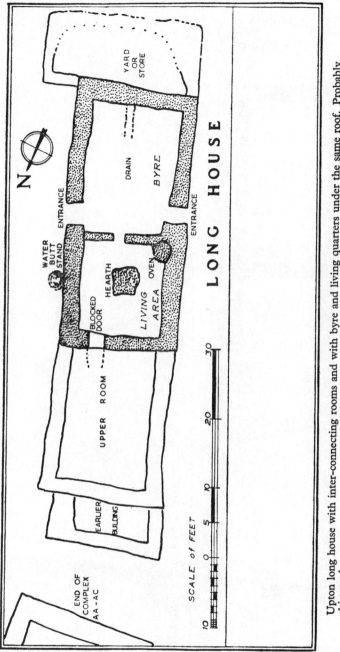

LONG HOUSE

Upton long house with inter-connecting rooms and with byre and living quarters under the same roof. Probably thirteenth century.

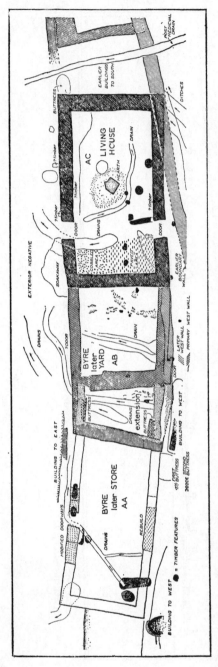

UPTON COURTYARD HOUSE

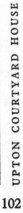

(*Below*) Timber-framed House, Defford.

NOAKE'S COURT, DEFFORD.

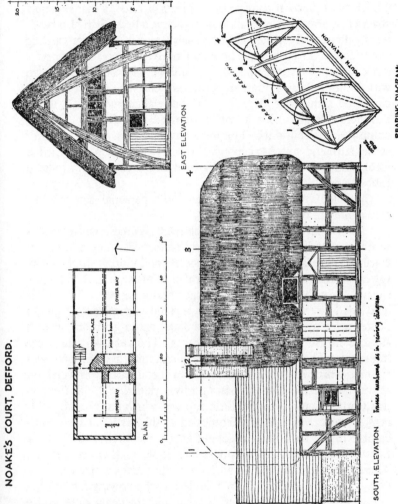

EAST ELEVATION

REARING DIAGRAM

SOUTH ELEVATION Trusses numbered as in rearing diagram

PLAN

HOUSE-PLACE

LOWER BAY

UPPER BAY

inserted beam

M.G.

to the goods and chattels of John Thresscher who had been arrested on suspicion of felony.[19] They consisted of a horse with saddle and harness; a green cloak with a red cloth lining; a striped gown, lined with white woollen cloth and with a hood; a sword and a buckler; a piece of canvas, three pieces of linen, a blanket and a coverlet; a brass pot one gallon in capacity; a brass dish also holding a gallon; a tripod; a spit (? *tourne*); a pair of cards for carding wool: eleven sheepskins; a bow and twelve arrows; a hatchet; a stack (? cap) of straw and fifteen shillings in cash. The woman with whom he was living had two tunics one with a hood, a lined cloak and something illegible. The total valuation was £2 3s 1d, not inconsiderable. But it will be noticed that there is no agricultural stock mentioned. This man may have been a farm labourer as his surname suggests; his woman may have spun and carded wool; and he seems rather well armed, so perhaps he was also a robber, and this was his felony.

The felon's chattels include the most personal things. The *principalia* are by no means personal.

A fairly well-to-do peasant at Wolverley (Worcestershire), at his death in 1346 left the following *principalia*.[20] Farming equipment consisted of a cart, a plough with coulter and plough share, a harrow, a scythe, two axes, a spade, a flail, a mattock, a fork for the sheaves, a bush hook, a gimlet, a sack and a hopper. The household goods were a vat, a little cup, a stand, a brass pot, a pan, a board, a cloth, a chest, a trough, a small vat, a gridiron, an iron stool, a measure and a wooden beam. The relative values are interesting. The most valuable piece of agricultural equipment was the cart, worth 7d. The plough, with the metal parts, was worth 4d as was the harrow. But the brass pot was valued at 2s 6d, the pan was worth 1s, and even the little cup was worth 6d. Not all holdings, however, were as well equipped as this. It is, in fact, comparable to the farm and household goods which vicars of Vale of Evesham churches were supposed to leave to their successors. These were: a plough with all its accoutrements, a fixed oven, a boat, a chest, a spade, a fork, a ladder, a whinnowing fan/sail ?, a brass bowl, a basin and ewer, a table and trestle, a cloth and a towel, a rake and a scythe.[21]

The documentation of the earlier period is very scarce. An enquiry in 1271 reported in an Evesham Abbey cartulary suggests that some tenants could be desperately short of chattels. The enquiry was made in the church at Abbots Salford by the vicar and two other clerics. It followed a discussion at Evesham between the abbot and some of his obedientiaries. The problem concerned the mortuary or payment to the parish church of one of a dead parishioner's chattels. In the case discussed at Abbots Salford, it appeared that a man called Richard Herberd had transferred his land to his son before his death. This was a common occurrence. At the date of transfer his only piece of movable property was a cow worth five shillings. He kept this until he died. His son Robert at the time of the transfer only owned a broken-down (*debilem*) horse which he had bought from his brother for 1s 6d and resold during his father's lifetime for 8d. The jury who were reporting on all this to the committee of clerics said that neither father nor son had made any profit out of any of their goods the whole of their lives, and that the only possible mortuary from Richard's goods that the abbey (as rector) could claim was an overtunic which had in fact already been handed over. However the abbey claimed a half share in the cow, the other half to go as the lord's death duty (heriot).[22]

Worcestershire court rolls contain a lot of lists of *principalia*, mostly rather short. It is interesting to compare the contents of these lists with the normal furnishings of peasant houses which are found during excavation. The chief difference is that brass pots and dishes are hardly ever found on excavated sites, whereas earthenware pottery is hardly ever mentioned in chattel lists, though it is found in enormous quantities on sites. The point is of course that excavations of medieval houses are of sites which have been abandoned and from which, almost certainly, everything of value has been removed, except for broken pots, and lost objects. The pottery which has been found suggests that the bigger peasant households not only had a considerable stock of local coarse ware for everyday use, but finer decorated pottery made at considerable distance, some perhaps even imported. Such wares, and occasional metal objects such as elaborate locks and keys, show that at the end of the thirteenth century even small villages were in touch with the market. Goods of organic material have normally perished, so the lists of confiscated chattels are among our best sources for clothing and wooden furnishings. Other lists suggest that furnishings were very simple, wooden tables, benches and lock-up chests. The poorer and richer households probably differed in the possession of these goods only as to quantity rather than as to quality.

More important than tables and benches was livestock, but unfortunately none of the west midland counties has any of those original tax returns (mostly of the 1290s) listing the taxpayers' stock which was the basis of the subsidy assessment. These are indeed very rare and have only survived for parts of some eastern counties, such as Suffolk and Bedfordshire, for south Wiltshire and for one village in north Wiltshire.[23] The conclusion which can be drawn from them however is no doubt applicable also in the west midlands, that except for a few favoured persons the villages were very much underequipped both as regards draught animals and as regards breeding stock. In those parts for which their figures have survived at least three-quarters of the taxpayers had no more than one draught animal and one cow. Those who were too poor to be taxed almost certainly had no animals at all, except perhaps some poultry, a pig or a sheep. Now the east midlands was a good deal more densely populated than the west midlands and it is possible that the peasants in our area were rather better off than those of Suffolk and Bedfordshire. A list of the chattels of three men who were involved in an affray at Halesowen in 1271 shows that one of them had five oxen, another three and a calf, the third, two cows, and that each of them had some sheep.[24] But it would seem that the wretched men over whose stock the Vale of Evesham clerics were arguing were probably by no means unique in their poverty.

How in this case did they manage to plough their land? All the examples that we have of full plough teams come from the lord's demesne. On Cirencester Abbey's Gloucestershire manors in the thirteenth century the demesne plough teams consisted of ten beasts, whereas in Berkshire and Dorset there were only eight beasts. This may have been due to the hilly country, for Cotswold soils, though stony, are light.[25] A twelfth-century plough team, however, in the heart of the Cotswolds at Hawling had six oxen.[26] On the Worcester church estates, both episcopal and conventual, the normal demesne plough team was eight. Two references will show that this team of eight was certainly the team which actually pulled the plough. In 1290, a tenant ploughman doing his plough boon-work at Minchinhampton was distrained for only ploughing one and a half acres when every plough whether equipped with three or with four pairs of animals (*de iii iugis sive iiii*) ought to plough three acres.[27] In 1367 at Harvington in the Avon valley the reeve was charged in the manor court with ploughing with six instead of with eight oxen, and selling the other two.[28] This does not mean, however, that the individual tenants had a team of six or eight beasts. Both for acquitting their demesne ploughing services and for ploughing their own land they would have to borrow, and indeed provision was frequently made for this in schedules of labour services. At Radway in south Warwickshire just below Edge Hill, four customary tenants were expected to contribute to a plough team, that is providing two beasts each.[29] Co-operation in matters such as this was inevitable in a technically underequipped society.

The livestock for which our region was best known was the sheep. Cotswold wool has become famous, but rather because of investigations into its fifteenth- than into its thirteenth-century history, although these hills were already sheep country early on. The other parts of the region also held sheep on the village open fields and rough pastures. Both the bishop and the cathedral priory of Worcester had flocks on their Avon and Severn valley manors, and in fact none of the considerable wool clip which formed an important part of the income of the Worcester cellarer and chamberlain in the 1280s and 1290s came from Cotswold manors. Those same sheep however almost certainly travelled up to the Cotswold manors for the summer pastures, even if they were shorn and wintered in such places as Cropthorne and Alveston; and as we have seen, Westminster Abbey's Cotswold flocks wintered at Hardwick and Knowle. Here, however, we are concerned with the peasant flocks, as in all other matters much less well documented than those of the demesne.

Our starting point must be outside the west midland region, the assessment for the fifteenth of movable goods of 1225 in south Wiltshire, a region where chalk upland pastures (analogous to the limestone uplands of the Cotswolds) are varied by old settled valley villages. An analysis of this assessment shows that the average number of sheep *per taxpayer* was between one and thirty-six, that is from village to village, according to the prevailing type of husbandry, or an average of fifteen over the whole area.[30] In the village of Minety, seven or eight miles south of Cirencester (once in Gloucestershire, now in Wiltshire), the average according to a return made in 1313 was 13·4. These averages, which would probably differ little in the Cotswolds, conceal great differences between rich and poor tenants. At Minety, two taxpayers who had plenty of livestock of all sorts, also had flocks of sixty sheep each; four had forty each; one man had twenty sheep but no other chattels; fifteen taxpayers had no sheep at all. The median figure was ten.[31] But in spite of the differences they conceal, these average figures nevertheless have a meaning in the context of adequate husbandry practice for the maintenance of the general fertility of the soil. For it must be remembered that important as sheep may have been as providers of wool, milk and meat, they were even more important as distributors of dung, the principal soil fertilizer known to medieval man.

This use of the sheep was well known to west midland farmers in the middle ages. One of the most resented of the lords' privileges was that they tried to make the tenants fold their sheep on the demesne instead of on their own land. A peasant in Minchinhampton who was accused, in 1272, of repeatedly removing his own sheep from the lord's fold back to his own was amerced for doing so.[32] But quarrels about the disposal of the sheep dung were not confined to lords and tenants. It was a matter of dispute between landowners of equal status. For example, a dispute of 1303 between Thomas Lord Berkeley and the abbot of the Cistercian Abbey of Kingswood was settled, by the mediation of friends, to the effect that the abbot was to fold 240 sheep on Berkeley's land at Simondshall between the beginning of May and the beginning of November, allowing only three days off for the shearing. The only conditions on which the abbot was allowed to evade this obligation were, if the rot had eliminated all his sheep at his granges of Edge, Osleworth and Caldecote, or if Lord Berkeley and his tenants between them had more than 800 sheep at Simondshall.[33] The value of manuring land by folding sheep on it was 2s an acre at Temple Guiting in 1327, a cost which the bishop of Hereford (or his land agents) had been willing to pay on sixty acres of demesne.[34] The difference in productivity of manured land and that which was not was measured by Worcester Cathedral Priory in a demesne lease at Wolverley, in north Worcestershire in 1315 to twelve tenants. The tenants had to pay half of the grain produced from manured land, but only a third from that which was not.[35] The reason why manure was treasured was that it was scarce, and it was scarce because of the shortage of animals. It has been calculated that in the area covered by the 1225 Wiltshire subsidy return already quoted, the number of animals per acre of cultivated land was only a quarter of the number per acre in the middle of the nineteenth century.[36]

Some peasant flocks certainly must have been adequate for the mixed pastoral and arable husbandry of the region. A tenant at Minchinhampton was amerced in 1294 for having a hundred sheep in the lord's oats. Three tenants of the cathedral priory were amerced in 1337 at Overbury, on Bredon Hill, for having four hundred sheep on the lord's common;[37] but most amercements of this type in fact concern trespasses with less than a dozen animals of any type. It is of course only possible to estimate the minimum size of peasant flocks and herds from reports of the number of them caught trespassing. However, in view of the shortage of any sort of reliable evidence about peasant livestock, we are bound to use it. And since in some court records, year after year we have this sort of information, the impression it gives is not worthless, particularly if every now and then, as we ought to expect, the larger herds or flocks of the well-to-do make their appearance. Let us quote a typical example. At a manor court of the Abbot of Pershore, held at Hawkesbury near Chipping Sodbury in July 1291, seventeen persons were accused of allowing their animals to trespass in the lord's corn and private woods, the animals being impounded by the manorial hayward. They were as follows: one pig; one horse; two cows; two cows; nineteen sheep; two oxen; eight oxen; six pigs; eight lambs; five lambs; six lambs; three sheep; five lambs; two stots; one horse; one horse. We cannot of course suppose that each man's impounded animals constituted his whole livestock holding. Strictly speaking, the only firm conclusion we can come to is that one man had a flock of at least nineteen sheep; but it is worth mentioning that trespass figures seldom include numbers even as moderate as this.[38]

Even in areas where one would have thought the availability of pasture and its profitability to the lord would have made possible greater individual peasant stock holdings, we have evidence of the same shortages as are revealed by other documents. In the middle of the thirteenth century, a survey, or 'regard' was made of various misdeeds, encroachments and other invasions of royal rights in Feckenham Forest.[39] Among other things, a list was drawn up of men who had put up sheds for animals in the forest. Almost all must have been peasants, though in some cases the persons

reported were big landowners, such as the Bishop and the Prior of
Worcester, the Abbot of Bordesley, the Knights Templar, or local
gentry such as Richard Pauncefot of Bentley. Some of these important persons were shown to be pasturing big flocks and herds. The
bishop of Worcester's encroachments (*purpresture*) from his manor
of Northwick had buildings which housed three plough teams of
oxen, sixteen other draught animals and two hundred sheep; the
prior had a hundred sheep in the forest attached to his manor of
Stoke Prior; the Templars had sixty sheep at their fine new farm
buildings (*pulcram curiam*) at Feckenham. But there are some
hundred and seventy names in all in the return, the total numbers
of various types of animals being as follows: two hundred and
eighty draught beasts (*averia*, oxon or horses); a hundred horses;
twenty-five mares, a hundred and fifty-four oxen; forty cows;
a hundred and thirty-five goats; five hundred and fifty sheep
(including the big flocks mentioned); and a hundred and twenty-
two pigs. The average holding of each person, apart from the big
manorial flocks mentioned, was quite small. No one had more than
three horses, the overwhelming majority had only one each; the
majority of sheep flocks contained less than ten, though there were
in fact only twenty-eight flocks; few people had more than half a
dozen draught animals, the median figure being three; most had
only one cow; the median figure for goats was five; that for pigs
was three. The small numbers of pigs is interesting since this is
often thought of both as a typical forest and a typical peasant's
animal. But in fact, this fits in with other evidence about pigs, such
as manorial presentments for trespass and payments for pannage.
These show that few peasants had more than half a dozen of the
animals. Upper-class persons may, however, have had bigger herds,
lords of manors certainly. In 1330, the parson of Minchinhampton
was accused of a trespass in the seigneurial closes with sixty pigs.[40]

Diet

Even where the pastoral aspect of the west midland economy was
strongly marked, as in the Cotswolds and the Forests of Feckenham and Dean, this was more an aspect of the lord's demesnes than
of the peasant holdings. The medieval peasant was essentially a
cultivator rather than a herdsman. This was inevitable in a rural
economy where the bulk of the product went directly to satisfy the

needs of the producer and his family without being put on the market. What were these subsistence needs, towards the end of the thirteenth century? There can be little doubt that the mass of the population lived primarily on a carbohydrate diet consisting mainly of foodstuffs and drink made from barley and oats. Although the peasants grew wheat, and sometimes even ate some, wheat was primarily grown for sale, so as to pay the rent. In addition, a few peas and beans provided a leguminous element in the diet, which was made tastier principally by the addition of onions and garlic. Although the protein content of the peasant and workman's diet in the fifteenth century may have been fairly high,[41] this was certainly not true in the thirteenth century. Meat and cheese (made from the milk of ewes) were scarce because livestock was scarce. Eggs were probably a more important protein source than either.

How can we know about the daily diet of the masses? No conclusions by analogy from what we know about the feeding habits of lords, or town gildsmen, are permissible. There are however many sources which throw an indirect light on what the peasants ate. First, the court rolls and cartularies include many settlements by sons on their parents when those sons took over the family holding from a failing father. The principal element in these settlements was grain for food. Secondly, farm labourers' wages were largely paid in grain and we have details about these in the demesne grange accounts. Thirdly, some monasteries gave or sold corrodies (as we have seen above) which were in effect old age or disability pensions or annuities. These were often based on ration scales applicable to monastery servants and give an idea of the normal composition of the well-to-do working man's or middling peasant's diet, in kinds of foodstuff, if not in quantity.

The provision for aged parents was even laid down as a general rule for the tenants of Worcester Cathedral Priory. If an heir took over a half-yardland holding with his mother's agreement she was to have three cronns (that is twelve bushels) of rye, one of barley, and a quarter of oats payable yearly between Michaelmas and Christmas. She was to lodge on the holding, but without a kitchen garden (*curtilagium*) to herself because her 'potage' was provided.[42] The normal rate of wages in kind paid to the more important demesne farm servants was a quarter of mixed grains every twelve or thirteen weeks, additional to their money wage. Their money wages at the end of the thirteenth century, in the west midlands were 4s a year, considerably less than the value of the grain liveries. This is more than the widow's provision, of course, for there is no reason to assume that the demesne ploughmen, carters, shepherds and so on were unmarried. Finally this emphasis on the overwhelming part played by the bread grains in the medieval lower-class diet is strengthened by some of the Winchcombe Abbey ration scales embodied in their late thirteenth-century corrodies.

These corrodies varied considerably according to the social status of the corrodian. A woman who had bought herself a somewhat lavish corrody in 1317 for the considerable sum of 140 marks down (£93 6s 8d) got a daily ration of two monk's loaves at the old (pre-1316) weight; a small white loaf; and two gallons of convent ale. Every year she had six pigs, two oxen, twelve cheeses, a hundred stockfish, a thousand herrings, and 24s worth of clothing. But the ration scale for the social class we are considering here is represented rather by that which was given to John of Staunton, reeve of Hazleton. This man in 1317 paid £10 and all of his wordly goods to the abbey and declared his willingness to accept any employment the abbot should choose for him. His rations were: six bushels of grain (three of wheat and three of the manorial livery, i.e. barley or oats), every eight weeks; two mutton carcasses and two pigs a year; pottage with the other abbey servants; and two acres of grain. He was allowed first choice of the two acres, presumably in the manor where he served, should he happen to be appointed reeve; the second choice if he was not. John of Sherborne, to whom we have already referred, in the 1270s was put on the same scale as the middling servants of the abbey, and got one monk's loaf daily, a gallon of beer, and a dish from the abbot's kitchen. This is almost identical with a Worcester Cathedral Priory corrody granted in 1306. But in addition, John got a robe a year like the other middling servants, 6s 8d for linen and shoes, and was allowed two days' board a year for his wife should she visit him. It is worthwhile mentioning that the Winchcombe loaves in question weighed about 2½ lb and that one monk's loaf a day through the year would use some two quarters five to six bushels a year. A more meagre corrody is found at the cathedral priory at Worcester in 1317. It was to be paid to a servant (*gordarius*) who looked after the weir, after his retirement, provided he paid ten marks for it. It was to consist of a weekly allowance of four servants' loaves, six gallons of beer and an allowance from the kitchen which he had during employment, probably a *ferculum* (a dish of mixed pottage).[43]

Even the poorest of the Winchcombe and Worcester corrodies were almost certainly more lavish than the normal peasant or labourer's diet. But even these relatively lavish dietary provisions show a heavy predominance of carbohydrates, for the pottage provided to supplement the bread ration was made mostly of barley or some other grain. The ale, of which vast quantities were drunk, was of course brewed from barley or more likely from oat malt. A diet lacking protein was almost certainly contributory to those high mortality rates of the thirteenth century which are rightly blamed on the undernourishment of the considerable population of smallholders and casual wage labourers.[44]

The Peasant Holding

What then, was the nature of the holding which furnished both the peasants' subsistence needs and the meagre surplus which, after the deduction of tithe, had to be sold in order to pay the rent, taxes, customary dues, court amercements, and to buy those things which could not be made in the household? They varied, of course, considerably within the village and between one part of the region and another. In the Cotswolds, for example, where the soils were light and easily eroded, demesnes and peasant holdings alike tended to be bigger than in the valleys, for the course of husbandry throughout the whole of the middle ages in the Cotswolds required half of the arable area to be fallow in any year. However there were also not a few villages in vale and plain where in the thirteenth century this two-course rotation involving a fifty per cent fallow was also the rule. More important than variations in the size of holding due to soil differences were those which were social in origin.

The holdings of the peasants were almost invariably expressed in yardlands, or in multiples or fractions of yardlands. This is a somewhat elusive thing to define, for it was more than a mere measurement of land, it also embodied a claim to common rights of meadow, pasture, access to woodland and so on. It was a quarter of a hide, which was a measurement of land, common in pre-conquest sources, whose Latin translation was *terra unius familie*. This would be a considerable amount of land, for a thirteenth-century family. But no doubt the *familia* of Anglo-Saxon times, including perhaps retainers and slaves, was bigger than the later peasant family, and in any case the amount of land available was greater. Be that as it may, five-hide estates in the Anglo-Saxon land grants from the west midlands were clearly equivalent in terms of human settlement to a hamlet, and after the conquest, five hides in Worcestershire and Warwickshire was regarded as being equivalent to a knight's fee, the endowment of the mounted warrior.[45] The term 'yardland' reveals that the origin of the unit was in the system of open field cultivation. In theory, if seldom in practice, it was imagined that one quarter of each of the acre parcels which constituted the hide in the open fields would be subtracted to make the separate yardland. Each of the long acre parcels, ideally, was composed of four ridges or lands, and the width of each ridge was a *virga* or yard, the basis in reality of the statute rod, pole or perch of sixteen and a half feet. From the later middle ages onwards, the term 'yardland' could be used as a measure of land whether in the open fields or not, but in the thirteenth-century surveys, the distinction between holdings described as yardlands, or half, or quarter yardlands and those described as so many acres of assarts or as crofts or in any other way, was a distinction between land in the furlongs of the open fields and land recently taken in from the waste and held in severalty.

By the end of the thirteenth century the yardland was the holding of the well-to-do peasant. On the manors of the Bishop of Worcester and of the Berkeley lords round about the year 1300 only a quarter of the tenants occupied a yardland or more. Forty or fifty years earlier the proportion of these better-off tenants on the Gloucester Abbey estates was nearer one-third. The difference in the figures may reflect a process of peasant impoverishment in the second half of the thirteenth century though it may simply result from a different social structure on the Gloucester estates, or even a different method of surveying. Of the remaining three-quarters, or two-thirds, the majority on the Worcester bishopric estates were tenants of half-yardlands, with a very substantial number of small-holders. On the Gloucester and Berkeley estates there were considerably more smallholders than half-yardlanders. But since the half-yardlander was, as we shall show, living on the very edge of subsistence, and the smallholder could only live by being a part-time wage worker or craftsman, it is clear at first glance that the majority of peasants must have lived more like the undernourished masses of contemporary Asia than like the idealized countrymen of Merry England.

What then constituted the yardland or half-yardland? The basic content, as we have implied in our reference to the open field origin of the yardland, was a certain quantity of arable land distributed about the fields. The amount of arable in the yardland varied from place to place, although surveys, describing the holdings in terms of yardlands seldom state its acreage. But medieval estate surveyors were of course aware of the area of the arable in the yardlands. They were also aware of the variations. In the Worcester Priory Register of 1240, the list of items that had to be included in manorial surveys include the question: How many acres make a yardland in various places? (*quot acrae faciunt virgatam secundum diversa loca*), though unfortunately the answer is seldom given. Four centuries later, another estate steward, the historian and topographer, John Smyth of Nibley, on the basis of his study of the ancient charters of the Berkeley family concluded that the yardland was forty acres in 'the ritcher soil of this (Berkeley) hundred; but in the wolds or hilly part thereof, a yardland is somewhat more'. In Warwickshire and Worcestershire, however, the yardland was more commonly between twenty-five and thirty acres. This means that the majority of peasant holdings, as far as their arable component is concerned, contained fewer than fifteen or twenty acres.[46]

Although in the forest areas in particular, there was a certain amount of land held in severalty, the majority of peasant cultivators grew their crops on widely scattered parcels in the open fields. Although this scattering meant that the good, bad and indifferent land might be more fairly distributed than if holdings were consolidated, the distances which necessarily had to be travelled from parcel to parcel must have meant that much time was wasted. One of the reasons why peasants sublet portions of their holdings to each other may have been to avoid dispersal by this method of re-arrangement. We have already given some examples of this scattering in the first chapter. This is how it worked out in the village of Rodmarton in Gloucestershire. A charter of about 1200 transferring a yardland describes it as it was distributed among the furlongs of the fields.[47] There were two main fields: the north and the south fields. Their distribution is perhaps best shown in tabular form.

This Rodmarton holding is, of course, the large Cotswold yard-

| NORTHFIELD | | SOUTHFIELD | |
Furlongs	Parcels (acres)	Furlongs	Parcels (acres)
Capital messuage	2	Warfurlong	1
Putaker	1	Dichecrundle	1½
Between Putaker and		Towards Dichecrundle	1
Hockeburi	3	Hamme	1
On Hockeburi	1½	Hamme	1
Wodewaideslade	1	Midelhulle	1
Towards Wodewaie	1	Nerweslade	1
Bradeberuwe	1	Towards Culkerden	1
Walbercrundle	1	Headland Culkerden	4
Soneberge	1	Portwey	1½
Dune	2	Cattesbrech	1
Muleweye	1	Cattesbrech	1
Muleweye	3	Towards Culkerton Field	1½
Heselhemedene	3	At Culkerton way	1½
Wodhull	2½	By Langeberge way	1
		Crauput	2
		Athethorne	1
		Chestle	1
Total	24	Total	24

land. The fragmentation appears not to be as far advanced as in many cases, but the holding was sufficiently broken up for a special provision to be made in the charter recording the transfer. 'If any acre which is not named here', it states, 'should belong to the said land, let the above mentioned Philip (the grantee) make an enquiry through law-worthy men of the village, and then have it.' The fact was that even parcels as big as those mentioned in the description tended to get lost in the vast patchwork of intermixed holdings. In the case of a transfer of twenty-six 'londes' in Kingshill, near Stoneleigh (Warwickshire) at the beginning of the fourteenth century,[48] where fragmentation had gone much further, such a loss was even more likely.

A holding consisting only of arable land was not viable under medieval conditions. Peasant holdings needed draught animals at least, and draught animals had to be fed. Therefore each peasant holding, in addition to the arable, had a share of meadow land, and of pasture, both on the fallow and on the rough grazing. Meadow

116

TWENTY-SIX 'LONDES' IN KINGSHILL

	Furlong	Parcel (acres)		Furlong	Parcel (acres)
Brook Field	Verinhom	1	Small Field	Huyrn towards Finham Green	2 roods
	Middelfurlong	2 roods			
	Brodemedowe	1 ?		Le Breche	1
	Beselowe	1		Longelont	2 roods
	Portbrug	1½		Sledefurlong	½
	Lowfurlong	1½		Baginton road	1 'bot'
	Scortforlong	2 roods			
	Brocforlong	2 roods	Wood Field	Under Foxenhull	2 roods
	Nethul	2 roods		In the Mor	½
	Bregeyate	½		Above Voxenhul	½
	Brocforlong	1 acre indivisim		Under Voxenhul	2 roods
				Above the Otlont	½
	Brodelont	½		Ruycroft	½
				Blakemor	½

Two entries are missing

was scarce. There were no sown meadows in medieval England, so they were the natural product of rivers and streams. The amount of meadow probably decreased in the thirteenth century, as the amount of ploughed land grew with the increasing population. An acre of meadow was rented at six to ten times the price of arable land, and as may be guessed, the proportion of meadow to arable was much higher in the demesnes than on the peasant holdings. The estate of the bishop of Worcester was, as we have seen, fairly typical of the whole region, being composed of valley, woodland and Cotswold manors. The demesne acreages are all given in the 1299 survey and the meadow was a little more than ten per cent of the whole (i.e. arable plus meadow). The bulk of the pasture was in common, not expressed in acres. If it were possible to calculate the area of pasture, the proportion of meadow to the total area in use would seem even smaller. But this acreage conceals immense variations. At Fladbury, a manor on the river Avon whose documentary history goes back to the eighth century, the meadow was twenty-eight per cent of the whole, whereas at Bibury in the Cotswolds it was rather under two per cent. These low meadow acreages were characteristic of the Cotswolds.

In the extents where peasant holdings are described as a quarter, a half or a full yardland, it is tempting to assume that, just as, without it necessarily being mentioned there, the yardland had pasture rights attached, so it must have had rights in the meadows. But this is not necessarily so. It is clear that in upland villages where there was a great shortage of meadow, many holdings must have had no meadow. What did they do for hay in this case? They bought it, usually from the lord, and usually as it grew, so that the purchaser had to mow it himself. 'Sales of herbage', as they were called in the manorial accounts, were therefore hardly distinguishable from short-term leases of grassland. However the lord also sold cut hay, mown, prepared and stacked by his servants and customary tenants. The early fourteenth-century extents of some of the Berkeley estates tell us how many acres of arable were in the tenants' yardlands and indicate that some meadow was also included; but we are not told how much. Mathilda at Yate, a tenant of half a yardland at Cam has twenty acres of arable, 'and meadow'. William Colewick, a tenant at Bradley, has a yardland which 'contains sixty acres of arable and meadow'. However in the case of some of the freeholdings, the amount of meadow is stated. Of the sixty-two free tenants at Cam, seven are listed as tenants of meadow land but only one, with one and a half acres, had more than an acre. Only nineteen of the tenants hold yardlands, or fractions or multiples thereof, which might have had meadow included. Thirty-six of the free tenants, in other words, were holding arable only. The demesne meadow, however, was twelve per cent of the total demesne acreage.[49] The 1240 Register of Worcester Cathedral Priory conveys the same impression. Holdings are described in terms of yardlands, occasionally a tenant also takes a small piece of meadow, but references to other than demesne meadow occur very seldom. It is only the occasional charter which describes the meadow component in a holding. Such a one comes from the Register (in the English language of the original) of the nunnery of Godstow near Oxford. It describes a holding at Meysy Hampton in Gloucestershire, round about the year 1300.[50] There was a messuage, a croft, thirteen acres of arable and an acre of meadow. The many similar charters which describe holdings without mentioning any meadow throw this particular description into relief. And yet the meadow is less than ten per cent of the total area of this holding, not counting pasture in the total.

The most important source of animal feed for the thirteenth-century peasant was not hay but the grazing rights which he had as a member of the community of settlers. These took two forms. First, the peasant's animals were allowed access to the meadows after the hay had been cut, and to the arable after the corn had been reaped. Both meadow and arable were privately appropriated in parcels until the moment that the crop was garnered, but then the private appropriation of arable parcels and of 'doles' of meadow was temporarily suspended, the fields and meadows became common and the animals of the commoners were put to graze in proportion to the size of their arable holding. Second, there was always more or less rough grazing on the common wastes of the village, that is such land as, for various reasons, was not put under the plough or kept as meadow. These common wastes suffered a good deal of encroachment in the twelfth and thirteenth centuries by both peasant and demesne plough teams, although their importance as pastures was fully realized by all parties. Scarcity produces restriction and definition and consequently we have written evidence of attempts to control the number of animals that tenants were allowed to put in the commons. The need to restrict pasture according to the size of the holding is, in fact, explicitly referred to in a Gloucester Abbey Cotswold (Coln St Aldwyn) charter of c. 1264.[51]

We have already referred to a holding in Meysy Hampton in connection with its meadow land. The charter which tells us about its thirteen acres of arable and one acre of meadow also states the number of animals from the holding which were allowed to use the common pastures. These were, four beasts (draught oxen), one horse and thirty sheep, an indication of the number of animals expected on such a holding, but, as we have seen, a maximum rather than a probable figure. For the Cotswolds this is not an over-generous stint. At Staunton, near the Corse Wood, in the Severn valley a yardland's share in the common pastures of both wood and open land was sixty sheep, eight oxen, four cows and pigs and goats without limit of numbers. This relative lack of restriction is clearly related to the abundance of adjacent woodland, and is paralleled elsewhere in the wooded parts of the region. In the Forests of Dean and Feckenham, men of the forest villages had almost unrestricted rights of pasture, sometimes with, sometimes without payment. Lands granted to the Abbey of Bordesley in the Arden country during the same period (mid-thirteenth century) show a high stint in relation to the amount of land granted, such as pasture for 360 sheep with the twenty acres of assart at Bearley (between Stratford and Warwick); for six-hundred sheep with a couple of furlongs between Barford and Tachbrook; for 240 sheep with eleven acres at Songar between Bearley and Wolverton. But the donors were well-to-do free men rather than poor or middling peasants, so these figures are only indicative of woodland conditions in general.[52]

Common pasture rights were not the only needs satisfied by the waste and the wood. Peasant communities also needed material for fencing their enclosed fields, for making and repairing timber buildings and for firewood. These were the common rights, rather than pasture, which were at issue in an inquiry at Stoneleigh (Warwickshire) in 1273. The sworn jury said that certain ancient tenures in Stoneleigh had the following rights in Stoneleigh wood, except within enclosures, game reserves and piggeries: enough thorn and oak branches for fencing between Martinmas and Easter to last for two years, and dead wood for domestic fires, for baking and brewing.[53] This right to firewood and wood for fencing was known as the right of *estover* and naturally the owners of woods attempted to control access in order to conserve the wooded cover. The main problem however, with regard to the preservation of woodland as of any other sort of pasture, was the encroachment of the plough to which we have referred many times, and which presented a problem in the relatively well-wooded west midlands as it did elsewhere.

The pasture that was available for the village livestock on the common wastes clearly varied greatly in extent from village to village, and (according to the progress of the assarting movement) from time to time. It is unlikely that the animals found much keep on the stubble and weeds of the fallow field: they were put there rather for what they could give in the way of dung than for what they could get. The keep would be better on the mown meadows after Lammas (1 August), but would not be available for long, if, as often happened, there was a second cutting. On the rough grazing and in the woods the winter keep would be extremely thin for pigs and sheep and hardly possible for bigger animals. On the demesnes, animals were stall fed with hay, oats, peas and beans. Even here extreme care had to be taken. 'No useless animals', says the Gloucester Abbey *Scriptum Quoddam*, 'are to be wintered on hay and forage', the definition of useful and deserving animals being the plough oxen and the breeding cows. And as we have seen, the hay was measured out parsimoniously by binding cords of fixed length in each byre.[54]

Even at the meagre rate of a bushel of oats per ox every three weeks (as recommended by Walter of Henley),[55] this would make serious inroads into the peasant household's reserves of grain. Great variations in the rate of feeding animals are shown on Knowle manor home farm in 1301. Some thirty draught animals, mostly oxen, were given only one-third of a bushel every three weeks, whereas two cart horses who were doing heavy work carrying timber and stone were given half a bushel of oats a night between them.[56] If, as on some demesne farms, they fed their sheep with cakes made from peas, and their lambs with beer or milk, human beings would literally be sacrificed to beasts. In fact, the peasants must have been unable to keep the same standard of winter feed for animals as did the lords, and therefore they were obliged to keep the number of their livestock to the minimum we have already noticed. This would happen without recourse to the legendary autumn slaughter of stock, for which there is no evidence.

There is no certain way of calculating the real budget of the medieval peasant, since, although we can get some idea of the expenses of the average household we have no direct evidence of the income. We say 'average', meaning the half-yardlander, but in fact innumerable factors from village to village and from region to region must make the very concept of an average almost meaningless. Variations in the fertility of the soil, in the number of working hands, in opportunities for supplementary income by sales of poultry or other small livestock, in opportunities to earn extra money by day labour or by engaging in some craft, are infinite and untraceable. There were, however, certain basic features of the income-producing factors on the holding which are worth considering when estimating the peasant standard of living. The amount of arable land that the solid core of peasant households possessed in the manors of the estates of the bishop or cathedral priory of Worcester, or of the major Benedictine abbeys of the Avon and Severn valleys, or of the principal lay landowners, such as Beauchamp or Berkeley, is well enough known. It was about half a yardland, or about fifteen acres in the vale, or twenty to twenty-five acres in the less productive Cotswolds.

It is quite feasible, and permissible as an exercise of the historical imagination, to take such a household and its holding. We will select a half-yardlander at Kempsey in 1299. This was a manor on the Bishop of Worcester's estate, about four miles due south of Worcester on the banks of the river Severn, an anciently settled part of the diocese of Worcester, but one in which nevertheless there had been a considerable expansion of cultivation in the twelfth century. In 1190 the king had pardoned the bishop for assarting 160 acres (the large forest acre) or roughly 240 statute acres. These were probably demesne assarts, but the survey of 1182 shows that tenants were assarting too. This expansion is likely to have continued in the thirteenth century; the number of small-holders, for example, nearly tripled between 1182 and 1299. By the end of the thirteenth century, in fact, the majority of tenants were, according to the extent at any rate, holding half a yardland or less.[57]

What was this half-yardland? Unfortunately, the acreage of these holdings is given only sporadically, whether on the bishop's estate or on the estate of the cathedral priory. In the 1182 survey of the bishop's estate, the few examples seem to have a fiscal rather than a real agricultural meaning. The acreage of a yardland simply does not appear in the 1299 survey. But judging by the fuller data of the 1240 survey of the priory estate, it seems safe to assume a yardland of about thirty acres. Now in estimating the annual pro-duction of a holding we need to know how much land was kept fallow each year, and in the absence of detailed manorial accounts this is difficult enough for the demesne, let alone the peasant hold-ings. However the bishop's survey states that at Kempsey, as indeed in most villages of the west midlands at this time, the arable was divided into two fields. One of these fields was called the wheat field, but was also sown with oats; the other, the rye field, could also be sown with barley, peas or vetch. This is clearly not a description of the rotation system, but an indication of the most fitting grains for the soil of either field. The fact that both winter and spring crops were grown on either field, and that there were only two main fields, suggests that half the arable was left fallow each year. A half-yardlander would therefore only have about eight of his acres under crop each year.

Yields, even on the better equipped demesnes, were normally very low at this period, seldom exceeding five times the seed sown. On peasant holdings an average yield of three to four is much more likely. If our Kempsey half-yardlander produced a crop of wheat, rye and barley on his eight acres, and fed himself and a family of three (after having paid the parson his tithe), he might have enough left to sell for 12s or 13s, at the average prices obtaining at that period. His rent was 5s in money and labour services valued at 10s 6d, so if he had to pay all his obligations in cash, as was done for instance during the vacancy of the see three years after the compilation of the 1299 rental, his grain sales would be insufficient to cover him. Furthermore, he would have other cash needs. He would almost certainly be amerced or fined in the manor court; he might be contributing to the Parliamentary subsidies of 1297 and 1301; he might well need to buy things which he could not make in the Worcester market. His cash income therefore would have to be made up in ways impossible for us to guess at—sales of poultry or wool, the earnings of a wife or daughter spinning or of a son working as a hired labourer. But if we assume, as we are entitled to do, that the main marketable asset was his grain, he must usually have been on the edge of destitution and must often have reduced his family's subsistence in order to sell more of his product for the money he needed to pay to the lord and others.

If our Kempsey half-yardlander had been a free tenant he might well have had much the same income, but his outgoings would have been considerably smaller. In particular he would only have had a money rent of 5s a year to pay. Nor would he have had to suffer the disadvantages of the legal condition of villeinage which was the lot of the majority of the peasants of the west midlands. Hitherto we have distinguished peasant households only according to the size of their holding in the village fields. Now we must consider peasants in relation, not to the natural unit of settlement and work, the village, but in relation to the unit of overlordship and jurisdiction, the manor. For it was the manorial system which produced the legal, as distinct from the purely economic distinction between one villager and the next.

CHAPTER 5

THE PEASANTS AND
THE MANOR

The manor was the organization through which the lords, on whichever rung of the tenurial ladder they might be, ensured the flow of income, partly from the demesne, partly from the tenants. The rents paid by the tenants could be in money, in kind or in the form of labour services. The tenants themselves could be free men holding freely, free men holding customary tenures, villein tenants holding either free or customary tenures and cottagers of both free and villein status. We have already sketched this pattern in outline,* but manorial organization must now be described in more detail.

The manor has been thought of as being virtually identical with, or at least a special aspect of, the village itself. This was sometimes, but by no means always, true. There were parts of England where it was hardly ever true. In the north of England the manor was normally a sort of confederation of hamlets unified by the jurisdiction of the lord, whose interest was in the tenants' rents rather than in the demesne. In East Anglia, the fragmentation of overlordship had gone so far that most villages had several manorial lords. It was the midlands that was usually thought to be the region par excellence of the 'typical' manor whose boundaries coincided with those of the village. But those parts of our region where the documentation allows us to estimate the relationship between manor and village clearly do not fall into this category of typicality. The Hundred Rolls of 1280 are the best possible source for solving this particular problem since they were drawn up village by village, but aimed to describe the manorial layout.[1] As we have already shown, they are unhappily only extant for the south and central Warwick-

* Chapter 3, pp. 65-6.

shire hundreds of Stoneleigh and Kineton. Fortunately these two hundreds include parts both of the anciently settled and manorialized Felden country south of the Avon, and of the Arden country of the upper Avon valley and to the north. Out of ninety-five villages, village and manor coincided in only forty-five. For other counties we can often get something of an impression of the number of lords to a village (though less precise than from the Hundred Rolls) from the *Nomina Villarum* of 1316, a list drawn up following a promise by the knights and barons of Parliament that a foot-soldier would be provided from every village in the kingdom for the war against the Scots. In addition to the names of the villages, the names of the lords of the village are given. The returns that were made for some counties are very full of this information. The returns for the county of Northampton are an example. Unfortunately, however, the value of the returns varies from county to county, probably according to the diligence of local officials. That for Warwickshire, showing only three villages out of forty in Kineton Hundred with more than one lord is clearly valueless, for its falsity is revealed by checking it against the Hundred Rolls. There is no return extant for Worcestershire, but there is for Gloucestershire. This clearly does not give a true picture of the villages and their lords in the county. It underestimates the total number of villages, as well as the number of lords in each village. In the 1334 tax return 425 places are named, but the *Nomina Villarum* gives only 212. This is because many hamlets, many of which were sub-manors, are included in the main village. However, this means that the number of villages containing more than one manor is probably underestimated. Even so, this inadequate return gives ninety-seven out of the 212 villages where there was more than one manorial lord.[2]

The *Nomina Villarum* cannot of course provide the same insight into the complexities of manorial structure which we can only see from the Hundred Rolls. No better example of this complexity could be given than the village of Harbury, five miles south-east of Leamington. In 1280 there were six manorial lords in the village, the Cistercian Abbot of Combe, the Augustinian Prior of Kenilworth, the Master of the Knights of the Temple, the Benedictine Prioress of Nuneaton and two lay lords, Eustace of Hethe and Geoffrey fitz Otto. In addition to these six who are designated as 'lords', there were three others who were in fact 'lords', Robert of

Ladbroke, Hugh of Charneles and the Hospitallers of Grafton. There were six demesnes described as such, belonging to the Abbot of Combe (about two hundred acres), the Prior of Kenilworth (about a hundred and fifty acres), the Master of the Temple (about sixty acres), Hugh of Charneles (a hundred acres), Eustace of Hethe (three hundred acres), and Robert of Ladbroke (sixty acres), but in addition Geoffrey fitz Otto had about two hundred and fifty acres in hand, not leased out to tenants, and which were in fact probably in demesne.

If the presence of these lords with their demesnes must have caused some confusion in the Harbury village community, this was undoubtedly made worse by the tenurial structure. The Prior of Kenilworth not only had his own demesne and free and servile tenants (the latter owing some labour services) but he was himself the undertenant of three of the other lords for a third of his demesne and fifteen out of his twenty-five tenants. Hugh of Charneles, who had four servile tenants as well as his demesne of a hundred acres, was the sub-tenant of the Master of the Temple for the lot. Robert of Ladbrook had a demesne, but no tenants. The Prioress of Nuneaton had tenants but no demesne. By contrast the adjacent manor of Bishops Itchington had a simple structure. The only lord was the Bishop of Coventry and Lichfield. He had a demesne of some five to six hundred acres, and seventy-five tenants. Most of these tenants were of villein or servile status. There were twelve yardlanders, thirty-five half-yardlanders and a tenant of a quarter yardland. All except ten owed fairly heavy labour services, that is three days a week on the bishop's demesne as well as seasonal labour. The other ten only owed seasonal works. The sixteen cottagers were all free tenants, and there were also eight more substantial free tenants of yardlands. Most of their rent was money, but they also owed a few seasonal labour services. There were four free sub-tenants. The only aspect of the village's manorial structure which was at all unusual was that the parish church itself was well enough endowed to have a minor manorial organization of its own, consisting of a demesne of a hundred acres and eight free tenants, who owed no labour services.[3]

Evidently the relations between lords and tenants must have been rather different in these two neighbouring villages. The bailiff or reeve at Bishops Itchington may very well, at this time, have organized the cultivation of the demesne mainly by full-time servants, but he could call on substantial reserves of servile labour at harvest or haymaking. One demesne would be matched by one manor court, the organ of seigneurial control which nevertheless from another aspect was the assembly of the whole village. In Harbury there were sixty-seven free tenants to fifty-one servile tenants, and if these serfs had ever owed week work it had by this time been commuted. None of the unfree tenants here owed any other than seasonal works. It seems pretty clear that the demesnes in this village must have been worked almost entirely by wage labour. In any case the obvious fragmentation of authority would have made it difficult to maintain labour discipline through the manorial courts, such as they were.

The west midland evidence generally supports the conclusions of E. A. Kosminsky that the large manor, usually part of an old-established estate, which coincided with the village area, tended to have the highest proportion of servile tenants, with the greatest labour service element in their total rent obligations. On the whole, the type of manorial organization which we saw at Bishops Itchington, is repeated, with variations of course, on the principal manors of the old ecclesiastical estates further west in the Avon and Severn valleys. The other type of organization is found most particularly in newer settled areas, like Feckenham Forest, and on estates of knights and the bigger freeholders. But since it was the old estates which dominated the life of the region, especially in its central and western parts, it was their characteristic social structure which gave the west midlands its special stamp.

Peasant Status

By the end of the thirteenth century, the customary tenants of the manor had become universally regarded in the eyes of the law as of unfree status.[4] The process by which they were reduced to this condition was complex, and was not accomplished without considerable resistance by the tenants. It is not easy to trace the stages of enserfment and the task is made more difficult because of the fluid nature of medieval social terminology. For example, it is from the word villein, Latin *villanus*, that we have the word villeinage, normally taken as the English equivalent of serfdom in the thirteenth century. Yet in an early twelfth-century law code, the *Leges Henrici Primi*, the word *villanus* is equated with the Old English *ceorl* with a specific statement that villeins or ceorls were free. *Villanus* of course comes from the word 'villa' or 'villata' and originally meant simple 'villager'. The twelfth-century west midland surveys are full of different terms for peasant tenants which were descriptive simply of the type of holding which the tenant held or of his function. In the surveys of the manors of Minchinhampton and Avening belonging to the nuns of Caen and of the manors of Evesham Abbey, a certain category of smallholder is referred to as *bordarius*, a word of Norman-French origin which was used in Domesday Book and means much the same as cottager. In the same two surveys there were also cottagers, or *cotres, coteri*. At Minchinhampton, on the Evesham estate and on the Bishop of Worcester's manors there were *bubulci* and *bovarii* that is, oxherds, or possibly ploughmen. There were *bercharii* (shepherds) and *porcharii* (swineherds) on the Evesham manors. On the Worcester bishopric manors there were *arkmen* or *avercmen* who also seem to have been ploughmen. These functional names were given to tenants because they were holding their land in return for services as ploughmen, shepherds, swineherds and so on. At Minchinhampton the word *operarius* (workman) was used for a substantial number of the tenants, and simply meant that the principal rent for their holdings was work (*opus*) in the lord's demesne. The word *villanus*, is found only at Minchinhampton in the west midland surveys of the twelfth century, but we find an even more socially neutral word *rusticus*, that is, countryman, on the Evesham and the Worcester bishopric manors. On the manors of the knights of the Temple the tenants are simply called *homines* (men), as are some of the Minchinhampton tenants. In fact the only terms applied to tenants which in themselves undoubtedly imply unfree status are found in the Minchinhampton surveys: *servi, ancillae, mulieres serviles*, all originally meaning 'slaves', and applied in the surveys to a minute proportion of the peasant population.

This terminology which in itself does not imply servility continues to be employed in the thirteenth century. The only change of significance is in the Hundred Rolls, a document of royal, not seigneurial, origin. Here, the word *servus* is commonly used where the manorial surveys would use *villanus* or *custumarius*. But between the first group of surveys, datable between about 1150 and 1185, and those of the second half of the thirteenth century it had become accepted legal doctrine, based on the precedent of a large number of cases fought in the courts, that the customary tenant, whether he was called villein, rustic or peasant (*peisaunt*),[5] was unfree. This meant that he had no recourse at law against his lord in any court but the lord's manor court; that he could not leave his holding without permission; that he could not sell livestock without permission; that he must get permission and pay a fine to give his daughter in marriage; and that he might be tallaged (that is taxed) by the lord at will. These were the principal consequences of unfree status. But there were other aspects, not so much of unfree personal status, as of the unfree tenure of land, which were just as important, and which tended to become tests of personal status even though they had not originally necessarily been connected with it. The most important of these aspects of unfree tenure was the performance of heavy labour service as part of rent.

Before looking more closely at those conditions of unfree tenure which were so important in villages where the old estate organization was entrenched, we must draw attention to the fact that even here free tenure was by no means extinct. Even if we did not have the lists of estate tenants, the great number of free charter witnesses in the monastic cartularies would emphasize their presence. The majority of the witnesses to the thousands of thirteenth-century charters were men who simply because they were valid witnesses, must have been of free status, though never aspirants to knighthood. The free men were of as varied origins as the customary tenants we have been discussing. Some of them had just managed to escape the net which brought the majority of the customary tenants into serfdom, by arranging an early commutation of their labour services. Some held fractions of knights' fees by military tenure, even though never rendering military service. Some were smallholders who may well have come recently from other areas as settlers, especially since, in parts of the west midlands, there was a relative abundance of uncultivated land. Others had very ancient roots in the district, and were of considerable local social importance.

In an agreement dated 1296 between the Bishop of Worcester and the Prior of Kenilworth concerning suit to the bishop's hundred court of Pathlow with respect to priory lands in Loxley (Warwickshire), the man who was assigned to do this suit, in the words of the agreement, was 'commonly called a Rodknyt'. This term appears in Domesday Book and in some later documents, usually applied to tenants of sizeable holdings. The word 'radman' is sometimes used with the same meaning. The two terms are found most frequently in the diocese of Worcester. At the end of the twelfth century they are still to be found in Fladbury, Ripple and Hanbury (Worcestershire), and two radmen's holdings on the bishop's estate were converted into small military tenures in the middle of the century, one at Gotherington (Gloucestershire) and one at Tredington (Worcestershire). In the same century, Roger of Gloucester, among other benefactions, gave as tenants to Gloucester Abbey two 'rodknyztes' living in Coln Rogers (Gloucestershire). The name suggests some connection with Bishop Oswald's famous leases to members of his retinue in the second half of the tenth century for, among other things, riding services. Some cathedral free tenants at Hallow, Grimley and Charlton (Worcestershire) in the 1240 register owed riding services (*equitatura*). In an eleventh-century law code the radknights were given a status classification intermediate between free and noble, as 'sixhyndmen'. The type of tenant, however, by the thirteenth century, is more frequent than the name, which was by then an archaic relic. But in many villages on the Worcester bishopric or the Gloucester abbey estate there were free tenants with holdings of fifty acres and more, whose main if not only conditions of tenure were suit of court to the hundred on the lord's behalf. Some examples from the Cotswold manors of the Abbot of Gloucester illustrate the type.[6]

In Aldsworth, near Burford, where there were twenty-seven ordinary servile holdings and four cottages, we find three families settled on holdings of half a hide (or ninety-six acres) each, paying low money rents that bore little relation to the actual area of the holding, and with special services of an 'honorable' character. These included suit to the abbey's 'free court of Gloucester' as well as to the local hall moot, and the payment to the lord of the military heriot (or death duty) in the form of armour, as contrasted with an ordinary peasant heriot of the best farm animal. In the neighbouring village of Eastleach, besides the thirty odd average-size peasant holdings there were again three large free tenements, two of ninety-six acres and one of nearly two hundred acres. Money rent, a commuted hunting service and attendance at the hall moot were their principal obligations, but one of them also attended the Cirencester Hundred court on behalf of the Abbot of Gloucester as well as attending the abbey free court.[7]

On the other hand, the poorest people in the village were often free men. Cottagers (both free and villein) were sometimes more numerous than the peasants with holdings adequate for family subsistence. In south Warwickshire a third of the peasants were cottagers, and two-thirds of these cottagers were of free status. These smallholdings were by no means uniform in type. One would naturally expect lack of uniformity amongst a class of squatters composed of wanderers from other parts of the country, younger sons, craftsmen and others who had perhaps known better days. More than half of the holdings in the Bishop of Worcester's big manor of Kempsey, on the banks of the Severn, were smallholdings of one sort and another. Some were mere 'curtilages', that is yards or gardens attached to a cottage; some were 'forlands', odd pieces of land in the fields which did not fit into the strips of the furlongs; and in some cases the holding consisted of four or five acres in the open fields. The names attached to some of the odd smallholdings indicate how their tenants tried to live. Some were known as 'gooselands' and others as 'swinelands', the rents being originally in kind to swell the bishop's larder with poultry and pork. By 1299, these smallholdings were not all in the possession of smallholders. Some of the richer peasants were taking them on lease, either to increase their own holdings, or (in the case of cottages) to provide accommodation for members of their own family or for hired men. Some of these smallholders were certainly of servile status, but many (as in south Warwickshire) must have been free.[8]

The Burden of Labour Service

The estate of the Benedictine abbey of St Peter's, Gloucester, had manors in Gloucestershire and Wiltshire, in vale, wold and forest. They were surveyed by the cellarer, R. of Sandhurst and Thomas of Tyringhame, prior of the daughter house of Stanley in Wiltshire, in 1266 and 1267. The demesnes of the two Wiltshire manors Littleton and Linkenholt are described but for some reason not stated, the Gloucestershire demesnes are not. The services of the tenants however were set down in detail. The reason for making this particular survey is not known. It may simply have been to enable auditors to check accounts; it was possibly part of a general financial overhaul at the beginning of the abbacy of Reginald of Homme (1263–84) who found a debt of 1,500 marks at his accession. It may have had the same object as an estate survey made in 1251 by Richard of Clare, Earl of Gloucester, at the same time as he was trying to raise money from his military tenants. This survey was sufficiently remarkable to have been noticed by the Tewkesbury Abbey chronicler who said that the earl had an estimate made of the land in villeinage, and an annual money valuation of the services, *ad maximum detrimentum possidentium*.[9] The services and customs that were demanded from tenants on the abbey estate had a basic similarity from manor to manor, as indeed did those on other estates, indicating a rationalizing pressure by the estate administration. Let us take as an example the rents and services in the manor of Buckland in the Avon valley at the foot of the Cotswold Hills, about six miles south of Evesham. The manor was one of a group of manors which formed the endowment of the abbey chamberlain, all near to each other, the others being Clifford Chambers near Stratford-on-Avon, Hinton-on-the-Green between Buckland and Evesham, and Guiting up on the wold. The tenancies at Buckland consisted of thirty yardlands (containing thirty-six acres of arable) held by single tenants; seven yardlands, each held by two partners; and some twenty-three smallholdings. It cannot be assumed of course that the actual occupiers of the whole of each holding were the actual tenants, in view of the widespread habit of sub-letting and other forms of illegal or semi-legal peasant interchange. But the rent burden on the holding of course remained, whatever unofficial redistribution had taken place.

The services of the individual yardland were divided into two sections, those to be performed between the end of one harvest and the beginning of the next (29 September to 1 August) and the autumn works themselves, which were of course the heaviest. With few exceptions all the works were valued. The first set of works to be specified in the first section were the general week works, known as manual works. Four days' work, every other week, by one man valued at $\frac{1}{2}$d a day were required. Then came the specialized works, only some of which were included in the manual works. First, the ploughing, one acre of demesne land at the winter ploughing, for the winter sowing; one acre at the spring ploughing, for the spring sowing; and two acres of fallow, to kill the weeds and air the ground. This amount of ploughing service would not of course be sufficient for the whole demesne but there were four demesne plough teams working, each with ten oxen and one spare. The whole of the ploughing done by the yardlander was valued at 20d (5d an acre). There were next various works suitable for the season after the harvest. These included three forms of threshing service. If instructed, the tenant had to thresh two bushels of wheat, peas, beans or barley or four bushels of oats. These presumably were the grains normally grown on the demesne. Next, it seems that the abbot was expected to visit the manor three times a year, and the yardlanders had to thresh in anticipation of this visit. This threshing was valued at 1½d, whereas the valuation of the first threshing works was omitted. Then the yardlanders threshed two bushels of seed wheat, the work being valued at ½d. Carrying the stacks of corn into the barn when necessary was valued at 2d.

Hoeing had to be done in the demesne corn for six days (½d a day), but any additional hoeing counted among the manual works. When the sheep were shorn, the yardlander had to help with the washing and shearing for two days (½d a day). Then just before the beginning of the harvest works, all the haymaking had to be done. When instructed, the yardlander had to mow in the lord's meadow for at least four days, work valued at 3d a day. Another four days (not to be allowed among the manual works) was to be spent lifting and gathering the hay (½d a day), and he had to lend his cart, or half his wagon for carrying it. This was allowed as a manual work. This was not, however, the most serious of the carrying services. On the fifth day of every other week the yardlander had to be prepared to go with loads of whatever produce was given him to Gloucester, Tewkesbury, Evesham, Chipping Campden, Clifford Chambers or Worcester. This service was valued at 1½d a day, and was unpopular. One of the articles in the *Scriptum Quoddam* states that manorial reeves were not to allow themselves to be bribed to exchange these carrying services for manual works. This instruction also suggests that the carrying services were often exacted, rather than commuted, as many other services might be. The mobilization of peasant carts and wagons for taking loads of grain and other produce to market and the monastery must have been a considerable economy for the lord.

The next group of works at Buckland were those which were owed during the harvest period, that is, between 1 August and the end of September. During this two-month period the yardlander had to work in the lord's harvest (*in messe domini*) five days a week, each day's work being valued at 1½d. In addition to these five days, two men had to come to the 'bederips' twice a week, this work being valued at 6d a week. The 'bederips' were boon works, additional to the labour rent, supposedly done voluntarily. But however they originated they had become assimilated into the general body of labour services. The normal practice which distinguished the day of boon reaping from ordinary days' labour was that the lord provided food. Similarly, at Buckland, tenants who spent a whole day binding the sheaves got a sheaf each of the grain on which they had been working, and a similar present when they had been carrying the grain. This service of carrying grain counted as one of the manual week works.

Such were the labour services which constituted the greater part of the rent from the tenants at Buckland, as indeed on most of the Gloucester Abbey manors. The total monetary value was 11s for the works between Michaelmas and the beginning of August, and 9s for those during the autumn, that is during the harvest period.[10]

This was not the end of the yardlander's obligations to the lord, even according to the extent. At Christmas the yardlander gave the lord a hen worth 1d. Every time he brewed ale for sale he paid 1d or gave the lord the value in ale. This was not a negligible provision for either side, for many village households brewed enormous quantities of ale and seem regularly to have set up a sign, a bush for instance, so that they could sell their surplus ale to all comers. Walter Beauchamp's tenants at Wickhamford and Murcot were prepared to pay ten marks to be quit of a similar toll.[11] The lord also charged a fee of 1d, known as pannage, for every pig over a year old, and ½d for every pig younger than a year, after it was separated from the sow. This fee was for the right to pasture the pigs on the acorns and beech mast of the commons. A licence fee had to be paid if the tenant wanted to sell an ox or a horse. If he wanted to let his son leave the household, or to marry off his daughter, he had to pay another fee. This last payment was called merchet. At death, the lord was to have a heriot, the tenant's best beast, just as the parson took a mortuary, that is, the second best beast. These last obligations were known as unassessed customs (*consuetudines non taxatas*) because, of course, they occurred irregularly, varied in value each time, and could not therefore be included in the annual valuation. Some surveyors, such as those of the Bishop of Worcester, made an estimate of what they would be worth in normal years (*communibus annis*), but the St Peter's surveyors apparently did not think it worthwhile.

The full meaning of this extent does not appear on the surface. There were two apparently, but not really, contradictory tendencies at work at this period. On the one hand, the amount of labour service that was being demanded from tenants was increased each time the estate surveyors made an extent, as in the case of the Earl of Gloucester's survey of 1251. This can be seen on estates all over the country where twelfth- and thirteenth-century surveys of the same manors survive to be compared. In the west midlands it can be seen by comparing the Bishop of Worcester's surveys of 1182 and 1299. But as we have attempted to show, it was also a period of increased need by estate owners for cash incomes. Now, it is true that an increase in cash income could be, and was achieved by increasing demesne production, and that this meant the employment of extra labour on the demesne. But the most stable source of cash income was always rent. The apparent emphasis on labour services in the thirteenth-century extents must not lead us into thinking that the manorial administration was reverting to a form of natural economy where obligations were acquitted not in money but in services. All of the labour services were valued so that, if the reeve or bailiff preferred, the money could be taken from the tenant instead of the service. But even if many of the services were in fact used, the later thirteenth-century manor was by no means dependent on them. Most of the year's work was done by permanent servants; it was when there was a pressing need for extra labour, at ploughing time, and in summer and autumn that labour services came into their own. This explains the importance universally attached to summer and autumn boon works. On the Worcester Priory estates, not only must younger sons who were not 'immediately' helping their parents go to the three boon reaps, but outsiders (not tenants) living on the estate must do so as well.[12]

Had any manorial accounts from Gloucester Abbey manors survived, it is probable that they would have given evidence of a considerable sale or commutation of labour services, since there were so many at the reeve's disposal. The situation would vary, not only from estate to estate but from manor to manor within one estate. Indirect evidence in default of adequate manorial material from the estate of Worcester Cathedral suggests that while on most of the manors boon services in summer and autumn were the only works to be retained, on a group of Avon valley manors week works also being used. These were the combined manors of Cropthorne and Charlton on the south bank of the river, between Evesham and Pershore, Netherton between the river and Bredon Hill, Overbury on the other side of the hill and Sedgeberrow and Teddington between Evesham and Tewkesbury. They were old-established, highly organized manors, long geared to arable production on the demesne. It is not surprising that labour services should have been used on a large scale for so long.[13]

But on other manors of typical structure, less of the total rent by the end of the thirteenth century was being taken in the form of labour services. On some of the Westminster Abbey manors, for instance, the labour services that were available were relatively few, largely because there was less week work throughout the year, at any rate by this period. But boon ploughings and work at the haymaking and harvesting seasons remained important. Although the boon ploughing was no substitute for the work of the demesne ploughs, it was used on all the Westminster west midland manors. At Pershore, tenants from as far afield as Wick, Pinvin and Pensham had to come with their plough-teams to work on the demesne, supplementing the work of the two demesne teams. Similarly, tenants on all the manors turned up to the haymaking and harvest boons. No doubt this was an irksome duty when they wanted to devote their labour to their own lands, and they had to be encouraged by being given free food, probably more lavish than they would have got at home. At Knowle, for instance, boon day meals included not only bread, cheese and ale, but bacon. Not all of the available works were used of course; more than half of the Pershore works (1,494 out of 2,729) were sold in 1317; but the crucial boon works were usually kept.

The manorial accounts do not give details about the number of hired workers taken on from time to time, but payments in addition to the money spent on entertaining the boon workers were considerable enough to suggest that casual labour was also needed at the peak periods of activity. The amount spent on weeding, mowing, haymaking and reaping the corn at Bourton-on-the-Hill in 1280 suggests that at least three hundred days' hired labour was paid for, while at Todenham two years later enough was spent on haymaking, reaping and binding to account for at least eighty days' labour. But however important from time to time and from place to place the casual labour may have been as a supplement to the boon works, it was the work of the permanent hired servants, the *famuli*, which constituted the vital contribution of hired labour to the working of the demesne. The number of full-time servants varied from nine at Pershore to twenty-four at Hardwick. According to special circumstances, part-time servants would be taken on, for the summer months for example, and there were often four or five of these. The most important of the full-time servants were those ploughmen (*tenatores*) who actually guided the plough, better paid than the *fugatores* who drove the plough animals. Carters were normally equivalent in status to the chief ploughmen, then came the cowman, the swineherd and the dairymaid. Full-time shepherds were of high status, but quite often shepherds would only be taken on for periods of less than a year, such as for the winter or summer visit of the flock to a manor. Or they could be hired for a specific task, as when in 1307 the Hardwick reeve paid two shepherds who brought 180 sheep from Todenham and Bourton-on-the-Hill, and drove them across the river Severn at Deerhurst to their winter pastures in Corse Wood.[14]

The involvement of the peasants in the cultivation of the manorial demesne must not be over-simplified. We can be sure that by the end of the thirteenth century, the regular week works throughout the year which are carefully listed in the descriptions of labour obligations, were often, perhaps normally, remitted for a money payment, for the farm servants could be relied on to do this work. But at those seasons, particularly haymaking and harvest, when there was a sudden need, at short notice, for extra labour to get in the hay and the corn, the wise reeve did not rely on casual labour alone but mobilized the tenants' boon services, which they were not, of course, in a position to refuse. Less urgent perhaps were the boon ploughings, especially in a manor like Hardwick where there were sixteen plough servants, enough that is for eight ploughteams. All the same, the plough boons were useful even if they only accounted for a small proportion of the arable.

At the same time that a flexible use of available services was being made, there was a trend towards a longer term commutation than the year by year sale of works that we have described. Evidence from the records of Gloucester Abbey shows that well-to-do customary tenants, for substantial sums down, were converting their holdings into life tenancies for money rent, without however losing their personal status as villeins.

The records of some of these conversions are copied out into the abbey's cartulary. Others have survived in the original, preserved among other documents of St Peter's Abbey at Gloucester Cathedral. Since the original transaction was an agreement, and each party had a copy, the one preserved by the abbey is sealed with the tenant's seal. This fact is of great interest, because most of the tenants were unfree villeins and in theory were not supposed to have seals, a symbol of legal personality. A good example of one of these agreements is from the Cotswold manor of Coln Roger. The abbey made an agreement with William, the reeve of the manor, and his wife by which they took for their lives two-thirds of one yardland and half of another. They were to pay money rents of 10s and 8s for these holdings, and were excused from ploughing, harrowing, carrying, reaping, mowing and manual works. But they were still to be burdened with pannage, brewing toll, the toll on the sale of stock and other customs owed by the other serfs (*nativi*). Their personal status was to remain as before (*sanguis eorum nullatenus immutetur*, their blood may in no way be changed) and their heirs after them were to be of servile condition. These life leases not only involved the payment of substantial money rents, but the payment down of high cash premiums. At Upleadon on the edge of the Forest of Dean, for instance, premiums of £5 were paid for two life leases of half-yardlands, whose rent was to be 13s 4d a year. These peasant lessees must have been moneyed men; the situation of which they were able to take advantage was clearly the financial need of their lord; what made all possible was the high level of monetary transactions.[15]

A half-way house to this situation had existed on some estates for some years. For example, the Evesham Abbey surveys, drawn up in the second half of the twelfth century, give the alternative for all customary holdings that they could be held *ad opus* or *ad censum*, that is, for work or for money rent. The same situation seems to have existed at the same period on the Templars' estates and is mentioned in the Worcester Priory survey of 1240 and that of the bishopric of 1299. It was an alternative which the lord could choose, and the alternative *ad censum* was not as far reaching as the individual bargains made by the Gloucester Abbey tenants. For it involved the commutation of the ordinary manual works through-

out the year, but the retention of many of the haymaking and harvest works. Thus the lords kept their labour reserves in hand for
difficult times. Nevertheless the existence of this choice shows how
far the payment of money rent by customary tenants had gone as a
feasible (and no doubt frequent) alternative to the performance of
labour services. By the middle of the fourteenth century most of
the holdings on the ancient estate of the Abbey of Winchcombe
had become holdings *ad censum* although tenure *ad opus* was still
vaguely remembered. It is improbable that Winchcombe was
unique in this respect.[16]

The type of estate organization which generated villeinage of the
the type described above has sometimes been regarded as peculiarly characteristic of Benedictine estates. This is simply because,
especially in the west midlands, the Benedictines were the principal
big landowners. Similar conditions are, however, found on manors
of the wealthy earls and barons. The Beauchamps' manors in
Worcestershire and Warwickshire had customary tenants whose
labour services were available when required, even if, as was generally the case, most of them were commuted from year to year.
The thirty-seven customary tenants at Salwarpe, near Droitwich,
for instance, were responsible during the year for 2,786 works on
the demesne besides tribute of hens and eggs and other miscellaneous payments. At Brailes in south Warwickshire, by 1280,
most of the winter and spring works seem to have been already
commuted for a money rent of 27d, seven bushels of oats and a hen
from each yardland. But there was still week work left in hand
from 24 June to Michaelmas, as well as mowing, reaping, carrying,
and ploughing services. Commuted labour services bulk large in
the inquisitions post mortem of Gilbert Earl of Gloucester which
describe his principal west midland manors in Gloucestershire and
Worcestershire.[17]

An interesting situation appears in the earliest of the extant
Beauchamp manorial accounts, just before the great dividing line
of the Black Death. This account, for 1345–6, is for their principal
Worcestershire manor of Elmley Castle. It would be risky to assert
that the situation would have been the same fifty years earlier, but
all other evidence suggests that it well might have been. Here we
find that the 4,286 works owed by the customary tenants are recorded on the receipt side of the account as sold, that is commuted.
But under various headings on the expenses side we find that

nearly 1,500 of these works were re-used again. The form of this, and subsequent, accounts shows that the money for the labour services was probably collected as a matter of course with the other rents. The customary tenants were not in fact made to use the recalled services entirely on the agricultural works for which they had been designed. About half of them were used to provide un-skilled labour for building craftsmen working on repairs and extensions to the castle. One suspects that they were paid back the price of the work with the other hired men. But of course they were not as other hired men, for their labour could be commanded by the lord because they were his villeins, and they could not refuse.[18]

Manorial Variants

Villeinage was the condition endured by most of the peasants on the highly organized manors of the big estates. It was a condition which, as a result of pressure by the lords of manors in the courts, had by the thirteenth century become part of the common law of the land. But the manorial structure, which was the primary cause of this villein unfreedom, was not of itself by any means universal. Even on the St Peter's estate there were manors which did not resemble those in the vale and on the Cotswold plateau to which we have already referred. In the deeply indented and wooded plateau overlooking the Severn valley, abbey property at Standish was not of the traditional manorial type.[19] The nuns of Caen at Minchinhampton in similar terrain may have conducted a con-siderable demesne farm, but many of their tenants were not sub-jected to the usual obligations of villeinage. The survey of Cam, a manor of the Berkeleys, which we have already quoted, shows a great majority of free tenures and smallholders as does that of the other Berkeley manor of Wotton-under-Edge. But more striking departures from the manorial structure which we have been con-sidering are to be found rather in the properties of the lesser landowners and in more recently occupied land.

A well-known family in Feckenham Forest was Strech. There were two branches, one of which held the hereditary post of forester-in-fee in that division of the forest known as Werkwood (mod. Walkwood), the other held a similar position in Berrow Wood in another part of the forest. Robert Strech, forester or woodward of Werkwood, died in 1262 and an inquisition of his estate was made by a jury of other forest landowners. He held most of his land from the king (who was lord of Feckenham), the equivalent of four yardlands, together with seven acres of meadow and nine and a half acres of 'new', that is assarted, land. But he also held land from Robert of Morton, from the Abbot of Bordesley, the Prior of Kenilworth, the Prior of Sandwell, and the Countess of Lincoln. He had a number of free tenants holding four and a half yardlands and paying him negligible amounts of money rent. But as far as one can make out from the laconic statement of the inquisition, most of his land, perhaps eight or nine yardlands, or about 250 acres of arable, with woodland and meadow in addition, was in demesne. Whatever oppressions the foresters may have perpetrated as foresters (and they were many), they had little opportunity to practise the traditional oppressions of manorial lords.[20]

Some of the recently established religious institutions played a role as landowners which was nearer to that of the gentry than to that of the old Benedictine or baronial landowners. The early endowments of Bordesley Abbey, for instance, consisted largely of untenanted land, crofts, assarts, portions of donors' demesnes, pastures and tithe rights, in three main areas of concentration; around Bordesley itself and especially in the eastern part of Feckenham Forest; in the vicinity of Bidford-on-Avon; and in the Arden country north-east of Stratford-on-Avon. These lands were organized in the characteristic Cistercian fashion, in granges whose land was worked, not by customary labour, but by that of the lay brothers and hired labourers. We know, from charter evidence, something of the composition of these granges.

Bidford Grange, for instance, was based on the donor's manorial demesne. It was a gift which excluded the land of the villeins of Bidford. In 1285, when the abbot was accused of having established an illegal court leet and assize of bread and ale, the jurors said that this followed the earlier establishment on the original demesne of a number of free tenants. Unfortunately the abbey has left little documentary evidence about the running of its estates, but there are some accounts of a small grange at Wickhamford (Worcestershire), between Evesham and Broadway, in the late 1320s. This grange was probably based on the glebeland, for the abbey had appropriated the parish. There was no income from tenants and the demesne land was entirely worked by wage labour. The grain receipts from tithe and from the demesne land was considerable and were almost all dispatched to the abbey.

In areas where the abbey nevertheless acquired subordinated tenancies, these were mostly of a non-manorial type. The abbey was lord of a considerable area in the parish of Tardebigge, a district of hamlet settlements including what was later to become the town of Redditch. The Tardebigge court rolls, like all of their kind, contain records of the land transactions in the area of the abbot's jurisdiction including descriptions of the terms of tenure. Between 1274 and 1342, when the social forces making for a strengthening of the servile aspects of villeinage were strong, none of the Tardebigge land transactions show any of the characteristic signs of villein tenure as we have seen it on the Gloucester Abbey estates. Rents, whether for customary or free holdings are almost entirely in money. On the only occasion on which a labour service was mentioned it was a day's boon reaping a year. Many of the tenements were customary, but the main aspect of customary tenure which appeared was the payment of heriot at death.[21] These special features of the Bordesley estate were not so much the consequence of the peculiarities of the Cistercian Order as of the social and topographical situation in which the estate was created. This is well demonstrated by the estate of Bordesley's daughter house of Stoneleigh in Arden near Coventry.

Although there were some outlying properties on Edgehill, the bulk of Stoneleigh Abbey property was in or near to the large parish of Stoneleigh, a partially colonized area of woodland given to the monks by Henry II. By 1280 there were eight granges and tenants in nine hamlets. An aristocracy of the tenants, referred to as sokemen, enjoyed the privileges of all tenants of lands that had been crown domain in 1086, the so-called ancient demesne of the crown. The principal privilege was that the existing lord was not to increase rents and services, and that the sokemen could, if he did so, implead him by a writ from chancery entitled 'Monstraverunt'. The other privilege was that tenants could litigate about the ownership of land in the manor court by means of a royal writ known as 'the little writ of right close', or sometimes the 'assize of freshforce'. In practice these legal rights might not matter as much as the fact that the rents were low, at 2s 6d a yardland, or 1d an acre. Other obligations were few, suit of court and attendance in a supervisory capacity at the abbot's bederepe. But this group of sokemen, thirty-seven families in all, was but a minority of the whole tenant population. The rest of them, nearly two hundred, enjoyed fewer privileges than the sokemen (such as free access to woodland pastures), but were nevertheless very different from ordinary manorial tenants. Apart from attendance at the manor court and at the abbot's harvest boon their obligations were entirely monetary.[22]

We have already referred to the fact that the Warwickshire villages whose descriptions are in the 1280 Hundred Rolls usually contained more than one manor. This was a county of small manors, owned either by lay lords or by small religious institutions of recent foundation. In this, it was vastly different from the rest of the region with its large and highly organized Benedictine estates. The effect on the mass of the peasantry was significant, and as we should expect from the cases analysed above, resulted in a high proportion of free or money-rent paying tenants. In Stoneleigh Hundred, half of the tenant population was free, the villeins were just over a quarter and the cottagers, many of whom, as we have seen, were of free status, were just under a quarter of the whole. This situation is what one would expect in an area of recent, indeed of continuing, colonization in the woodland. But even in the old settled Felden of south Warwickshire (Kineton Hundred) nearly a third of the peasants were free tenants, nearly a quarter were cottagers and less than half were villeins. In neither hundred was week work of any significance in peasant labour obligations, and the maximum amount of labour service that could be exacted was less than one-third of the total value of the rents. In practice, with annual sales of works, it would be considerably less. The fact is that the fragmentation of lordship was common to both hundreds; in neither hundred had the manorial structure been stabilized in the framework of the large, long-lived monastic estate: more than two-thirds of the manors in both hundreds were quite small, less than five hundred acres of arable, including both demesne and tenancies. This social and political factor was thus at least as important as geography in determining the character of the peasantry.

The Burden of Cash Payments

Twelfth-century estate surveys contain remarks which make clear that many tenants, probably the better off, were anxious to convert their labour services permanently into money rents. The latest of the Minchinhampton surveys (*c.* 1180 perhaps) tells us, for instance, 'Roger the Big holds a yardland for 5s, it used to be held for labour services, but he made up to Simon of Felstead (the steward) so much and afterwards to other people that he had held it for 5s up until now'. Similar statements occur in the roughly contemporary surveys of the manors of Evesham Abbey, such as, 'Randulf, in the time of kings William and Henry used to do labour services and all customs, but at the request of prior Elricus he was made free, and this unjustly . . .'[23] Yet it should not be imagined that the conversion of labour services into a money payment was necessarily an advantage for all tenants. We have seen that the Kempsey half-yardlander would have had a real struggle to pay his money rent. But if he had strong sons he would have been able to acquit the equivalent of his money rent in labour without imposing a financial strain on his household economy. Everything depended on the peasant's resources in land, cash reserves, and manpower. For tenants with substantial holdings commutation might certainly be an advantage, as we can see when we have details of the acreage of the holding.

Let us re-examine the survey of the Berkeley manor of Cam. The reason for using this survey is that it gives us the rent and acreage of both customary and free holdings. The customary yardland of sixty acres paid an annual money rent, which must certainly have been largely a commutation of services, amounting to 43s 5½d. Of this sum, 10s 8d is described as 'aid'. This customary payment, also known as 'tallage', was imposed only on villeins. The total rent burden works out at 8·7d an acre. Some of the free, money rent paying tenures in the same manor were paying nominal rents. These would be either ancient freeholdings, or holdings acquired by purchase for a sum of money high enough to compensate the seller for loss of rent. But many of the free tenures at Cam were clearly held at competitive rents, and none of these had as low a rental per acre as the customary yardland. The lowest was about 9d an acre, a sixty-nine-acre holding; the highest, an eighteen-acre holding, paid nearly 3s an acre. Similarly at Wotton-under-Edge, a customary yardland paid 6·2d an acre whereas among the free holdings a forty-acre holding at 20d an acre is found.

On the estates of St Peter's Abbey, the services due from the customary holdings, all similar to those at Buckland which we have described, work out at 4½d to 6½d an acre, based on the money equivalent of labour service of 18s to 20s a yardland. To this amount should of course be added the monetary burden of the *consuetudines non taxatas*. This could be considerable, but owing to the fact that there are no manorial accounts or court rolls surviving from the St Peter's estate we cannot estimate their effective addition to the burden of rent of the tenant. For this we must turn to the evidence surviving from other west midland estates. This is quite legitimate since in spite of inevitable variations from the norm, the monetary valuation of labour services together with already commuted money rent seems to work out quite generally at anything between 4d and 10d but mostly around 6d an acre. It is to this figure that the burdens which were not a direct payment for land held, but were rather the monetary consequence of villein status, must be added.

On reading the manorial evidence for this period, what strikes one most about the villein customs, as contrasted with the relative stability of the rent, is their arbitrary character. It must have been this, as much as their actual weight, which caused resentment among the tenants. Arbitrariness did not always work to the tenant's disadvantage. Entry fines and heriots were sometimes relaxed when a tenant was too poor to pay. But alternatively, when it was known that the tenant had money, the fine was increased: the serf or neif (*nativus*) on the Worcester Priory estate was to pay as much as he could (*sicut poterit*). In the early 1270s, on the manor of Minchinhampton, fines could be as much as 1s an acre, or 20s for a mere twelve-year lease of a yardland. Unfortunately we are seldom told either the acreage of a holding or its annual rent, so we cannot gauge the relative weight of the fine, but on the whole, in this period, they were fairly low, rarely more than half a mark (6s 8d). This is the case two decades later, but by about 1320 fines seem to have increased considerably, half-yardlands paying a full mark, and bigger holdings more than 20s. This rise in entry fines between the last decades of the thirteenth century and 1320 or thereabouts has also been noticed on the estates of the cathedral priory. Earlier on, fines were irregular, but by the later date half-yardlands were charged as much as 26s 8d. Another type of fine, purely personal in character, which seems quite arbitrary in its fluctuations, was merchet, the licence fee for marrying off a son or daughter. These varied at Minchinhampton between 1s 6d and 6s 8d.[24]

The Minchinhampton accounts sufficiently distinguish rent, customs and fines for us to get an impression of their relative value to the lord, and burden to the tenant. By the beginning of the fourteenth century the assize rent of free and customary tenants during the first three decades of the century was about £20 a year. Between 1330 and 1380 there are no account rolls, but in 1380 the assize rent stood at £33. Part of the £5 increase must at least be partly made up of the value of such labour services as had not been commuted by 1330. Compared with this rent payment of £20, and the possible performance (which need not be entered on the account) of a number of labour services, there were the additional payments, mostly flowing from the lady's power over her villeins. In 1307 a series of items entitled 'consuetudines' (customs) amounted to £1 8s 4d. A substantial part of this sum was payment for pannage, but other items included stall rents on the market, which might legitimately be included as a straightforward rent payment. The profits of jurisdiction in the manorial court came to £3 1s 6d. These consisted of a whole range of customary payments and amercements which fell largely on the villeins. Listed separately are the fines, which were mostly entry fines, amounting to £1 7s 8d. There are also some items in the section of the account entitled 'Exitus munerii' (issues of the manor) which are customary payments by tenants rather than profits of the demesne. These include further pannage payments for pasture in Minchinhampton woods amounting to £7 6s 2d. The 'sales of pasture', which amounted to £1 9s 7d should also be included among the rent and customary burdens on the tenants, since this again is not sale of demesne produce but lease of grazing land to the pasture-hungry peasants. These financial levies, which would not appear in any rental or survey, amount to half of the total amount of rent. In 1311 the amount of extra payments dropped by nearly a third owing to a reduction in pannage payments, and was further reduced to only a fifth of the assize rent in 1316. In 1321 it rose to a quarter of the assize rent. But in 1330 the customs, pasture sales and profits of jurisdiction equalled the total amount of assize rent.[25]

Some figures from the account rolls of the Westminster Abbey manors show variations from place to place in seigneurial profits. At Todenham in 1293, money payments by tenants extra to their formal rent obligations were considerable. Money rents amounted to about £6, but tallage was £5 and the lord's profits of jurisdiction were £4 10s. At Bourton-on-the-Hill rents overtopped tallage and jurisdictional profits, £7 5s to £3 10s. Where there was a large number of tenants, particularly, one suspects, where their numbers were swollen by smallholders and assarters, the straight money rent increased in importance. At Hardwick in 1307, court profits were £7 compared with £52 rent; £6 10s compared with £30 rent at Knowle in 1302; and (with tallage) £8 compared with £100 rent at Pershore in 1313. The proportion of seigneurial profits to rent sometimes dropped quite low, but it was always there.[26]

The incompleteness of extents which show the regular rents and labour services but do not value the profits from the *consuetudines non taxatas* is also illustrated by the accounts of a couple of manors in lay hands. The Bigod earls of Norfolk were lords of Chepstow at the mouth of the river Wye, and had some property in and just outside the Forest of Dean, not far from Chepstow. One of these manors was the now disappeared village of Alverston in Aylburton parish. In 1280 the profits of the manor court, the pasture sales, herbage sales, pannage and beer toll slightly exceeded the total value of the assize rents; in the following year the court profits alone (of which entry fines were the most substantial element) exceeded the assize rent; and five other extant accounts in the last two decades of the thirteenth century show that these customary and jurisdictional payments were either greater than, or very little less than, the rent payments. The same situation can be observed on the Berkeley manors of Cam and Coaley. In 1297 the rents of both manors should have brought in £57, but allowances and deductions reduced it to £35. 'Aid' taken from the tenants amounted to over £14, pasture sales, pannage and ale toll to £3 13s, and perquisites of courts to nearly £13, so that customary and jurisdictional extras were not far short of the regular rent payments.[27]

The level of money payments extra to the assize rents fluctuated according to a number of factors. The exaction of entry fines was the lord's way of compensating for rents which tended to get fixed at a low, non-economic level by the influence of custom, and the amount he could get depended to an appreciable degree on the demand for land. The level of demand also determined the profits from pannage and pasture sales. But an essential condition of the exactions was the lord's power over his subjects, a power which was inextricably linked to but not identical with his rights as a landowner over his tenants. Merchet payments, licence fees to sell stock, brew ale, or leave the manor, and the profits of the petty police jurisdiction of the manor court are even more clearly the direct consequences of seigneurial power. This power was enjoyed in a moderate degree by the Abbess of Holy Trinity, Caen, acting through her steward at Minchinhampton. Other west midland landowners had much greater power, partly because of the greater extent of their private jurisdiction, partly because of the greater weight of their presence, based on the size of their estates. We can be sure, therefore, that the extra money, on top of the rent and commuted labour services, which the villein tenants of St Peter's Abbey, Gloucester, or Cirencester Abbey, or the Beauchamps had to pay must have been at least up to the level of the payments of the region whose evidence we have just quoted.

CHAPTER 6

THE VILLAGE COMMUNITY

Most of the aspects of the peasant's life that we have so far discussed arose from his relations with his lord, as tenant of the lord's land and as subject to the lord's jurisdiction. There are two reasons why this aspect of his life is bound to bulk large. First, the documentary evidence which we have is the by-product of manorial administration; second, since most peasants' households must have been primarily occupied in producing enough, additional to their own needs, to pay the rent and the customary dues, their attention must necessarily have been fixed on the lord, his steward, his reeve and his rent collector. However, the medieval village was also a community, though it was by no means a community of equals. The collective element in agriculture was much greater than in modern times, both in the common arrangements about pasture on stubble and fallow and in co-operation to fulfil the lord's demands for labour on the demesne. The manor court therefore was not simply an institution to exercise labour discipline, or to register the terms of tenure of land held from the lord, it was also an assembly in which villagers discussed affairs of their own. But as we have seen, many villages had more than one manor, and therefore more than one manor court. If there were to be an assembly of the villagers, then one manor court would be an insufficient framework. In any case the doings and discussions of villagers among themselves were often hostile to the lord's interests. It was probably the parish, therefore, which was the institutional focus of such peasant business as transcended or violated manorial interests, and the parish church which was the meeting place.

The parishioners, unfortunately, leave records only in stone, the nave of the church for whose upkeep they are responsible.

Otherwise the parish is seen as the incumbent and his revenue. But where manor, parish and village coincide, then we can see something of the inner life of the village in the records of the manor. Just as the working of the agricultural routine of the village required the frequent collective activity of the villagers, so the working of the machinery of the court imposed common rather than individual pursuits. Offences against the lord or against neighbours were reported or 'presented' at the court by spokesmen for tithings, groups of adults who stood mutual surety for each other. Sometimes the tithings were groups of ten or more in the village, but in the huge manor of Halesowen, which contained a large number of small hamlets, it was the whole hamlet which presented as a tithing. The village of Oldbury, for example, in 1280 presented Richard, the son of William of Cernhul, for trying to kill his brother and another man. As a result of the affray the hue and cry was raised (*hu. et cri levatum fuit*), and in fact this ancient method of putting a stop to a fight was one of the main reasons for hamlet presentments.[1]

The villagers referred to themselves as 'communities'. In 1281 Walter the Archer complained that five men at Romsley had falsely presented him in the Romsley court, and had him punished in his absence, for putting his animals on the common pasture. The five defendants said that Walter was not of their community and had no holding entitling him to common rights. They warranted their original presentment both on their own and on the community's behalf (*tam pro se quam pro communitate ville*). The upshot was that the Halesowen court, to which Walter had appealed, upheld him, but the abbot's court's contrary judgement cannot have lessened the sense of community at Romsley. Another word often used, as well as 'community' is 'neighbour'. This is not a matter of sentiment but of fact. Open field cultivation meant that one man's injury was everybody's, even the lord's. In 1280 the sworn jurors of the Halesowen court said that seven persons, whom they named, had failed to keep their fences and that consequently the corn of the abbot and of other neighbours (*bladum Abbatis et aliorum vicinorum*) in Hales field had been damaged. These were the fences which every tenant who had parcels on the perimeter of the open fields had to keep up when the corn was growing, to prevent the animals getting in, not merely into his own corn, but, since the fields were open, into the corn of all who had parcels in that field. At Minchinhampton, the right of the peasant community to choose its neighbours makes its appearance. At a court held in 1317 it was reported that two tenants had sold land to two buyers, but that a suit concerning these purchases was to be postponed until the next court because they had not yet been admitted by the tenants. That the tenants referred to were not simply the two sellers but the whole community of tenants, is made clear by an entry in a court in 1329 where a man claiming land in his wife's right is accepted by the court, both free men and villeins (*tam per liberos quam per villanos*).[2]

Collective Action

Historians have recently written much about the matters on which villagers took common action, reacting against earlier theories of peasant individualism, which in their turn had been reactions against unsupported nineteenth-century theories about primitive village communism. These matters were largely those for which the government attempted to find some person or institution prepared to take responsibility for raising taxes or soldiers, and which are therefore frequently mentioned in central government records. But what was the constitutional machinery through which this action was taken? Was there an assembly of all villagers, of all householders, of all tenants or merely of the richer men? In the fourteenth century there began to be written into the manor court records of a series of rules, mostly, though not entirely connected with the regulation of the harvest, called 'by-laws'. Earliest extant codified by-laws in the west midlands are entered on the court rolls of the Beauchamp manor of Elmley Castle in 1373 and here we are told that the rules were made 'by the assent of all the lord's tenants both free and servile'. Earlier references to by-laws occur in the Halesowen court rolls between 1300 and 1302, clearly in a slightly different sense, and sometimes as 'benlaw' rather than 'bilaw' or 'belaw'. The by-law referred to here seems to be some sort of court or gathering which makes judgement about matters in dispute (the felling of an oak, the obstruction of a road) between men of different villages on the probably imprecisely defined boundaries between the villages. It seems to be used in a similar sense, too, in a description of the boundary between the Bishop of Worcester's manor of Alvechurch and the king's manor of Bromsgrove and King's Norton. The boundary is described from point to point, with occasional comments on the points in order to identify them, such as 'Apultonesford where the third sheaf of the tithe is paid to the lord rector of Alvechurch'. Another boundary point, called Crokedebrugg (Crooked bridge) is described as 'where the *binlaues* are usually held between the above mentioned manors and where the hue for robbery and theft is usually taken and received from franchise to franchise'. This looks much like the Halesowen by-law or 'benlaw', that is a session which is common to adjacent settlements. It is perhaps not quite the same as the later harvest by-laws but it has the same implication of being an affair of villagers rather than of lords of the manor.[3]

The boundary perambulation just quoted is written in a late thirteenth-century hand, and is probably not much earlier than that period. Another document in the same cartulary tells us something about one of the village communities just mentioned in action and indicates who were the active participants. It is an agreement between Godfrey Giffard, Bishop of Worcester, and the community of King's Norton, dated September 1287. In the agreement the community releases to the bishop and his tenants of Alvechurch its right to common pasture in Dodenhaleshcye in exchange for ten marks (£6 13s 4d) and continuation of their common rights in West Heath. The bishop added his seal and twenty named persons add theirs on behalf of the community of King's Norton. Of these twenty, fifteen can be identified in the tax list of 1275, out of a list of 147 Norton taxpayers. It is most unlikely that the missing five were so poor as to be exempt. Some may be disguised under other surnames, some may be dead. For on the whole, the representatives of the community were those in the top bracket of assessed movable wealth: only two of them were in a low bracket, and even so there were thirty or so paying less than them. If we had manorial court rolls surviving from the date of this agreement it is very likely that we should find that, apart from two clerks who seal, the others would be the jurors and the manorial officials, posts which usually revolved among a restricted circle of the richer tenants. The point here, however, is that in the absence of the lord (the king) the *communitas* takes over, and that it is spoken for by a relatively small number of its more prosperous members.*

* We will not go far wrong if we say that the upper bracket of taxpayers paid 10s or more. There were eight of these among the fifteen identified sealers. Five paid

152

This brings us to another aspect of the common action of the villagers, acting not so much independently of the lord as collectively replacing him. When Worcester Cathedral Priory was still leasing out its demesnes at the beginning of the thirteenth century the lessees, as we have seen, in some cases were the villagers.[4] What was called the 'West' land, for instance (presumably demesnes west of the city) was leased in 1201 for fifteen years 'to the men of those villages'; Henwick in 1206 was leased for fifteen years to the men of the village (*hominibus villae*); Harvington in 1207 was leased to the men of the village (at an increased rent), and again in 1230. In 1239, too, the men of Phepson took the lease of their village for eight years. When the lease of the manor of Cleeve Prior lapsed on the death of the lessee, William Norman, it was let out again for five years (less the mill) to the men of the village. When the survey of 1240–2 was drawn up, nine of the manorial demesnes were leased out, about a quarter of the total number. But this was not all. In four cases, in addition to the demesne the total farm rent paid covered the value of the tenants' rents and customary dues as well. In the case of Cleeve Prior, the phrase used in the document is simply that the whole village, except the church, was put to farm. Now in every case, it was the villeins of the village, not an individual farmer, who took on the farm. In the case of Boraston and Grimley the leased demesne was divided and let, apparently under priory auspices, to individual villeins, for their names are given, with the rent of the portions of demesne, and there is no lump sum as a farm payment for the whole demesne. The villeins of Hallow on the other hand took the demesne arable and meadow, profits, heriots and tenant land (*villenagium*) for a farm of a hundred quarters one cronn of wheat, a hundred quarters of oats, eighteen cronns of rye and seventeen cronns of barley. But although they paid two quarters of rye in common (*in communi*) for the demesne farm buildings, the grain rent was allotted to each villein for his portion of demesne, and is entered in the rental, again as if this were done under priory supervision. But in all the other cases any subdivision of the leased land was done by the villagers, and the priory's only concern was the collection of the whole rent.[5]

The practice of leasing the demesne, or the whole village, to its

more than 5s, still an indication of reasonable wealth. A clerk paid 3s and two others 2s 6d. Not a few manorial lords in other villages paid 10s or less.

inhabitants, to dispose of it at their will, was not new. It is found in Domesday Book, and it continues into the fourteenth and fifteenth centuries, though the later tendency was towards leasing to individual farmers. Nor was it confined to ecclesiastical estates. Thomas Beauchamp, Earl of Warwick in 1358, leased not only the demesne of Barford, near Warwick, to six tenants, but the perquisites and other profits of the court. The earl's steward, however, held the court.[6] It was not the custom, earlier or later, for the lord to lease his jurisdiction to his tenants, whatever he did with his land. All the same, the fact that the lord could negotiate with the village community as such, confident that it could find the farm rent, and usually willing to leave the details of working out the disposal of the demesne lands to the tenants themselves, implies that villagers' assemblies, however inadequately documented, must have been normal features of village life.

Rebellion

The lords and the peasant communities could not, in the nature of things co-exist in a state of natural harmony. The lord's ownership of his soil and its villein occupants was firmly established in law too recently to be accepted without question. The aristocratic structure of society, the institution of lordship, and the ownership of great estates were of course accepted as if they had existed since the beginning of time. But within this aristocratic framework, ancient peasant communities still doubted the legality of the absolute disposal by the lord of the commons, still doubted whether any men except slaves could be treated as unfree, still doubted whether lords had the right to increase or change rents and customary services. The lords lived by taking the product of the peasants' labour, or the labour itself. The directness of this appropriation meant that any attempt by lords to increase their income was felt immediately. The claim to the waste meant that any extension of cultivation by lords, or by wealthy free men, was felt at once as deprivation of pasture. Consequently most thirteenth-century court rolls give the impression (exaggerated no doubt by the nature of the record) that village life was a continuous series of guerrilla actions by the tenants, partially but clearly not completely checked by the hierarchy of the lord's officials, bailiffs, reeves, beadles, haywards, woodwards, park keepers and so on.

154

Let us take at random the proceedings of one of the sessions of the Abbot of Pershore's manor court at Hawkesbury, held on Saturday, 21 August 1290. After the usual presentment of essoins (apologies for non-attendance) and defaulters we begin with a report of tenants' sheep in the corn before the fences were taken up. Then came an accusation against certain persons for putting their beasts out to graze on the lord's pasture at night. Next, an obscure complaint by a man referred to as *dominus*, who was probably a cleric, about a woman and his son and a plot to kill another man and bury him in a wood. Seven gleaners were presented for gleaning against orders. A man from the hamlet of Hawkesbury Upton was accused of keeping his children away from labour service for the lord at the harvest, and for denying his condition (presumably that he was a villein) in an attempt to avoid sending his family to the harvest. Other persons are presented for sheltering strangers, some of whom were said to come and go at night carrying bundles. Some again were presented for not doing their harvest labour services; others for theft; another for marrying outside the manor. The final presentment is for failure to repair a wall on a holding. Now manor courts were usually supposed to be held every three weeks, but seldom were. The Hawkesbury record is incomplete, but where a complete year's record exists it looks as though up to nine courts could be held. The record quoted may then represent only the affairs of the last five or six weeks, and undoubtedly reported only a fraction of the offences actually committed. Furthermore not all types of offences would be presented to every court; the one we have quoted does not for example have the presentment of offenders against the assize of ale (in effect a licensing system for ale brewers) which fill the record of some courts.[7]

It is difficult in many cases to decide whether conflicts between the peasants and the lord would have arisen because of frictions between the individual and any reasonably constituted authority or whether they were inherent in the nature of the economic and social relationship between the two sides. But in many cases the element of class conflict is obvious. There are surviving records of some fifty Hawkesbury manor court sessions during the reign of Edward I and, in addition to the sort of items already given as a sample there is a substantial number of cases of tenants refusing to do labour services, or doing them deliberately badly. Examples include a female tenant who, in 1294, refused to do such services as carriage of wheat and weeding the beans on the lord's demesne. Others in the following year were accused of not doing their ploughing services. The same sort of troubles occur at the same period on the Worcester Cathedral estates. Twenty tenants at Stoke Prior, near Bromsgrove, were amerced in 1297 for not doing the ploughing services they owed for the demesne land they had on lease. The reaction by the tenants which is recorded on the court roll expresses the outlook of peasants at this period well beyond the west midlands 'All and singular', it says, 'asked that they should be able to have the customs which they used to have in the days of Richard of Feckenham [Prior 1274–86] which were written in a book of the customs of the manor of Stoke and granted to them by the Lord Prior'. There seems to have been no settlement, since Stoke Prior tenants were still refusing to do their ploughing services in 1321. On another cathedral manor, that of Teddington near Tewkesbury, it was reported in 1336 that the whole village of Teddington, with its hamlet of Alstone had failed for a long time to do its accustomed services. A royal letter of 1325 says that twenty-six discontented Stoneleigh Abbey sokemen left their holdings, a manipulation by the abbot to get greater control of their frccholdings.[8]

Resistance to the lord, then, was another, no doubt potent, stimulus to common action among villagers. It is true that on the whole, the west midland region did not see as many village rebellions as the southern and eastern counties, frequent in the two or three decades before and after 1300. In spite of the local grip of the great ecclesiastical landowners, notorious for their bad relations with their tenants, social conflicts were less frequent because the pressure of population on the land and the shortage of pastures was less acute in our region than further east and south. Even so there are two striking examples of sustained revolt which, though written about elsewhere, must be fitted into this picture of independent peasant action. They were movements, in both cases, by the tenants of ecclesiastical lords, the abbeys of Cirencester and Halesowen, and both concerned the fundamental issues of thirteenth-century social struggle, personal freedom and the increasing burden of services.

The case of Cirencester is somewhat complicated by the fact that there were here effectively two communities: one of merchants and artisans and the other of agricultural tenants. Both communities were fighting for a higher social and legal status than the abbey was prepared to give them. The burgesses, like those of many other towns with church lords, wanted simply the elementary juridical rights of an urban community, already enjoyed by many towns on the royal demesne. The agricultural tenants wanted a limitation of services and a recognition of free status. While we are not concerned here with the claims of the burgesses it must be emphasized that in all probability burgess and peasant communities overlapped, in that the abbot attempted to involve members of the urban community in the agricultural affairs of the manor. But it would be unwise to treat them as one. Gloucestershire had many seigneurial boroughs smaller than Cirencester with burgess and peasant communities which were clearly separate. It is not conceivable that the wealthy merchants of Cirencester town would rub shoulders with the tenants working on the abbot's demesne.

Cirencester was originally a royal manor, not farmed to the abbey until 1155, twenty-two years after the house's foundation. As in so many other cases, this fact was used by the tenants as a reason for resisting increases in services. As a starting point, we should look at the history of the struggle from a late phase of its development. This is described in a document of 1241. Tenants of the village of Minety, a member of the Cirencester manor, complained before the royal justices itinerant at Gloucester that the abbot had demanded services beyond those in force when the king was lord. The abbot countered their plea, not by denying the increase in services but by saying that since Minety was part of Cirencester manor, and all the men of Cirencester were villeins, paying merchet at the will of the abbot, he was not obliged to answer their plea. The proof of the villeinage of the Cirencester tenants, he said, had been given earlier by a jury of twenty-four knights.[9]

But the question of the Cirencester villeins was not so simple. A return of tenants' services at the time of the farm of Cirencester to the abbey lists nearly forty who did some sort of work on the demesne and another eighteen who were paying 1d rent. It is unlikely that there were burgesses in this group of whom it was said 'none is so free a man that he must not plough and carry with waggon or cart'. The burgesses are referred to some twenty years later in a writ of Henry II ordering the abbot not to vex the men with free tenements in Cirencester, nor to demand more services of them than they had rendered the king. But this does not mean that agricultural tenants were unfree. The very fact that the phrase 'none is so free' is used, demonstrates (what can be demonstrated from other evidence of the same date) that freedom was a relative concept, and that in spite of the fluidity of its meaning, even the least free were still not serfs. The degradation of these men, as the abbot admitted in 1241, came later, at the end of the twelfth or at the beginning of the thirteenth century, a period of crisis in the legal status of the English peasants.[10]

In John's reign (1199–1216), possibly in the early years, some events about which we are uncertain resulted in another statement by a sworn jury of the customs and services of the men of Cirencester. Forty-one tenants and holdings are listed, one or two with rather 'honourable' services, such as attending the king's hunting, or escort duty. But the rest render labour services of one sort and another, though only one is allotted week work. All of them have by now an obligation to pay merchet when marrying off their daughters, a custom considered a mark of servility, though not mentioned in 1155, and, in general, only recently used by lawyers as a servile test. The hay and harvest boons are expected not only of the tenants but of all people dwelling in the manor. In effect this meant all members of each tenant's family as well as their hired men. This was in every sense a boon for the lord but not for the tenants who also had to get their hay and grain in from the fields.

This declaration of custom is almost contemporary with a movement, not so much of insurrection as of protest, in the Gloucester county court by the young men of Cirencester, and the outsiders dwelling temporarily in the town. They complained about being made to do the three harvest boons, so persistently that a jury of inquiry was empanelled. This jury, of course, gave the right to the abbot (otherwise the record of the case would not have been published in the abbey cartulary). But it mentioned certain concessions. The young men need not come to the boon as long as they were, as we would say, 'minors', in their phrase 'under the rod and power and in the mainpast of their father and mother', so long as the boon was acquitted by their parents. As soon as they were free of their fathers' power and made their own living, were what the jurors called 'sulfodes', then they must attend the boons.

In return they were to have access to Cirencester market with freedom to buy and sell without paying toll, on payment of 2½d 'cheping gavel' (lit. 'market rent'). Any stranger living in Cirencester from the night of St John the Baptist, and during the period of the harvest, was also to do the three boon works.

Which came first, the protest of the young men or the inquisition into individual rents and services ? The protest of the young men comes first in the cartulary, and the inquest which firmly asserts the right of the abbot to the labour of all persons dwelling in the manor immediately follows. It may have been provoked by it, rather than the other way round, for in 1225 another dispute between abbey and tenants provoked the repetition, in the king's court at Westminster, of the first detailed statement of tenants' services. This was the declaration of the jury of twenty-four knights which was quoted to the tenants of Minety in 1241 as proof of the villeinage (that is, by now, serfdom), of the Cirencester tenants, and consequently as proof of their own villeinage.[11]

The Cirencester case is a mirror of the history of the peasants, that is the slow erosion of their personal status and the increase of their services by the joint pressure of the lords' and kings' courts. The resistance of the young men was partial and ineffective, though time was to show that the Abbot of Cirencester had not finished with trouble at home. But next time it was to be the burgesses. Meanwhile a sterner example of peasant organization for resistance was being shown at the other end of our region, in the manor of Halesowen.

As in the case of the Cirencester tussle, a good starting point for the Halesowen story is a late phase in the history of the struggle between the abbey and its tenants. The court rolls of the manor in the year 1279 tell us that Roger Ketel was fined 100s because he had entered into a conspiracy with his neighbours falsely to implead his lord the abbot in the king's court. In return for the 100s the abbot promised to remit his indignation against those insolent tenants, while they in turn admitted that they were servile. This was a victory for the abbot and he, in fact, conceded very little, for this was nearly the end of a case that had been going on for forty years.[12]

Peter des Roches, Bishop of Winchester, one of King John's closest advisers, had with the king's help founded the Premonstratensian Abbey in 1215 and, in addition to the large manor of

Hales, had endowed it with extensive franchises including exemption from the jurisdiction of the hundred and county courts. The grant of all jurisdiction over tenants except for those cases for which the punishment was death or mutilation (*excepta sola justicia mortis et membrorum*) was made at the height of the landlord pressure on the rights of the hitherto free villein tenants, and was bound to produce a clash. We do not know the nature of the clash, but there was a dispute between abbot and tenants which ended in 1244 with a settlement largely in the abbot's favour. The level of labour services was to be fixed at the existing amount but the sums to be paid in merchet and entry fines were to be at the abbot's will. Being a former royal manor, tallage was limited to those occasions when the king tallaged the rest of the royal demesne, and it was established that so long as the abbot's mill was in working order, the tenants must grind their corn there. The abbot agreed not to demand extra labour services, and made one or two minor concessions. But in fact he did increase services some time in the early 1270s, for the Shropshire jurors in answer to the inquiries of 1274 said that he had done so beyond the level obtained in the reign of Henry III (d. 1272) in spite of his agreement that they should remain unchanged. An enquiry two years later seemed to stabilize the position in the tenants' favour, and embodied no statement as to whether they were free or villein. This was an important point, because a decision in favour of their villeinage, under the law as it was by then, would mean that they were at the abbot's will. So the abbot petitioned the king's council to prevent the tenants from using the argument that the manor was of ancient demesne, which strictly speaking it was not.* The council told him to test his point at law. This he did. As so often happened in these cases, the tenants did not turn up, whether due to coercion or not we can only guess, and the abbot won the case by default. But they had obviously tried, Roger Ketel being their spokesman, as the private record of the Halesowen manor court tells us. It is even possible that they in their turn had tried coercion, for the Bishop of Worcester ordered the excommunication in 1278 of those who had laid violent hands on the abbot and his retinue at Beoley (Worcestershire). Was this when he was on his way up to Westminster to complete his tenants' enserfment? The abbot in any case won

---

* It had been in the hands of the crown, but not at the time of Domesday Book. *Domesday Book*, I, p. 308.

hands down, for he got another judgement against his tenants in 1286 to the effect that they were villeins for ever (*in perpetuum*).[13]

Peasants as Lessors and Employees

So far, in showing the life of village and manor from the point of view of the peasants, we have emphasized those occasions when they acted in common. We must not however give a false picture of social harmony within the village. While the gulf between the peasant class as a whole and the lords was greater than any divisions within the village community, these must not be minimized. They were of course primarily economic in character, though remarkably fluid all the same. Enough has been said about the division of the tenant population between the relatively few free and customary tenants of a yardland or more, the middle core of half-yardlanders, and the mass of cottagers and other smallholders. This is a division which emerges clearly from every rental and survey which has survived. But we have also insisted that the picture of a tenant population evenly divided between these categories is, from the standpoint of the actual occupation and working of the land, quite false. Formal differences in the size of holdings, as shown in the lord's rental, were both exaggerated and minimized by the working of the peasant land market, a market in which the lord's presence might or might not be acknowledged, but which in any case probably made little difference to the process of redistribution.

All the west midland court roll evidence which is extant for the late thirteenth and early fourteenth centuries contains plentiful indication of this inter-peasant leasing, and fits into a pattern which was found everywhere in England at this time. The Halesowen rolls are full of examples from 1275 onwards. One of the earliest entries in the extant record shows seven tenants fining* with the lord concerning land illegally transferred among tenants. At the same time as these tenants paid money for these past lettings, a rule was made that henceforth such leases were only to be made with the abbot's special permission. And, in fact, subsequent references to these transactions show that some were licensed and others not. An exchange of land, for instance, in 1280 was licensed for 6d. In 1281 John of Haslebury had to fine with the lord 3s for taking small parcels of land on lease for eighteen years from four other tenants.

* That is paying a sum to end (*finire*) a dispute.

On the Worcester Priory manors many leases between tenants were licensed, ranging from complete holdings to tiny parcels. A widow at Stoke Prior in 1297 leases for nine years to another tenant all her land except the croft. the sub-tenant doing all the services except the boons and paying as rent the crop from one ridge. On the other hand, in the same village, in 1305 a sub-tenant takes only 'two days ploughland' (*dieta* or *arura unius diei*), perhaps an acre or an acre and a half, for four harvests. The licence fee here was 12d, but the rent from sub-lessee to main tenant is not mentioned. At another priory manor, Overbury on Bredon Hill, there seems to have been a lot of unlicensed sub-letting. In some cases a fine was imposed, but at Overbury in 1315 and at nearby Teddington, land so let out was taken back into the lord's hands. The practice of leasing without licence was also forbidden on the Abbot of Pershore's manor of Hawkesbury, though there are very few cases on the court rolls. At Minchinhampton, some tenants clearly have sub-tenants. William Jameson's tenants, who owed customary rents to the lady of the manor of hens and eggs, were to be distrained by two oxen, so they could not have been in the poorest group of villagers. But, as at Hawkesbury, there is no evidence, either through licences or through prosecutions for illegal sub-letting, of peasant land transactions which by-passed the manor court.[14]

But at Minchinhampton the peasant land market could have operated in full legality as it did more obviously at Tardebigge, during this period, by the surrender of the land in question into the lord's hand with the provision that it should be leased to a person named by the surrenderer. The indications that this may have happened at Minchinhampton are when surrendered tenements are immediately taken up. But there is no proof that this was arranged. At Tardebigge, on the other hand, while there is evidence of ordinary inter-tenant leasing for short terms (for example, for two, eight and twelve harvests) in 1273, surrenders of land into the lord's hand by A *ad opus* B (that is so that B can take the holding), begin in 1295, though not becoming common until after the Black Death.

The difficulty about the peasant land market is that while we know from court rolls that it existed, we do not know what was its overall consequence. In many places, the leases were for short terms of years, in fact the phrase used for these transactions in the Halesowen court rolls is 'sale of terms'. Hence not merely from generation to generation but from year to year, the amount of land actually worked by each tenant, as distinct from formal holding in the lord's eyes, must have changed. The lord of the manor, as well as the historian, may also have found it difficult to keep up with the changes in peasant occupation. As we have seen, in some cases they were prepared to license these alienations, but sometimes things went too far. At Stoke Prior, for example, we are told that a half-yardland was subdivided so extremely (*vehementer*) that the services and customs from it could be neither fully nor properly performed on account of this dispersal. Consequently the holding was taken into the lord's hands. It was for this reason, and because the lord risked losing the financial profits of alienation, that on two estates which represent extremes of types in the west midlands, the same veto was imposed on the free peasant land market. On the manors of St Peter's, Gloucester, 'it is not permissible for customary tenants to make any exchanges of lands, meadows or any sort of holding without licence, and in the hall moot'. At Stoneleigh 'if anyone, having obtained the lord's consent and fined with him, wishes to give his holding to anybody (*ad opus alicuius*) he must come to the court and surrender the holding into the lord's hand, without any charter for the buyer or grantee, and the lord's bailiff, having taken the heriots and other rights of the lord, will issue to the buyer or grantee to hold according to the custom of the manor. And the said recipient will fine with the lord as soon as they can agree.'[15]

We often find that peasant lessors are widows. At Stoke Prior in 1294 a widow and her son leased their holding for twelve years to another tenant for an annual payment of mistil (mixture of wheat and rye), oats, peas and vetch. This sort of lease suggests that a small family like this might dispose of the holding for a period, in return for their sustenance, because for the time being they had not the manpower resources to carry on. The lessee on the other hand might want the extra land, either because his family was too numerous to be fed from his existing holding, or because he saw the chance of making more money by increasing the area under cultivation. Both reasons were no doubt operative, so that while some adjustment of size of holdings to size of families would be made, the peasants with cash or grain resources, and with ambitions, could thrive even further. The rise and fall of family fortunes in the peasant community was part of the constant rhythm of rural life, a rhythm punctuated, however, by many discordant notes. The many pleas of debt which occur in every court roll are eloquent testimony to the presence of the Christian usurer, the man who lends to his neighbours in a bad year and prosecutes for his debt in the next. The type was even recognized in the presentments to the itinerant justices under the rubric *De usurariis Christianis*. Such was Miles of Evesham who sold corn dearer than it was worth in order to conceal the interest on a loan.[16]

Another and more archaic way by which men climbed on the backs of their fellows is illustrated by events in the parish of Stoneleigh during the twelfth and thirteenth century. One of the Stoneleigh hamlets was Canley where by 1280 there was a population mainly of cottagers, but with a core of four ancient sokeman holdings much sub-let. They were all the Abbot of Stoneleigh's tenants or sub-tenants, but the situation only fourteen years earlier had revealed an interesting history of usurpation. In 1266, probably as part of the national inquiry into the usurpation of royal rights after the defeat of the baronial party, the king issued a writ to the sheriff of Warwickshire ordering him to summon a group of Canley tenants to Kenilworth to show why they had robbed the Abbot of Stoneleigh of rights which the king's ancestors had given them. It appeared that all but one of these tenants were paying their rents for their holdings at the regular Stoneleigh free rent of a penny an acre, with a higher rent for some assart land. They were paying, not to the abbot, but to one other tenant Robert of Canley, and in addition were each giving him 1s 6d a year for the suit of court which they should have done to the manor. Robert of Canley said the reason for this was that in the time of Henry II his ancestor, Ketelbern, had been the lord of Canley and that the ancestors of the present Canley tenants had been enfeoffed of their holdings by Ketelbern. A different story emerged from the statements of sworn jurors. According to them Ketelbern was simply a neighbour of the other tenants. They, however, were not rich (*exiles in bonis*) and Ketelbern, being better endowed with both lands and sense (*fuit maior et discrecior*), offered to collect their rent and take it for them to the royal manor. Ketelbern's son married the sister of the constable of Kenilworth Castle, and the constable sanctioned both this diversion of the other tenants' services and the performance for them of their suit to the court of the royal manor. The next stage in the usurpation must have been quite recent and throws curious light on cases in the royal courts by which free men were depressed into servitude. For the Robert of Canley who was answering the charges of 1266 had brought a writ *de navitate* against his neighbours at the last tour round the county of the justices itinerant, by which he had tried to have them declared of servile status. The writ had, however, failed. It is in fact possible that the failure of this suit had led to the whole case against Robert of Canley, because it was not simply a question of a wealthy villager subordinating his neighbours, but of offending the superior lord as well. When the superior lord was the tenant of an ancient demesne manor in which the king still took a lively interest, the local usurper met his just deserts. But if these peculiar circumstances had not been present it is quite likely that by the end of the century the villeinage of the other Canley tenants would have been accepted without question.[17]

The manorial court rolls show us that rich peasants were employers of labour. The labourers worked on the peasant's holding and from time to time were sent on to the demesne to acquit the peasant's labour services. It was accepted as a matter of course that yardlanders, perhaps even half-yardlanders, would have servants. In the lists of labour services on the Bishop of Worcester's manors in 1299 a common stipulation is that the yardlander will attend the three boon reapings on the demesne with all his household (*familia*, a word implying servants as well as relatives) except for his wife and his shepherd. Sometimes the court rolls reveal the ingenuity as well as the enterprise of the peasant employer. William the Parker of Avening (part of the Caen nunnery estate near Minchinhampton) was presented in 1273 for stealing (or perhaps borrowing, since his name may imply an official position on the manor) a bushel of demesne oats to sow on his own land. More than this, at least three, perhaps more, Avening men (and one woman) were presented at the same time for going to work on William's land when they should have been working on the demesne.[18] But these do not in fact look like permanent, but casually hired labourers. In spite of the large numbers of smallholders who must have been available for hire, in spite of the not infrequent casual references in manorial records to such a peasant's *famulus* or *famuli*, it is remarkable how little mention is found of troubles between employers and employed in the records of both manorial and public courts, which otherwise record innumerable examples of uninhibited conflict. The conclusion is inescapable that at the peasant level a number of factors, at this period, prevented the development of serious social divisions. Most important, even wealthy peasant households seldom acquired holdings so big that they needed more than one or two permanent hired hands additional to the labour of the family. Secondly, the high mortality rates even among the relatively well fed prevented the establishment of long-lived rich peasant dynasties. Occasional exceptions, when compared with the total number of non-surviving families, only prove the rule. Thirdly, the policing of the manor, however harsh the penalties imposable for flight, was in fact really ineffective. There was a good deal of mobility of labour, as the lack of regional variation in wage rates shows. And if employment, or the chance of squatting on somebody's waste, did not provide alternatives to starving in the village, the king's wars did.

There was social conflict during this period. But it was first of all a conflict between tenants and lords, and secondly between peasants and officials. Some say that the lawlessness of the age had no social content, that bandits could be from any social group, that hostility to officials is found in all social strata. A careful reading of the manorial and especially the national court records does not bear this theory out. The peasants, tied to the routine of agriculture, in addition to being the victims of manorial exactions, were like all sedentary groups, the prey of the nomads. And the nomads were the gentry, the clerks, the officials and the soldiers, an incoherent, but recognizable set of oppressors.

CHAPTER 7

TOWNS, MARKETS AND MANUFACTURES

Medieval English society was composed mainly of peasants who provided their own means of subsistence. This does not mean that they were living in a purely subsistence economy, as the high level of cash incomes which was enjoyed by the upper class clearly indicates. For those cash incomes were mainly derived from money rents and profits of jurisdiction which came out of the pockets of the tenants and from profits from the sales of demesne produce. The peasants had to sell some of their agricultural products in order to get cash to pay rents, fines and taxes, and the lords sold their demesne produce in order to support their status, their standard of living and their political role in the kingdom. There was a certain amount of trade in agricultural products (in seed for instance) within the agricultural community itself, but the main market for the products of agriculture naturally came primarily from those who were not themselves agricultural producers. To a certain extent the nobility, gentry and clergy bought agricultural products, though much that they consumed came from their own estates and from tithes. Much more important was the demand from the artisans, merchants, lawyers and others whose incomes were in money, and who were primarily town dwellers.

The English towns at the end of the thirteenth century varied enormously in size, function and social structure. London with a population of perhaps 50,000 was comparable rather to one of the great towns of the continent than to any other English town. It was the focal point of a number of international trade routes, was the most important export port for England's massive trade in raw wool and was closely tied up both with the Baltic grain and timber and the Gascon wine trades. The next biggest towns after London were York and Bristol. These were provincial capitals, Bristol's population being reckoned at 17,000, York at about 10,000. They stand on their own, for the next group of towns, county towns for the most part, with a few ports or textile towns (such as Yarmouth, Boston, Lynn, Beverley, Coventry or Bury St Edmunds) seldom exceeded 4,000 and were often only 2,000 or 3,000 strong. After these, there was a very large number of small market towns, some of them nothing more than big villages, others with very definite urban characteristics, that is, a population mainly engaged in trade and industry. The function of these small towns was to enable the agricultural producers of the district to sell their grain, livestock, eggs, cheese and garden vegetables, and to buy manufactured goods in metal, wood and leather, wool and linen cloth, wax, and other commodities unobtainable in the village. Every English county was well supplied with these market centres, each serving an area of twenty or thirty square miles, that is, within an easy day's travelling distance from most villages in the region.[1]

The West Midland Urban Pattern

Although the west midland region was not as densely populated as some other parts of the country, and with its large area of forest could even be thought rather backward, it was nevertheless relatively highly urbanized. In the first place, of course, it contained, peripherally it is true, two major urban centres, Bristol and Coventry. The three county towns of Gloucester, Worcester and Warwick were of moderate size, but the first two at any rate had flourishing economies and social and constitutional features characteristic of the general run of English boroughs. Now, although our knowledge of all these towns is rather scanty for the thirteenth century compared with the later middle ages, we are fairly certain, in general, of their place in the urbanization of the region. It is when we attempt to construct a picture of town life outside these main centres that we face a number of obscurities. These, however, are not peculiar to the west midland region, for important though the small market town is in social and economic history, it has been much neglected in general owing to lack of historical evidence.[2]

There are several features which indicate a degree of urbanization. One obvious indication of urban status in the thirteenth century was that the place concerned should be called a borough (*burgus*), enjoy certain privileges by charter and be inhabited by burgesses (*burgenses*). Chartered privilege cost money, and if a community could raise enough cash to buy a charter from the king or the lord of the town, it is fair indication that there was present a concentration of moneyed wealth normally only found in a mercantile community. However, by the test of chartered privilege, Coventry, though at the end of the thirteenth century undoubtedly a bigger and wealthier town, was not so advanced constitutionally as Worcester, and Warwick was by the same test more backward than Droitwich. Another test of urban status is the proportion of assessed movables paid to the lay subsidy of 1334.[3] Rural communities paid one-fifteenth, towns one-tenth. Here again Coventry is treated with the rural communities, whilst villages, such as Stoneleigh, paid the tenth because they were of the ancient demesne of the crown. Another criterion is representation as a borough in Parliament, and here Coventry was counted as a borough. Yet another indication of urban characteristics is the presence of men holding burgage tenements. This again, as we shall see, is not a totally reliable sign of urbanization. In judging the degree of urbanization in the region at the turn of the thirteenth century we must bear in mind all these partial criteria, but in particular that which is, after all, the primary, real meaning of urban status, the separation from the rural hinterland, the specialization in non-agricultural occupations, and the presence of merchants and artisans. Above all, the existence of a market was essential, though we must beware of assuming that a market charter purchased by a lord of the manor is all the evidence that is needed to prove that a market existed as a going concern.*

In spite of the implications of our generalization about the distribution of market centres in the English counties, it must be stated that towns and markets in the west midlands were at this period unevenly distributed. The most urbanized part of the region seems to have been the southern Cotswolds. This is not surprising since the population density there was higher than most parts of the region except for the Avon valley. It was a very anciently settled and once highly Romanized area. Although its rural population, as in other peasant societies, lived in a largely subsistence economy, the characteristic agricultural surplus

---

* The presence of an annual fair is, of course, no sign of urbanization. They are often found in rural surroundings.

products, wool and barley, were objects of trade: by the end of the thirteenth century the wool was not only exported from the region as a raw material but was also being used in local manufacture; barley was used in enormous quantities for brewing ale.

Cirencester, in spite of the restrictions on its urban autonomy imposed by the abbey, was the principal town of the Cotswolds. Its taxation assessment in 1334 was nearly half that of Gloucester.[4] Its location, intermediate between the Thames valley to the southeast, the wool producing areas to the north, and the Severn valley to the west, made it particularly suitable as a centre of trade. Surrounding it was a constellation of satellite markets. Towards the upper Thames to the east were Fairford and Lechlade; towards Bristol were Minchinhampton, Tetbury, Marshfield, Chipping Sodbury, Wickwar, and Horsley; towards Gloucester were Bisley, and Painswick; and to the north and north-east, Northleach, Burford (just in Oxfordshire), and Stow-on-the-Wold. Not all of these places had urban characteristics other than a chartered market, and some villages whose lords had bought a market charter completely misfired as future centres of commerce. But there were groups of burgesses at Fairford, Lechlade, Tetbury, Chipping Sodbury, Painswick, Northleach and Burford; and the Evesham Abbey town of Stow-on-the-Wold had a lot of obviously non-agricultural tenants even though their holdings are not described as burgages. These little towns were living off the trade of the Cotswold plateau.

Closely linked to the Cotswolds, but also to the river valleys was another group of small nascent urban centres. These were sited just below the escarpment and commanded routes which connected the wolds and the lowlands. One of these, Winchcombe, was a very ancient town, once the county town of Winchcombeshire before that county was merged into Gloucestershire at the beginning of the eleventh century.[5] Besides being at the end of a valley leading up into the hills towards Andoversford it was the seat of an old abbey which, as we have seen, had properties in both wold and vale. Further to the north-east, Broadway in Worcestershire was a market and still-born borough. Chipping Campden, which was in a dip in the wolds rather than at the foot of the escarpment, already played an important part as a north Cotswold wool collecting centre and was to become more important still. At the same time it was connected with the Avon and Stour valleys, and with Stratford-on-Avon in particular. Moving now in the opposite direction south-west along the scarp foot from Winchcombe, we find other market towns linking vale and wold. The Bishop of Hereford's manor of Prestbury had a market and burgesses but was rather overshadowed by near-by Cheltenham, a borough in the lordship of the Abbey of Fécamp. There is somewhat of a gap along the western edge of the scarp, until we get to King's Stanley, where there was a market and a newly created borough. Next were Dursley and Wotton-under-Edge in the northern and southern edges respectively of a spur of the Cotswolds jutting out into the valley. Dursley was the seat of the elder expropriated branch of the Berkeleys and was one of Gloucestershire's oldest boroughs. Wotton-under-Edge, also a market town with a burgess population, was the possession of the younger and greater line of Berkeleys of Berkeley Castle.

As one would expect, the two main river valleys were the other main focus of the urbanization of the medieval west midlands. The urban centres were not so close together as in the southern Cotswolds, but they contained individually bigger towns than were to be found on or at the foot of the wolds. The general causes of urbanization here are obvious. The river routes, particularly the Severn, were main lines of transport for men and goods. Population and production, particularly in the Avon valley, were high, providing a surplus product and an available non-food producing population reserve.[6] The most important valley town was, of course, Bristol. Its original importance may have owed much to its protected situation between the two Severn tributaries, Avon and Frome, but its commercial connections with Ireland, the Atlantic coast of Europe and Iceland, with the midland and south-western counties by the river Severn and with Wales by the river Wye were the obvious causes of its great twelfth- and thirteenth-century expansion.[7] The importance of Gloucester and Worcester was due less entirely to commercial causes. Both were important as river crossings on the way to Wales. Both were sites of royal castles and centres of county administration. Both were packed with religious corporations, and Worcester of course gained extra importance as the seat of the bishop. But they were also important as river ports, and their quays were crowded with boats plying between Shrewsbury and Bristol or between intermediate ports, carrying grain, wool and vegetables to Bristol, and wines and manufactured goods to the

171

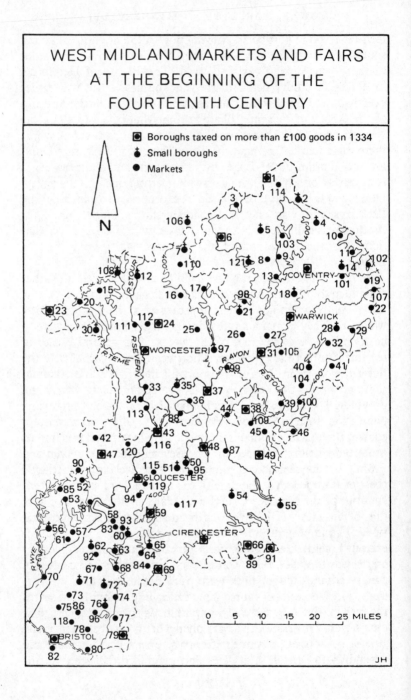

WEST MIDLAND MARKETS AND FAIRS
AT THE BEGINNING OF THE
FOURTEENTH CENTURY

◙ Boroughs taxed on more than £100 goods in 1334
♦ Small boroughs
● Markets

N

Markets and Fairs

The number, and relatively even spread, of chartered markets illustrates the considerable development of local and regional trade. (In the list, F = fair only.)

Key to the west midland markets

1 Tamworth	42 Dymock	81 Newnham
2 Atherstone	43 Tewkesbury	82 Redcliffe
3 Sutton Coldfield	44 Broadway	83 Alkerton F
4 Nuneaton	45 Moreton-in-Marsh	84 Beverstone
5 Coleshill	46 Long Compton	85 Bicknor
6 Birmingham	47 Newent	86 Frampton Coterell
7 Halesowen	48 Winchcombe	87 Guiting (1330)
8 Hampton-in-Arden	49 Stow-on-the-Wold	88 Kemerton
9 Meriden	50 Prestbury	89 Kempsford
10 Wolvey	51 Cheltenham	90 Lea Bailey (1343)
11 Monks Kirby	52 Mitcheldean	91 Lechlade
12 Kidderminster	53 Coleford	92 Newport (1348)
13 Balsall	54 Northleach	93 Leonard Stanley
14 Brinklow	55 Burford	94 Whaddon
15 Rock	56 St Briavels	95 Whittington
16 Bromsgrove	57 Lydney	96 Yate
17 Alvechurch	58 Frampton-on-	97 Alcester
18 Kenilworth	Severn	98 Beaudesert
19 Rugby	59 Painswick	99 Bidford
20 Lindridge	60 Kings Stanley	100 Brailes
21 Henley-in-Arden	61 Alvington	101 Bretford
22 Willoughby	62 Berkeley	102 Churchover
23 Tenbury	63 Dursley	103 Fillongley
24 Droitwich	64 Horsley	104 Tysoe (1341)
25 Feckenham	65 Minchinhampton	105 Wellesbourne Hastings
26 Aston Cantlow	66 Fairford	106 Dudley
27 Snitterfield	67 Tortworth	107 Hillmorton
28 Southam	68 Wotton-under-	108 Bewdley (1376)
29 Napton-on-the-Hill	Edge	109 Blockley F
30 Clifton-on-Teme	69 Tetbury	110 Clent F
31 Stratford-on-Avon	70 Beachley	111 Holt F
32 Bishops Itchington	71 Thornbury	112 Ombersley (1354)
33 Severn Stoke	72 Wickwar	113 Upton-on-Severn (1416)
34 Hanley Castle	73 Tockingham	114 Polesworth
35 Pershore	74 Hawkesbury	115 Churchdown F
36 Elmley Castle	75 Almondsbury	116 Deerhurst
37 Evesham	76 Chipping Sodbury	117 Brimpsfield (1354)
38 Chipping Campden	77 Tormarton	118 Winterbourne (1394)
39 Shipston-on-Stour	78 Pucklechurch	119 Kings Barton F
40 Kineton	79 Marshfield	120 Staunton (1347)
41 Burton Dasset	80 Bitton	121 Solihull

Note : Later chartered markets have been included (with dates) on the grounds that they may simply have been confirmations of existing informal markets.

interior. But apart from these big towns, the only other symptoms of Severn valley urbanization were slight. Between Gloucester and Bristol the market towns of Berkeley and Thornbury, in spite of their burgesses, were of purely local importance: north of Gloucester, the Earl of Gloucester's private borough of Tewkesbury acquired some extra importance, not only as the seat of one of the region's richest Benedictine abbeys, but because of the confluence here of the Avon with the Severn. Between Tewkesbury and Worcester, a market at Hanley Castle, did not indicate any real degree of urbanization in these middle reaches of the river. The markets of Upton-on-Severn, near Hanley Castle, and of Ombersley and Bewdley north of Worcester, were later creations.

The most important town in the Avon valley was Warwick. As the seat of the Earl of Warwick, and as the centre of county administration it had a certain pre-eminence. It is, however, doubtful whether its commercial importance equalled its social and administrative role, although John of the Gate (de Porta, de la Porte), a prominent real property owner in 1280 was also a wool merchant, having bought a licence to trade in wool in the kingdom, provided he did not export to Flanders.[8] It was backward as far as political autonomy was concerned, for the shadow of the castle seems to have been as inhibiting as the shadow of the abbey at Cirencester. Its tax-paying population within the walls in 1332 was considerably smaller than that of the purely urban part of Stratford-on-Avon, and its assessment to the 1334 subsidy was less than Stratford's.[9] There is the complication that Warwick was divided into that part within and that part without the walls, but other towns too had semi-rural suburbs whose recorded numbers and tax assessment we could add to the urban figures. Taking all these factors into consideration Warwick, unlike almost all other centres, urban and rural alike, hardly seemed to be growing in the thirteenth century. Stratford, a new town only a century old in 1300, was certainly growing, becoming an important regional market and river crossing. Further west, Evesham suffered the presence of a powerful lord, the Benedictine abbot, but in spite of lack of the administrative apparatus of borough status was clearly a flourishing little river port, rather smaller than Stratford. Pershore, divided between the abbeys of Pershore and Westminster, hardly got going, in spite of its market and the burgesses of whom we hear as early as 1086.

There were, of course, a number of centres with chartered markets outside the populous and commercially advanced valley and Cotswold areas. These were to be found west of the river Severn in the Forest of Dean and up the Teme valley, as well as in northern Worcestershire and Warwickshire. Some seigneurial boroughs, like Henley-in-Arden, dominated by the Montforts' castle at Beaudesert, hardly became urban in character; on the other hand the seigneurial borough of Kidderminster in north Worcestershire was becoming, like Worcester, a cloth-manufacturing centre. In the north of Warwickshire, Birmingham, on the surface a purely rural manor with a chartered market, was beginning to grow. Its tax assessment in 1334 was greater than that of Warwick within the walls. This early stage in Birmingham's growth is usually attributed to commercial rather than industrial development. As we have shown, there are indications that it was an important entrepot of the Welsh and North of England cattle trade in the direction of Coventry and the South. But in Birmingham itself, in the villages of the adjacent parish of Aston, and reaching as far as Coleshill and Walsall there are indications that some specialization in iron-working was already beginning. This industry was not, however, focused in an urban setting, and was for long to remain rural or semi-rural, like much of medieval industry.[10]

Worcestershire contained a genuine, purely industrial town, Droitwich. It was one of the main national supply centres of salt, the others being the brine springs of Cheshire and the coastal salt pans of the east coast, especially Lincolnshire. The Droitwich brine springs had been producing salt ever since Anglo-Saxon times, and production continued to expand, even after the beginnings of large scale import from the French Atlantic coast in the middle of the fourteenth century. Salt was in fact vital in the medieval economy not as a condiment but as the means by which perishable foods like meat, fish, cheese and butter could be preserved. This was its main use, much more important quantitatively than industrial uses, such as tanning. The Droitwich brine was measured out by the borough officials to private individuals who had property rights in it. The claims of these persons were measured out from the brine springs according to a measure called a 'vat', each of which produced about twenty quarters of salt a year. They paid dues to the borough, a right which the burgesses had been given by charter in 1215. It was the vat owners who, having drawn their allocation of brine from the pits, had it boiled and reduced to salt which they then marketed. Owing to the need for the borough authorities to keep records of payments of dues by vat owners we have quite good sources of information about salt production, but information about the marketing is much less abundant. However, the network of roads along which the salt was distributed to the world at large can still be identified by the names given to these roads, such as Saltway, Salters' Way and so on.

Droitwich was situated on an important highway from the Severn valley at Worcester which went through Birmingham to Lichfield and northwards. This was a position useful for its commerce. On the other hand it was set in the middle of Feckenham Forest, a rather thinly populated region. Not that this was a disadvantage, given Droitwich's special function, for the boiling of the brine made great demands on fuel. Since most vat owners were also lords of manors they were in a better position than others to acquire fuel from the woods. By 1300 then, Droitwich was a flourishing town, with municipal self-government and a chartered market to match its industrial importance. A lot of money must have been made there, because the burgesses had to pay an annual fee farm of £100 a year to the exchequer for their privileges, compared with only £30 paid by Worcester.[11]

Let us summarize our picture of the urban element in west midland society at the end of the thirteenth century before going on to describe the more important aspects of town life in greater detail. At either end of the region there were the two manufacturing and trading centres of Bristol and Coventry. Of the three county towns, Gloucester and Worcester were flourishing river ports and centres of manufacture, Gloucester (assessed for the subsidy in 1334 at £54) being larger than Worcester (assessed at £20). These two towns had the amount of municipal self-government characteristic of most chartered boroughs in the country. Warwick on the other hand, dominated by its earls, was stagnant. The only other royal boroughs in the region were Winchcombe and Droitwich. Constitutionally, Winchcombe was succumbing to the death-like grasp of the monastic house in its midst, whose abbot was more and more assuming the king's position in the borough and in the rural hundreds surrounding it. Droitwich, as we have seen, was a flourishing industrial centre though its capacity for growth was somewhat limited by the monopolistic attitudes of the borough government and the brine owners. Apart from these places, industry and trade, in so far as it was focused in urban or quasi-urban centres, was under the control of private lords. The market charters which had been acquired by about 1300, about one hundred and ten in all, had mostly been brought from the crown by lords, who realized the profit they could make from tolls and tallage fees by giving facilities to an existing traffic.[12] In some cases lords went further and attempted to plant communities of burgesses in these market centres, hoping that merchants and artisans would be attracted as permanent residents. In some cases the venture succeeded, in others not. The point to remember, however, is that while urbanization was impossible without economic growth, its setting was a society dominated by lay and ecclesiastical lords who took a share of the profits and gave their own special stamp to many of the towns, before loosening their grip–if they ever did.

The Towns and the Trade of the Region

The nature of the documentary evidence makes it difficult to find out about the day-to-day economic and social contacts between town and country. There are no details of tolls charged on goods for any of the west midland towns showing the volume, character or origin of commodities coming into or exported from them. There are none of those interesting contracts between country producers and town merchants, such as are found in continental notaries' registers. The only evidence of this sort of trade is indirect, occasional reference in manorial accounts to places where goods were bought and sold which unfortunately have no quantitative value. For example, the Elmley Castle building accounts for 1347 inform us that prepared timber was bought at Evesham and Worcester; that lath nails were bought at Evesham; and that lime was stored (having presumably come by river) at Saxons Lode on the river Severn near Ripple so as to be brought by cart to Elmley.[13] Such figures tell us nothing about the volume of trade or production. Carrying services owed by customary tenants are uncertain indicators of the currents of trade. On the Worcester Cathedral estate, from most of the manors, whether those between Worcester and the Hereford border, in the Avon valley, or the Cotswolds, there was provision of carrying services to Worcester. These reflect a traffic which was separate from normal commercial channels, although, as we have seen, the grain from the estate, by the end of the thirteenth century, was sold on the Worcester market rather than consumed in the priory. Carrying services from Cutsdean (Gloucestershire) to Evesham were however more likely used for sales or purchase on the Evesham market. The Bishop of Worcester's boatmen in Bishops Wick had to take loads of timber to various parts of Worcestershire by boat, and these journeys also might have been commercial in aim. As we have seen, carrying services from the Gloucester Abbey manor of Buckland near Broadway were to other places besides Gloucester, including Tewkesbury, Evesham, Chipping Campden and Clifford Chambers (near Stratford-on-Avon). These were almost certainly journeys for commercial purposes. Unfortunately few other lists of Gloucester Abbey labour services specify the places to which goods had to be carried, and where they do it concerns inter-manorial rather than commercial traffic.[14]

Although it cannot be measured quantitatively, there are some useful insights into the nature of the regional trade from sources which often show obstacles placed in the way of its normal flow. For example, the 1274 Hundred Rolls are full of reported incidents connected with the wool trade. We know, of course, that wool was being produced in various parts of the region for export as well as for local consumption, so it comes as no surprise to read about these incidents. They are usually described in complaints about wool merchants being mulcted by royal and even seigneurial agents as they took their wool to the coast during the period of a ban on the export of wool to Flanders after 1270. Sometimes bribes seem to have been taken to allow illegal export, but more often the merchants had government export licences but had to pay money to be allowed to proceed. The journeys which were impeded were not only those of merchants travelling with local wool but those of merchants bringing the high quality wool of the Welsh Marches. Henry of Abergavenny and others paid heavily as they passed through Westbury Hundred, presumably on their way to Gloucester bridge, for permission to take their wool through the county. The Cistercian Abbot of Tintern, a big wool producer, was said by the jurors of the Hundred of St Briavels in the Forest of Dean to have sold his wool every year to Flemish merchants, though they did not mention that he needed to pay any bribes to get his wool through. Brightwellsbarrow Hundred jurors in the extreme south-east of Gloucestershire also reported the famous Shrewsbury merchant, Nicholas of Ludlow, for taking his wool for export during the period of the ban. They cannot have known that in 1273 he had bought licences for the export of more than three hundred sacks.[15]

But much of the wool mentioned in the record must have been from Gloucestershire. According to the provenance of the local juries who reported incidents involving wool merchants we can locate the area from which the merchants started or through which they were passing, for the precise place is seldom stated, nor is the place of destination. However, jurors in south-east Gloucestershire refer twice to Southampton as the destination of some wool convoys, including wool taken by Nicholas of Ludlow. More surprising, a Bristol merchant, John le Long, also equipped with an export licence, was sending wool overland to Southampton. His load was intercepted by the bailiff of John Muscegros, a prominent landowner with manors in Gloucestershire and Somerset. But clearly, a good deal of wool was being shipped direct from Bristol, mostly by foreign buyers. Hence some of the wool which was the target of local extortion may have been going there. Reported stoppages in Winchcombe, Kiftsgate Hundred, Chipping Sodbury, Cirencester and Grumbalds Ash Hundred were probably of Cotswold wool which could have been going either to Bristol or Southampton, as also could the Marcher wool intercepted in the forest and in the hundreds on the west bank of the Severn.[16]

The evidence just quoted is insufficiently specific to allow one to draw conclusions about the organization of the wool trade. Clearly there was a substantial number of foreign merchants, from the Low Countries in particular, but it is impossible to say whether they were making direct contact with country graziers rather than frequenting the urban marts. Some London merchants were certainly making arrangements direct with the growers. These included Adam of Blakeneye, and Reginald of Toundesle or Thunderle, a draper, recently immigrated. They were buying Gloucestershire wool from the Westminster Abbey bailiwick of Todenham in the early 1290s. This perhaps was easy because of London's proximity to Westminster, but there were other Londoners, part of the same small circle of those interested in this trade, who were making direct contact with Forest of Dean (Flaxley Abbey) and Cotswold growers. Another was John of Burford, a pepperer and alderman with interests in the wool export. In 1315 he paid Worcester Cathedral Priory 160 marks for twenty sacks of good, well-cleaned wool and made arrangement to buy more in 1316, 1317 and 1318. Collection was to be made at the Avon valley manor of Cropthorne where wool from the Cotswold flocks of the priory would also be concentrated.[17]

But Bristol obviously was an active wool mart; nor was it the only one. A curious case at the Gloucester assizes in 1306 shows that some Cotswold marts, better known for their activity in the fifteenth century, were already centres of the wool trade. The Kiftsgate jurors presented William of Combemartyn, an alderman of London and the biggest of the London exporters, for spreading a rumour through a group of agents that the king was going to take all the wool throughout England, thus causing a drop in prices. These rumour-mongers were principally operating at the fairs of Northleach, Cirencester and Tetbury. William of Combemartyn's aim, of course, was to be in a position to buy up wool cheap. Neither he nor his agents could be found in Gloucestershire, but eventually he appeared before the judges in Oxford, where he offered a fine of 200 marks to get himself off. A local wool merchant in the district, buying up monastic wool in large quantities, was Geoffrey of Marston, burgess of Cirencester, who first makes his appearance in the records of Cirencester Abbey in 1306. A contract made between him and Lanthony Priory in 1319 is copied on to the flyleaf of one of the Lanthony cartularies. It shows that he had agreed to buy at the priory manor of Barrington 'good, dry and well cleaned wool' at $11\frac{1}{2}$ marks a sack to the total value of 100 marks. The wool was to be from priory sheep, but if the amount fell short the canons were to make up the value from other sources. Another local merchant, Richard le Mercer of Worcester, contracted in 1312 with the prior and convent at Worcester to buy twenty sacks of wool over two years for £103 6s 8d, and to buy the third year's wool at the slightly improved price of eight marks a sack.[18]

The grain trade must have been very active, operating for the most part over short distances. As we have seen the Bristol evidence shows fluctuations in grain prices which reveal considerable variations during the year in the supply of the commodity. This no doubt led to a certain amount of speculative buying and selling. The urban markets were naturally those which absorbed the greatest amount of the country surplus and where the conflicting interests of townsmen and country producers were brought to the surface. So, in 1274 we find men from the rural area near Bristol, in Henbury Hundred, complaining that when they went with their grain to Bristol and Sodbury to sell to the men of those towns, the buyers were trying to extract an illegal advantage by manipulating the half-bushel measures. A year later the jurors of Halfshire

Hundred in Worcestershire presented dealers in Droitwich and Bromsgrove for buying grain by a large bushel measure and selling it by a small one. It was in this year that Miles of Evesham, the Evesham grain dealer, was accused of concealing usurious loans in his dealings. We need not be surprised therefore at bad blood between buyers and sellers leading to violent quarrels. John de Ferrers of Chartley had just married the heiress of John Muscegros and acquired, amongst other properties, the manors of Kemerton near Tewkesbury, and Boddington, six miles north-east of Gloucester. In June 1302 he sent some of his men to Gloucester to sell grain, and two Gloucester men bought half a quarter, which they took to their house, but refused to pay 3s 4d demanded. The quarrel may have been about the price. There is a series of Bristol prices extant for this year, the highest of which was 5s 8d, probably near harvest time, most of them being below 5s. A price of 6s 8d a quarter in June does therefore look like extortion. A fight broke out between Ferrer's servants and a crowd of some thirty Gloucester men, following an exchange of blows with one of the buyers, Andrew of Pendock. The townsmen rang the town bells, and the countrymen had to retreat to Gloucester castle. They were joined later by their lord who had come to Gloucester to find out what was happening and was chased there by the town crowd. They were unable to get away until they were rescued by the sheriff and the king's bailiffs from the Forest of Dean.[19]

Most of the grain trade probably consisted of deals between country growers and local townsmen. There was undoubtedly a longer distance trade, as well as occasional exports. Grain was a bulky commodity, and transport by such rivers as the Severn would be cheaper than by road. A broken contract about which there was litigation is suggestive. The buyer, Robert of Sestenelode, had contracted in 1275 to buy the grain of two years from Master Walter of Bertun at Aust. Robert died and his son refused to honour the contract. Now Aust is on the east bank of the Severn estuary, opposite the mouth of the river Wye at an ancient river crossing. 'Sestenelode' is the medieval form of the modern 'Saxons Lode', a landing on the Severn between Upton and Ripple. It was used, as we have already seen, as a landing place for building materials needed at Elmley Castle. If Robert of Sestenelode and his son, as is likely, lived or worked at Saxons Lode, they may have been specialist dealers in grain and possibly other materials coming up river. The contract was for 35 marks 10s (£23 6s 8d), a big sum implying a commercial venture. Another case in the legal records shows long distance traffic by land to a district where there was probably a grain shortage. This was reported in 1305 and concerned a robbery committed in Studley (Warwickshire). A cart loaded with grain belonging to a merchant from Ashbourne in the Peak district was broken into by a local man who stole half a quarter of grain priced at 1s 6d. This was cheap and no doubt was the reason why the merchant had come so far to buy it.[20]

Merchants were, in fact, clearly prepared to invest considerable sums in buying grain. Letters from the Abbot of Westminster in 1285 and 1292 mention payments (perhaps in instalments) of £21 and 22 marks (£14 13s 4d) for the grain crops of Todenham and Bourton-on-the-Hill. The abbot, like such landowners as Ferrers, was also prepared to organize quick, small sales in order to raise cash, as when the serjeant and reeve of Todenham were instructed in 1293 to sell 40s worth of wheat and oats so as to buy cattle. He could, however, wait, as when in February 1295 he instructed the same serjeant to make advances of grain to local people at the price prevailing the previous Michaelmas, the money to be collected in the fortnight before the next Michaelmas.[21]

Presentments by town juries of offences connected with articles of sale frequently mention cloth sold against the assize (probably in reference to short measure), but at this period such evidence as we have about cloth concerns production rather than sale. There are also many incidental references to wine sales in the larger towns. Bristol was the main place through which wine entered the west midlands, though, judging by the exemptions from the custom on wine which are given in the constable's accounts, more than two-thirds of the wine imported into Bristol normally went to Wales and Ireland. There is no evidence about the local redistribution or about the relations between Bristol vintners and those of other towns. A presentment by the jurors of Halfshire Hundred gives a brief glimpse of the trade. It concerned an accident that happened in 1275, somewhere in the hundred, when a carter driving a cart loaded with a barrel of wine for Coventry was killed by the cart and its load falling on him. The cart, the animals pulling it, the harness and the wine were valued, since the carter's relatives were entitled to the 'deodand', the value of the inanimate killer. The total value was £3 14s 4d of which the wine and the barrel were worth

£2 6s 8d. The deodand had to be paid by the man to whom the wine was being taken, John of Ludlow. This man, or rather his heirs and relatives, appear as real property owners in Coventry in 1280. There seems no reason to connect him with the Shrewsbury wool merchants of the same name, but a later John of Ludlow who died in 1295 and held a manor in Chipping Campden may have belonged to the Coventry family.[22]

Urban Growth

Another source provides some evidence, not of commercial currents, but of the area of the recruitment of population from the countryside to the towns. These are the lists of names of townsmen in tax assessments and surveys. Surnames in the thirteenth century were seldom hereditary. A man's permanent name was what we would call his christian name, but since medieval parents were conservative in the names they gave their children (a boy often being called after his grandfather) it was necessary to identify a person more precisely. If he was not a native of the place in which he dwelt he would be called after the place from which he came. He also might be called by his occupation. And sometimes he was given a nickname, frequently a physical characteristic. The same man might be known by several different surnames. A note in the Stoneleigh Abbey Leger Book, concerning the ancestor of a man whose ownership of some land had to be proved, states: 'Memo that Robert the Heir, Robert the son of John of Stoneleigh, Robert de la Maree, Robert Wynrych was one and the same man.' This fluidity of surnames presents a lot of difficulties when one is trying to trace descents, but it has the advantage that, in a thirteenth-century list of names, if a man is called 'John of X', X is almost certainly the place from which he, or at the earliest his father, had recently arrived.[23]

Lists of names of inhabitants of some west midland towns yield some interesting results on analysis. We know from other evidence which were the towns that were reception centres for rural immigrants and which were growing only slowly or were virtually stagnant. As one would expect it was the already big centres of trade, industry and therefore of opportunity and (no doubt) excitement which took the most immigrants. The 1275 tax list of Worcester contains 314 names. Of this total, 117 surnames indicated an origin outside the city. In the 1280 Hundred Rolls for Coventry, 127 out of about 500 names are composed of place-names. In a Bristol tallage roll of 1312–3, there are 1,111 names of which 323 are place-names. A Gloucester tax list of 1327 shows that 110 people out of 257 had place-name surnames. In these four big and growing west midland towns then, only in Coventry does the proportion of place-name surnames fall much below a third of the total, the Bristol proportion being not much less than a third. But both the Coventry Hundred Rolls and the Bristol tallage roll tend to lay more stress on owners of real property (some of whom might have been non-resident) than do the tax returns. The 1327 tax return for Bristol and the 1332 tax return for Coventry both show place-name surnames as well over one-third of the whole. Now if it is true that these place-name surnames indicate, by and large, the recent immigrants, it is of considerable interest that in smaller places for which there is not other evidence of economic expansion, the place-name surname proportion is considerably lower. In the monopoly-ridden town of Droitwich in 1275 it was only one-tenth, in backward Dursley it was only a tenth, in Winchcombe it was only a sixth, in Painswick a fifth, in Henley-in-Arden a sixth, in Warwick a quarter. On the other hand, in Stratford-on-Avon (1332), a growing town, it was between a third and a half; in Newent on the northern edge of the Forest of Dean, a town replacing Dymock as the local market centre, it was a third.[24]

The big and the growing towns then, were growing by considerable rural recruitment. If we plot the place-names which are used as surnames on a map, we find, of course, that some come from other parts of the country, even from abroad. But these are in a minority. The great majority come from within a radius of thirty or forty miles at the outside. In the Worcester 1275 list, for example, eighty-three out of a hundred and seventeen place-names used as surnames are in Worcestershire or adjacent counties. But there is nothing surprising about this. Urban mortality rates were probably higher than those of the countryside, so towns could not expand rapidly merely by natural increase. In the thirteenth century, as we have seen, there is evidence of population pressure on the land. But in view of the difficulties of communication, the differences in local speech and custom it is not surprising that most rural emigrants from their villages should not want to cut themselves off completely from their place of origin, and would not, therefore, travel far.

Even the biggest towns kept something of a rural atmosphere about them. Coventry, Worcester and Gloucester all had common fields, that is arable and meadow in individual possession but over which burgesses were liable to claim pasture rights. The meadows were prominent, of course, in the riverside cities. Worcester had its Pitchcroft, Gloucester a whole row of meadows on the banks of the river Severn, such as Common Ham, Oxleasow, Archdeacons Meadow and so on. Coventry had its Lammas Lands by the Sherbourne river, commonable after 1 August by the freemen of the city. Every town had barns and byres and pigstyes within the walls. None were so built up that there were not innumerable gardens, crofts, curtilages and orchards interspersed among the buildings. According to the Coventry Hundred Rolls return of 1280 there were rather more than seven hundred properties described as burgages, messuages, cottages and tenements, and which might therefore be regarded as part of the built-up area. But there were also about a hundred curtilages, thirty crofts, a few gardens, even pieces of meadow and ridges of arable scattered among the built-up sites. Nor can it be certain that a holding referred to as a burgage was necessarily totally occupied by buildings. The term burgage meant a piece of land, subject to certain conditions of tenure which originally gave to the tenant his rights and status as a burgess. These burgage tenements could be quite large, upwards from half an acre. In Coventry some holdings that were described tenurially as burgages were, in fact, crofts. About a hundred and eighty out of two hundred and sixty burgages were still held integrally by one tenant and may therefore only have contained one dwelling house with its outbuildings. The capacity of the burgage is, however, shown by the fact that in thirteenth-century Coventry, two burgages could be divided up and sublet as thirty cottages and thirteen curtilages.[25] This is an extreme example, but the sixty burgages that were subdivided are testimonies to the building expansion that was under way. But it was nowhere near complete enough to fill up the empty spaces in the town.

The thirteenth century was an era when the urban areas proper were being filled up to house the growing population and when suburbs grew, not only to take the overspill (for there was still room enough in the towns), but to house those who were not allowed to share the privileges of the townsmen. Suburbs might partly be occupied by ordinary farmers and landowners, but they were also the refuge of the poorer labourers and artisans. Bristol, which became rapidly built up in the thirteenth century, had sub-burbs south of the Avon, east of the new course of the Frome and to the north. The chief suburbs of Gloucester were outside the North and South Gates, and were also developed during the thirteenth century. North of Worcester, the bishop already owned an extensive suburban development at Northwick as early as the end of the eleventh century. Its further development in the twelfth and thirteenth centuries is testified in the two surveys of the bishop's lands in 1182 and 1299. There were also suburban developments towards the manor of Battenhall on the south side and over the bridge on the west bank of the Severn. Warwick had its suburbs mainly to the east. Outside Coventry there were a number of hamlets in the Arden woods which gradually became, not so much urbanized, as suburbanized. But the woodland here was to a certain extent a barrier to early suburban expansion, as was Feckenham Forest at Worcester's East Gate and the river Severn west of Gloucester. Walls, however, more necessary for defence near to Wales than they were deeper in the midlands, seem to have made little difference to the proliferation of suburban dwellings. By the end of the thirteenth century, Bristol had four sets of walls where it was not protected by the moat formed by Avon and Frome; around the castle; around the original nucleus of the town; around the south-western suburb between the Frome and Avon; and around the Berkeley suburbs of Redcliffe and Bedminster. Gloucester had walled defences by the end of the thirteenth century partly superimposed on the walls of Roman Glevum. They perhaps did not entirely surround the city, protection on the west being given by the old and new branches of the river Severn. But they must have been adequate, for Robert of Gloucester's metrical history shows how Sir John Giffard of Brimpsfield and a companion during the Baron's Wars had to enter the city by deceiving the keepers of the western gate.* Worcester, too, only needed walls on the north, east and west sides, partly superimposed, as in the case of Gloucester, on pre-existing Roman walls. The west was protected by the Severn. Warwick's

---

* See below, Chapter 8, pp. 224–5.

walls enclosed the whole town (not including the suburbs), but Coventry did not have any walls until the end of the fourteenth century.[26]

The walls were not the town's only defences. Each of the county towns and Bristol had a castle. That of Bristol was occupied by royal castellans who also accounted for all royal revenue from the town as well as from the king's suburban manors. Gloucester castle was the home of the sheriff and therefore the focus of the county administration. Worcester castle, also the sheriff's headquarters, was in a sense a private castle since the shrievalty was the hereditary right of the Beauchamp family. But though they were hereditary sheriffs of Worcestershire and castellans of Worcester Castle (acting through an under-sheriff) they were not sheriffs of Warwickshire. Consequently the sheriff of Warwick, who was usually also sheriff of Leicestershire, had to do without a castle in the county town. Warwick Castle was the private possession of the earl. It was not, however, true that castle and town were always in harmony. The king, when displeased with the burgesses of Bristol, would place the rule of the town in the hands of his castellan, so that the castle became the symbol of oppression rather than protection. This was the case, too, during the Barons' Wars at Gloucester, when the baronial partisans, supported by the burgesses, besieged the sheriff in the castle.

The town walls, were they existed, may not have prevented the growth of suburbs, but they were all the same a manifestation of the division between town and country, especially since they were not the only symptom of this division. However rural the atmosphere of medieval Worcester or Gloucester might seem to be to us, there were distinctions between townsmen and countrymen which went far beyond simple differences in economic function. Furthermore these distinctions held good, or were expected to hold good, in towns much smaller than the big commercial, industrial, and administrative centres we have been discussing.

Urban Characteristics

In the twelfth and thirteenth centuries, when social status was still much influenced by the terms on which a man held land, one of the most recognizable distinguishing characteristics of urban communities was that the leading men of the communities held by burgage tenure, were governed by borough custom and were known as burgesses. Burgage tenure was a form of free tenure, and the individual burgage plot, as we have already mentioned, was quite sizeable as a building site, sometimes not much short of an acre, but was not meant to be agricultural land. It was held almost invariably by money rent only. This money rent was often as low as 1d or 2d in old boroughs, such as Gloucester where it was called 'land gable' (from *gafol*, Anglo-Saxon for rent). Newly created burgages, however, were often rented at as much as 12d, higher that is than arable land. But burgage tenure conferred on the tenant a whole number of privileges, such as free alienation of land, favoured terms in the borough market, preferential treatment in the payment of tolls, not to speak of political privileges, so that those who made their living by trade and manufacture were prepared to pay the heavier rent.

Burgage tenure was to be found in all the big and in some of the smaller towns by the twelfth century. The name is of Norman-French origin but although there were important borrowings of continental borough custom, through Normandy, it could not have been entirely a post-conquest innovation. In pre-conquest England, boroughs had a customary law peculiar to the urban mercantile communities, enjoyed by men whose status was primarily determined by their trading activities, but who, of course, in a land-owning society occupied houses and land in the towns. These urban building sites were often known as 'haws', and many pre-conquest 'haws' must have become post-conquest 'burgages'. The burgess communities of places like Bristol, Worcester and Gloucester are not therefore anything out of the ordinary, though it must not be imagined that all the towns' inhabitants held burgages or enjoyed burgess status. The burgesses were an urban aristocracy of traders, perhaps including the richer master craftsmen. It is also a matter of course to find burgages and burgesses in smaller but old established urban communities like Winchcombe, Droitwich and Cirencester. As we have seen, the rapidly expanding town of Coventry already had a large number of burgage tenements by 1280.

One of the measures of the urbanization of the west midlands before the end of the thirteenth century, in addition to the expansion of the main trading and industrial centres, is the proliferation of those small towns to which we have already referred. The deliberate creation by lords of new towns is a well known phenomenon over the whole of medieval Europe during this period of demographic and economic expansion, and it was done in many different ways. In our region it was for the most part done by the creation within the framework of an existing agricultural community of a group of burgesses, holding burgage tenements, with their own borough court and market. All of these new communities were founded by private lords, and in this way differ from the older towns, most of which were on the royal demesne.

There was a considerable range in the importance and size of the seigneurial boroughs. Strictly speaking, Bristol should be counted among them, for although it was in the hands of the crown by the period about which we are writing, it had once been part of the Honour of Gloucester, which did not fall to the crown until the reign of King John. Even after that there remained parts of the urban area in which seigneurial privilege was entrenched. Coventry too was a borough which did not throw off the seigneurial yoke until the middle of the fourteenth century. There is still disagreement among historians about the nature of that seigneurial yoke. It seems possible that at the end of the eleventh century the borough of Coventry belonged to the earls of Chester, successors to Godgifu of Mercia. However, only its agricultural, not its urban component, was recorded in Domesday Book, under the name 'Godeva'. Nevertheless, burgess tenants existed in 1129 at the latest and some time between 1129 and 1153 their lord, Earl Ranulf II of Chester, gave them the privileges of the city of Lincoln. Some time in mid- or late-twelfth century, the monks of Coventry's Benedictine Cathedral Priory forged charters which purported to give them lordship over a substantial enclave around the cathedral. This would have led to prolonged conflicts between the lords had not the Earl of Chester's heir, Roger of Mold, granted his lordship on lease, round about 1250, to the Prior of the cathedral. The Prior thus became lord of the whole of Coventry. By 1280, when the Hundred Rolls enquiry was made, the division into two lordships was clear. But the similarity of courts and market privileges in the descriptions of the separate parts, and the fact that many burgesses had property in both parts, suggests that there was basically one urban community. Recent interpretations argue that quarrels, once thought to have been between the Earl's tenants and the Prior's tenants, may rather have been between the burgesses as a body and the Prior. The debate continues.[27]

In many seigneurial boroughs the urban element hardly outranked the rural. Tewkesbury, whose burgesses had been given important privileges by the earls of Gloucester in the twelfth century, was, by 1307, a market town in which seventy burgesses held 146 burgages at the normal new town burgage rent of 12d. But there was also a manorial demesne of about 300 acres, a park, and 115 manorial tenants both free and customary. All these were included in the manor of Tewkesbury. Another borough and manor of the Earl of Gloucester, Fairford, was surveyed in the same year. The market town was inhabited by sixty-eight burgesses each holding a burgage, paying a 12d rent. There was a fair, a market, and a court for the burgesses, which are clearly grossly undervalued. But this description is overshadowed by that of the rural manor, which consisted of a very large demesne of some 700 acres, thirty-one free tenants and about eighty customary tenants and cottagers. Chipping Sodbury, another borough and manor of the Earl of Gloucester, shows rather a preponderance of the borough over the manor. There were 160 burgages, a fair, a market and a borough court, but only about fifty free and customary tenants of the manor. There was, however, a large demesne of some 700 acres. But the income from the borough was a third of the total Sodbury income, whereas at Fairford it was only reckoned at about a fourteenth of the whole. Most of these Cotswold seigneurial boroughs, like the ones just described, or Tetbury, or Northleach, or Chipping Campden eventually paid off whatever investment the lord had to make in laying out burgage tenements and attracting trades and artisans. For most of them took a lively part in the vigorous economic activities of the region, and two of them, Northleach and Chipping Campden, were later to become as famous even as Cirencester as wool markets.[28]

One of the most interesting and successful of the seigneurial boroughs of the region is Stratford-on-Avon. Its history shows clearly how the new borough community was inserted into the rural manor, and what were the topographical aspects of this new growth. The lord of Stratford was the Bishop of Worcester, and there is a fairly detailed description of the manor in the bishop's survey of 1182. It was composed then of three settlements, Stratford itself, by the river, Shottery to the west and Welcombe to the east. Bishopston and Clopton which had been part of Stratford manor were not at the bishop's disposal, as they were now sub-manors on their own. In 1182 the bulk of the population was concentrated in Shottery where there were nearly half of the named tenants of the manor. About a third were in Stratford and the rest were in Welcombe.[29] Now, as its name implies, the river Avon was fordable at Stratford, and was crossed, not only by a Roman branch road from the Fosse Way to Alcester (the *straet* of Stratford) but by routes along the northern Cotswold scarp, and up the Stour valley, going north and north-east. In 1196, John of Coutances, Bishop of Worcester, obtained a market charter from the king for Stratford, and immediately issued a charter to his burgesses of Stratford. Since there were no burgesses at Stratford in 1182, this was probably in effect the foundation charter of the new borough, for, in addition to confirming the heritability of the burgage plots, it lays down their dimensions, 3½ by 12 perches, the rent due from them, 12d, freedom from toll and the customs of the Norman borough of Breteuil, a common source for new town customs.[30] By 1252, instead of the eighteen peasant tenants in the Stratford of 1182, there was a borough community of some 300 tenants of burgages or fractions of burgages. About forty of them had surnames indicating an industrial craft, such as tanner, whitesmith, dyer, weaver or cooper, but most of them had place-name surnames. There was already the beginning, not only of the subdivision of burgages, but of their concentration in fewer hands. Robert the Tanner, for example, had five burgages and a piece of land. He probably sub-let most of this land, perhaps to other burgesses, perhaps to persons not appearing in this rental of 1252. But however the burgage plots were really distributed, it looks as if within half a century Stratford had grown until it was bigger than either Evesham or Warwick, its two Avon valley neighbours.[31]

Henceforth the rural manor was known as Old Stratford to distinguish it from Stratford borough. The original peasant community of Stratford itself seems to have been entirely eliminated by the borough, although, according to the 1252 and 1299 rentals, there were still some free tenants who were not burgesses. Shottery and Welcombe on the other hand nearly doubled their tenant population between 1182 and 1252. The remnants of rural Stratford were probably to the west of the urban area, in the vicinity of the parish church, the collegiate church of the Holy Trinity. This church is outside the boundaries of the borough since it was the centre of a large rural parish.* The urban area was, of course, easily distin-

* The only medieval church in the borough itself is the chapel of the Holy Cross Gild, built in the fifteenth century.

guished because it had been laid out in burgage plots of equal size, a regularity which reflected itself in the street plan, and which can still be seen.

The bishop's new town flourished, as did many of the borough creations of lords in other parts of the region. Not all were equally successful. The almost contemporary creation, probably sometime in the 1220s, by the Abbot of Westminster, Richard of Barking, of a 'new town' at Moreton-in-Marsh, hardly seems to have developed, in spite of its official market (1220) and fair (1253). In 1327 its taxed population was only one more than that of the neighbouring village of Bourton-on-the-Hill. Its taxation assessment was only a third that of Bourton. The growth of the new town, along the Fosse Way, and away from the 'old town' and its parish church, came much later.[32] There were, however, much more marked failures than this. In eastern Warwickshire, the village of Bretford, near to the Verdon castle at Brandon, was a member of the manor of Brandon. However it is where the Fosse Way crosses the river Avon, so in 1227 the lord, Nicholas de Verdon, either taking advantage of or anticipating some local commerce, obtained the grant of a market charter from the king. Although no record of an attempt by the lord to follow up the market charter with the creation of a borough community, as at Stratford, survives, something like this must have happened. For in 1280, according to the Hundred Rolls, Bretford's tenant population consisted of nineteen burgesses holding thirty-one and a half burgages, and 11½ acres of land in free tenure. The burgage rent was the 12d characteristic of newly formed boroughs and there was an acre of land for each burgage as well. However the burgesses had to do haymaking and reaping services, for the lord, Theobald de Verdon, had a demesne of two ploughlands. There was not enough land for subsistence, even though some men were tenants of two or three burgages. They may have been in some way involved in the manorial economy of Brandon, to which they owed suit of court. Certainly nothing came of the borough. Sir William Dugdale, who knew the Warwickshire Hundred Rolls and transcribed details about them from the Brandon entry in his *Antiquities of Warwickshire*, does not even mention the burgesses of Bretford.[33]

Another failed borough was Broadway, a manor of the Abbot of Pershore at the foot of the northern scarp of the Cotswolds. This was on the road between Evesham and Stow-on-the-Wold, close to Ryknield Street and to the White Way from Stratford-on-Avon over the Cotswold plateau to Cheltenham and Cirencester. The Abbot of Pershore bought a charter for a Friday market and a mid-summer fair in 1251, an expenditure he would not have made had he not been confident of profit on an existing trade. This charter is registered in a late thirteenth-century cartulary (unprinted) of the abbey together with other charters relating to Broadway land transactions. None of these land transactions give any inkling that the abbot had followed the current fashion of borough creation, but the earliest of the Broadway court rolls, dating from 1388, suggests that some time previously such an act of creation had taken place. Broadway, for the purpose of the presentment of offenders and all matters requiring court action, was divided into three tithings. Two were parts of the village, Upend and West End. The third tithing was referred to as the Portmoot, the normal name for a borough or town court. Land transactions in the Port-moot concerned burgages and there was a statement of custom to the effect that burgages could be alienated by portmoot charter. The existence of the Broadway portmoot suggests a borough crea-tion between West End and Upend, probably on the Evesham to Stow road near the bottom of the escarpment, where the Snows-hill road branches off. It is almost certain that the creation would be before the population collapse of the mid-fourteenth century. It is also clear that by the date of this first reference to burgesses and burgages, these tenants were as purely agricultural in calling as the customary tenants of Upend and West End.[34]

The Economy of the West Midland Towns

The essence of an urban community is not to be discovered by con-fining our examination to the tenurial conditions of the burgesses, and in fact tenurial qualifications were becoming less important by the end of the thirteenth century. The most important fact of men's lives is the work they do and the conditions under which they do it. The products of the towns like those of the villages were relatively unspecialized. Peasants had first to provide their fami-lies' subsistence, and they were all, therefore, to some extent, arable farmers, growing bread and drink grains and some leguminous crops. After that, they might specialize in a cash crop, like wool. Most towns served a regional market of varying extent, and therefore manufacture and trade was in a wide range of articles of clothing, leather, wool and metal goods which could not be made so well or so cheaply in the villages. After that they might specialize in producing or distributing certain products for the national or international market. Droitwich was the only really specialized manufacturing centre in the west midlands. All the rest produced, with varying emphasis, the normal range of urban manufactures. It is often said, however, that certain towns specialized in the manufacture of woollen textiles. But this is a matter of emphasis. Almost all medieval towns had weavers, fullers, dyers and other textile craftsmen, just as they had tanners, shoemakers, carpenters or smiths. Some towns began to produce more than the town population or the population of the regional hinterland could absorb, and when they did this, presumably in response to the wider demand, they became, to a certain degree, textile specialists.

Bristol, of course, differed from the rest because it was a great port as well as a regional market centre. Wine was a prominent import in the twelfth and thirteenth centuries, though during two years of the Anglo-French war in Edward I's reign, wine imports dropped to nothing (1295 and 1296). Otherwise imports were around two thousand tuns, and on the eve of the war, more than three thousand tuns. There had been an export trade in hides, wool and corn since the beginning of the thirteenth century at the latest, though by the beginning of the fourteenth century wool exports had become insignificant. This was almost certainly due in part to the home demand by cloth manufacturers to which we made reference in discussing Pegolotti's list of monastic graziers. For as soon as statistics of cloth exports by ports make their appearance, in 1349, we find that Bristol is exporting more (900 cloths) than all the rest of England's ports together (852), including London. This, however, was an exceptional year, the year of the plague. In the previous year (Michaelmas 1347 to Michaelmas 1348) when details of individual ports are not given, the country's total exports, still small compared with the later fourteenth century, were 4,423 cloths. On recovery from the chaos of the plague year, Bristol still appears as the leading port for cloth exports, and this position may have been achieved well before 1347. These cloth exports would probably include cloth manufactured in Bristol itself, for an analysis of the occupational names in the Bristol tallage roll of 1312-3 shows a considerable number of cloth manufacturing artisans.

They constituted the largest group of artisans, exceeding the numbers both of those in the building trades and in victualling, occupations whose members were always numerous in large towns. Some of those textile artisans (the dyers) were interested in the import of woad for which, unlike wine, there are unfortunately no figures. This raw material for blue dye was at first mainly imported from Flanders, later from the Toulouse area. References to it in early thirteenth-century documents show indirectly the importance, even then, of the cloth manufacture in Bristol and in the area of the import redistribution of woad.[35]

The volume of grain exports cannot be estimated, but it is certain that there was a considerable grain trade in the town. The king's mills were grinding between five hundred and a thousand quarters of wheat and mistil a year at the end of the thirteenth century and this must have been only a small proportion of the grain entering the town. Later regulations show that the town authorities were concerned to extend control of grain purchases to a wide area beyond the town itself, the object being to prevent the establishment of monopolies by persons buying up supplies of grain direct from the producers. Other items of local trade on which a toll was charged by the crown as the goods entered the town were wool, hides, cloth, butter, iron, tallow, grease, herrings and 'other vendible commodities'. The volume of this trade cannot be measured for no indication of the amounts of each commodity are given in the constable's accounts from which we have the information. The income from this toll brought in between £40 and £60 a year.[36]

This short list of customable commodities can be extended by reference to the royal charters which gave the town the right to charge a toll on goods coming into Bristol as a financial aid to various public works, such as walls, quays and pavements. These lists do not, of course, give any indication as to volume, but they indicate the commodities on which the town authorities expected to be able to charge a toll. Apart from goods already mentioned a murage of 1261 includes lead, cheese, sheepskins, skins of other animals, brushwood, sheep, goats, pigs and freshwater fish. A pavage of 1317 adds horses and cattle, their hides, salt and fresh meat, bacon, linen cloth, canvas, silks, ashes, honey, alum, copperas, argol and verdigris, onions, garlic, boards, faggots, turves, brushwood and coal, nails, horseshoes and cart-clouts, tin, brass

195

and copper, hemp, and oil (probably nut-oil). The bulk of the goods seem to have come into Bristol from Gloucestershire, since in the 1261 pavage, cartloads of imports from that county are mentioned separately from goods from other counties, which were charged at twice the Gloucestershire rate (1d as against $\frac{1}{2}$d per cart).[37]

Were there any special features about the economic and social role of the next biggest west midland town, Coventry? At the end of the thirteenth century, the town's industrial expansion, well documented only for the fifteenth century, was evidently under way. This is most obviously shown in the expansion of the town's population from obscure beginnings to perhaps five thousand by 1280.[38] There are almost no local records of town government and economy at this period, but references in the national records indicate the outlines of Coventry's progress. An analysis of the occupational names of tenants of urban property in the 1280 Hundred Rolls shows the beginnings of the later industrial pattern. For not only were craftsmen of the textile manufacture, weavers in particular, among the most numerous of craftsmen mentioned, but even more prominent were the craftsmen of the metal trades. Smiths, more numerous than members of other crafts except the goldsmiths, were the foundation of the metal trade, for it was from the roughly worked iron shaped by them that the locksmiths, needlers, lorimers and marshalls (shoesmiths) got their basic raw material. Many of these workers in iron were, no doubt, working up the metal for the multifarious needs of the rural and urban economies, but the cloth industry itself was an important market for metal products, of which the most important were the big cards, studded with wire bristles, which were used for brushing out the wool, after sorting, but before spinning. The needlers of the 1280 return may very well also have been making the wire bristles for wool cards. But the textile industry must have become or have been on its way to becoming the primary industry. This would explain why leading Coventry merchants, accustomed to dealing in the raw material of the cloth industry, played a prominent part in organizing the collection of wool on Edward III's behalf for financing the first stage of the war against France, in the late 1330s.[39]

Coventry iron could have come from Dudley, but the most important source of the metal in the west midlands at this time was the Forest of Dean. Before the iron reached Coventry, however, it came through the Forest to Gloucester. There was, in fact, a toll called 'chiminage' on the passage of the ore (and coal as well) to Gloucester, one of the crown's minor profits from the forest. Gloucester's connection with Dean's iron smelting is shown as early as 1086, for, according to Domesday Book, part of the annual render of the borough of Gloucester to the crown in 1066 was thirty-six 'dicres' and a hundred rods of iron for ship nails. Hence it might be thought that a special feature of Gloucester would have been a relatively large production of goods made from iron. Indeed, in a list of urban specialities from 'a lawyer's handy-book of the thirteenth century' which J. Thorold Rogers quotes (without precise reference), Gloucester is referred to as an iron mart. Not that this handy-book is all that trustworthy since it says Bristol's speciality was leather and Coventry's soap. The occupational names in the 1327 subsidy return are rather scanty and show no particular prominence either of metal or textile workers. But an analysis of the occupational names mentioned in the thirteenth-century charters relating to property in the town shows better results. These are the names of grantors, grantees, neighbours and witnesses, and if charters over the long period of rather more than a century (roughly 1180 to 1320) are taken, sufficient numbers give some statistical validity, even though changes during the period of the relative importance of different trades cannot be safely measured. Out of some three hundred persons with named occupations, metal workers (in iron) are certainly prominent, sixty in all, while the second class, textile workers, contains forty-five names. Skinners, tanners and leather workers (including girdlers) have thirty-six; merchants of various types, thirty-four; victuallers thirty-one; and wool workers twenty-five. Other occupations, some seventy names in all, include nineteen tailors and thirteen goldsmiths but few others have more than half a dozen, though parchment makers (seven) deserve notice.

The most numerous textile workers mentioned in the deeds are dyers (eighteen) and after them weavers (fifteen), fullers (six) and challoners (four). The large number of dyers mentioned in deeds may be due to the fact that they tended to be among the richer members of the industry and would, therefore, be more likely than poorer men to be involved in real property transactions. But it must also be remembered that finishing cloth tended to be a specialized urban function. It may be that Gloucester dyers were taking in not only Gloucester woven cloth, but white cloths from the country industry as well. It may even have been the case that the country cloth was also fulled in town, though, as we shall see, there were plenty of country fullers. Gloucester's fullers were prominent enough from the beginning of the thirteenth century for a street near to the Severn bridge to be called the street of the fullers (or Walkers Lane), just as there was a street of the smiths off Southgate Street.[40]

Worcester, a smaller town than Gloucester in the thirteenth century, had a midsummer drapery fair once a year which was established before 1223. But this did not mean that it was a cloth town. Fairs were held rather for outsiders than citizens, and other evidence suggests that the occupational structure of the city was quite unspecialized. Our chief evidence again consists of occupational names in tax returns and deeds. They are not as abundant as one would wish for, but the distributions in the 1275 subsidy return and in the thirteenth century deeds show a similar pattern. Metal workers, including bellfounders as at Gloucester, predominate slightly. There is a textile industry, but the evidence for it does not suggest that it supplied more than local needs. As in all towns where there was a large population of clerics, administrators and other non-producers, there were a lot of victuallers, especially bakers, and garment makers, especially tailors and girdlers. Leather workers, carpenters and other wool workers, parchment makers, horners and other such artisans occur in similar numbers. In spite of its glovemakers' street (*vicus cyrothecariorum*), the city seems a perfect example of non-specialization, a sharp contrast not only with near-by Droitwich which was of course a much smaller town, but probably with the seigneurial borough of Kidderminster. This place, divided between several overlords, took the opportunity to establish a modest form of burghal autonomy. Although its customs, drawn up sometime in the 1330s, emphasize the presence of an agricultural element in the town, they also make clear that there was a cloth industry. It was laid down that no man in Kidderminster manor or borough was to make broad or narrow cloths without the bailiff's seal. In as small a town as this, it does imply specialization. The same may be true of Stratford-on-Avon. References in its earliest deeds, in the second half of the thirteenth century, certainly emphasize its role as a country market town where sheep, pigs, hay, salt and honey were sold. But there was a street of the fullers (Walkers Street) as early as 1277, and one of the prominent burgesses of his period was William the dyer.[41]

In spite of salt at Droitwich, iron wares at Gloucester, cloth at Coventry, Bristol, Kidderminster, Stratford and at one or two of the small Cotswold towns, the west midland urban economy in the thirteenth century was on the whole unspecialized. Industrial specialization was not to be expected, except in particular circumstances, in a near natural economy like that of medieval England. There were, as yet, no English equivalents of thirteenth-century Flanders. Some relatively big towns may have had hardly any industry at all. In spite of Warwick being picked out in the thirteenth-century lawyer's handbook as a centre for the manufacture of cord, it seems to have been largely an administrative and market centre. It is true that in the middle of the fourteenth century there was, as in Stratford, a street of the fullers, but deeds recording land transfers suggest a prominent rural element. The 1280 Hundred Rolls give some 150 occupants or holders of urban burgesses and tenements in Warwick, of whom twenty or so have occupational surnames. These suggest no particular industrial development. In so far as such a meagre list can suggest anything it is that building craftsmen, such as masons and lead workers, were in demand. There was a Jewish community, which left its record in the street-name 'Jury'; two Jews were burgage holders in 1280. There were groups of Jews too at Worcester, Gloucester and Bristol. Their presence is, of course, by no means a sign of industrial or even more general economic development, for their main business was consumption loans to landowners. In any case, they were already disappearing by 1280 as a result of their persecution by Edward I. This king, who is notorious for his expulsion order of 1290, was also hanging them on the pretext that they were clipping the coin of the realm. An echo of this is to be found in the Bristol constables' accounts which refer to the dues from the confiscated property of the hanged men.[42]

Urban Social Structure

Although most towns were unspecialized from the industrial and commercial point of view, their class structure reveals great inequalities of wealth and power. Unfortunately, we depend entirely

1327 TWENTIETH OF MOVABLES: AMOUNT OF TAX PAID

Town	Number of taxpayers	10s–20s	20s–30s	30s–40s	Above 40s	Total Subsidy	1334 Subsidy	Remarks
Bristol	347	27	9	—	2	£80 12s 0d	£220 0s 0d	£220 is a fine (i.e. lump sum offered by the town instead of assessment).
Coventry	200	19	6	—	1	£40 13s 6d	£75 0s 0d	1334 figure adjusted from 1/15 to 1/10.
Gloucester	246	9	1	—	—	£28 4s 9d	£54 0s 0d	
Cirencester	92	3	5	—	—	£13 4s 3d	£25 0s 0d	
Warwick	84	3	1	—	—	£12 5s 6d	£18 13s 0d	Includes Warwick without the walls.
Worcester	95	—	1	—	—	£10 8s 2d	£20 0s 0d	Does not include suburbs.
Stratford	58	—	—	—	—	£10 2s 8d	£13 2s 0d	
Evesham	54	—	—	—	—	£5 3s 10d	£12 7s 9d	1334 figure adjusted as above.
Birmingham	75	1	—	—	—	£7 6s 0d	£14 0s 0d	ditto
Coleshill	44	2	—	—	—	£5 17s 6d	£6 7s 6d	ditto

on tax returns for our knowledge of these inequalities of wealth at the end of the thirteenth and beginning of the fourteenth centuries. These must be treated with caution, but it is fairly certain that underassessment was normal. Such were the complaints of contemporaries. For instance, in 1324 jurors of the county of Worcester produced, for the benefit of itinerant justices who were investigating complaints against officials, a long list of principal and subordinate assessors and collectors of taxes.[43] The principal assessors and collectors and their clerks were accused of having received bribes from the local collectors so as not to look into any irregularities. The local collectors were accused of not assessing their neighbours at the true value of their goods and even of omitting certain persons who should have been assessed. It does not require much imagination to realize that the susceptibility of tax collectors to bribery would result in the relative underassessment of the rich, of those, that is, who were able to bribe most effectively.

But even this flattening of the apex of urban wealth in the tax returns cannot disguise the extreme inequalities that existed in the possession of movable goods. Movable goods, on the value of which tax was levied, were much more important in the towns than in the country, for rents from urban land did not constitute an important part of merchants' income. As one would expect, the biggest concentrations of taxable wealth were to be found in the big centres of commercial and industrial activity. This is well illustrated by an analysis of the returns of the tax collectors for the twentieth of movable goods levied in 1327. The majority of taxpayers did not pay more than about 2s or 2s 6d and an even greater number of inhabitants did not contribute to the tax at all. We can tell this by comparing the number of Bristol contributors to the tallage of a fifteenth of 1312–3, imposed only on boroughs and royal demesne, with the number of contributors to the nation-wide 1327 subsidy. There were 347 taxpayers in 1327, but 916 tallage payers in 1313. There is a similar, though less striking, contrast between the 234 payers of a tallage in 1304. The difference is, of course, mainly caused by a lower exemption limit for the tallage. For the moment, however, we will ignore the majority and concentrate on the upper reaches of the taxpayers in order to see where are the greater concentrations of wealth, or perhaps we should say, revealed wealth.

Probably the most interesting fact revealed by this table is that in spite of its much smaller taxed population and total assessment, the concentration of wealthy taxpayers at Coventry was already comparable to that at Bristol, and much greater than that in older centres such as Gloucester, Worcester, Cirencester and Warwick.

Who were these rich taxpayers, this small minority of the towns-people? The period around the year 1300 is one of poor documentation for the internal history of the west midland towns, and we are largely reduced to guesswork. The leading men of a large town like Bristol were certainly merchants handling the principal commodities of the town's commerce such as wine, cloth, wood and grains. A cloth dealer, Richard le Draper, was both steward and mayor between 1279 and 1290. If he was the same man as Richard of Mangotesfield as has been suggested, he was mayor another four times. John of Kerdyf who was steward or bailiff of Bristol possibly in 1281 was concerned in the trade with Ireland in 1290, and a member of his family (probably his son) was a steward in 1308 and one of the biggest contributors to the tallage of 1312–3. This tallage was taken at a time of internal conflict in the town between two factions. The conservative faction, which was backed by the king and his local representative the constable of Bristol castle, was led by William Randolf, the mayor, who as we will see, suffered the attacks of the Berkeley retainers when about his business as a merchant at the fairs. He was once steward and four times mayor between 1290 and 1315 and paid a substantial sum to the 1313 tallage. Most of his wealthy supporters, such as Laurence of Cary, John of the Celer (or Seler), Adam Welischote, John Snowe, Robert of Otery, Thomas le Spicer, were at one time or another mayor or bailiff of the town. The same is true of the so-called popular party led by John le Taverner (probably a wine merchant) who was a steward in 1298 and three times mayor between 1308 and 1313. His supporters included William of Axe, John le Lunge (a mariner, and somewhat of a pirate if we are to believe a plaintiff to the Parliament of 1316), John of Kerdyf, Roger Turtle and others who filled similar official positions. MPs for the town between 1295 and 1306 also came from the same two groups. In spite of the apparently lower assessment of the Taverner faction's supporters as compared with the followers of Randolf, it would seem that the factional division was within the dominant group of office-holding merchant oligarchs rather than between distinguishable social groups. In any case, a lower assessment might be as much a reflection of political influence as of relative poverty.

These wealthy office holders and politicians of thirteenth-century Bristol paid their contributions to the tallage for the most part on the movable goods in their shops and houses. They were often also real property owners, as we learn from an assessment for the purpose of the tallage of their income. In most cases it was not a large income, but William Randolf, and a wealthy supporter called Richard of Welles (who seems to have evaded the burdens of office), had considerable incomes from rent (£20 4s 2d and £10 1s 1d net). Others with house property were only assessed at up to £5 in rent. In the Taverner party, William of Axe had £7 from house property, John of Kerdyf had over £16 (but was not assessed on movables), John le Taverner had about £8 in rents and Nicholas of Roborough (twice a steward of the town in recent years) had about £4, but few others had more than £1.[44]

, The history of the leading merchants of Coventry hardly begins before the period when Edward II and Edward III were mobilizing the English wool merchants to discuss policy matters concerning the wool staple and the raising of war taxation bond on the country's wool resources. By the late thirties of the fourteenth century, we can be sure that two Coventry families were prominent above the others, Shepey and Meryngton. Hugh of Meryngton (whose widow Alice was at Westminster with other merchants in 1338) had already attended wool staple discussions at the York council of 1322. Several members of the family were contributing heavily to the 1327 and 1332 subsidies, but do not appear to have taken either of the two leading municipal offices of the time, bailiff or coroner. No Shepey was at York in 1322, but it appears to have been an older established family than the Meryngtons since there was a Simon of Shepey who was tenant of part of a burgage in 1280. Lawrence of Shepey was one of Coventry's MPs in 1301 and the highest contributor to both the 1327 and the 1332 subsidies. The Shepeys, however, do not appear as municipal officials at the turn of the century.[45]

The busy men of municipal affairs in thirteenth- and early fourteenth-century Coventry would have appeared mainly in the records of the municipal courts. But these do not survive at this early period. Many charters by which property was transferred were, however, witnessed in the borough court, and it is from these witness lists that we get some idea of the names of early municipal officials, such as bailiff and coroner, and with them the other regular attendants at court sessions. Prominent here we find the Baker family (pistor, le Peschur). The name Henry Baker appears in these witness lists in 1287, and four years later he is described as bailiff. He was again bailiff in 1296. Robert Baker appears in the same post from 1299 to 1305. Whether these men followed the trade of their surnames cannot be said, but Henry in 1280 was one of the most considerable real property owners of the town. Other prominent persons in municipal business at this time were Alexander the Vintner and Anketil of Coleshill, the latter being an MP in 1295. But they, and others like them, hardly appear as more than names in witness lists. They were not real property owners like Henry Baker, and nothing is known about their mercantile interests. Although the wealthiest merchants of Bristol seemed to monopolize the top municipal offices, this does not necessarily seem to be the case at Coventry.[46]

Gloucester and Worcester seem to provide the same sort of contrast, in the public preoccupations of the wealthier members of the municipal community, as Bristol and Coventry. At Gloucester the leading officials of the town were the two bailiffs. The office was shared between a comparatively small number of men. For example, Walter the Seuare, between about 1277 and 1298, held the office of bailiff nine times. Alexander of Bicknor between about 1273 and 1304 was bailiff seven times; Roger the Herberare, five times between 1298 and 1313; Robert the Spicer, three times between 1300 and 1314; Walter the Spicer, four times between 1306 and 1312. Most of these persons and other bailiffs were all assessed among the highest in the town in the tallage of 1304. Furthermore most of the dozen and a half men who paid large sums to the king's tallage based on the assessment of their movable goods were also recipients of rent income on which they also paid tax. This is the sort of pattern we see in Bristol, a small merchant oligarchy, clearly set apart from the majority of even comfortably off townspeople by their wealth in movable property; recipients of rent incomes from land and buildings in the town; and sharing the highest municipal offices between them.[47]

Worcester, however, seems different, at any rate judging from its by no means abundant documentation. As in the case of Coventry and Gloucester, the names of the earliest municipal officials are to be deduced from the witness lists of charters concerning land transactions recorded, or at least notified, in the municipal court. In order to correlate the names of those busy in municipal affairs with such evidence as we have about the distribution of wealth, we have to look at a slightly earlier period than the turn of the century. We get an idea of who were the wealthiest persons in the town from the tax assessment of 1275. There were fifteen persons paying between 20s and 10 marks (£6 13s 4d), the average payment in the city being between 5s and 6s. Yet only one of these high tax payers appears as a bailiff in the deeds of the period, John fitz Osbert, who at 10 marks was the highest tax payer of all in 1275. It was not that the office of bailiff was widely shared, for there was the same tendency for a few men to hold the office quite frequently as we observed at Gloucester. We find William Roculf five times bailiff in the last three decades of the century; Pain Burgeys four times; William Colle five times at the turn of the century. But most of those men who were active as bailiffs around the period of the tax list, with the exception of John fitz Osbert, were small tax payers. Pain Burgeys was assessed at half a mark (6s 8d); John of Astley (four times bailiff) at 7s; Walter of Dorley (twice bailiff) at 2s; Walter Lenveyse (thrice bailiff) at 2s. William Roculf does not appear as a Worcester city taxpayer at all, though he was a bailiff both before (1272–3) and after (1296–7) the tax. The name does, however, appear in the list of taxpayers in the village of Rous Lench, otherwise known as Lench Roculf. A possible explanation of this is that the William Roculf of 1296 might have been the man better known as William Roculf, junior, thrice bailiff between 1311 and 1320. The older Roculf might have retired to his native village. But he was only taxed at 3s. On the other hand, William Roculf, senior, who, as bailiff, was an active wrongdoer under both Edward I and Edward II, may have also used his influence to escape being taxed altogether.*[48]

We cannot conclude much about the ruling class of these towns from their scanty thirteenth-century archives. That they were merchants rather than craftsmen seems certain, but although, as we have seen, we get some glimpses of their participation in the trade in commodities such as wool and wine, a full picture of their social and economic rule does not emerge. Even the curious variation of policy from one town to another in the attitude of the richer burgesses to municipal office holding is something we can suggest

* See below, Chapter 8, pp. 259–60.

rather than prove. When we try to look further down the social scale we are even more in the dark. We know from surnames and descriptions in tax lists and charters what was the range of urban occupations, and even that there were certain incipient tendencies towards specialization. But there is no evidence of the internal organization of the crafts until we have the ordinances of craft gilds or fraternities.

The word 'gild', an ancient Germanic word which probably originally meant a mutual benefit and drinking club, was, of course, known. In the bigger towns it was used for the organization, probably unofficial to begin with, of the leading merchants, the *gilda mercatoria*.* Smaller towns which did not have a gild merchant had social and religious gilds, such as the gild of St Mary and St John, which appears in Stratford-on-Avon round about 1260, and the more famous Holy Cross gild, which may be even earlier. A gild hall in Winchcombe is even referred to in the Winchcombe Abbey records as a possession of the men of the town in the second half of the twelfth century. Now the twelfth- and thirteenth-century merchant gilds may have included master craftsmen from the more important manual occupations. The social and religious gilds certainly did. But at this period we have no direct evidence of craft gilds. The indirect evidence must be used with care. In a charter by which Henry II confirmed the privileges of the Abbey of St Augustine, Bristol, there is a reference to a payment by the weavers of Gloucester of 20s a year to the abbey. In the inquisition post mortem of Guy de Beauchamp, Earl of Warwick, 1316, there is a reference to a customary payment made to him by all his shoe-makers and cordwainers of Worcester of two pairs of boots a year. These payments may well have been in return for protection or for privileges. But were they individual or corporate privileges? At the end of the thirteenth century the Bristol constable's accounts refer to annual customary payments made to the king by eight linen weavers, twenty-one cobblers, twenty-one bakers and fourteen greengrocers, also, no doubt, in return for privileges, perhaps the simple privilege of pursuing their calling. These payments are entered as if collected from each individual tradesman. There is no suggestion that the tradesmen paid collectively, as if organized in a gild, no indication of corporate organizations of craftsmen, though these may have existed unofficially in some trades.[49]

* See below, Chapter 8, pp. 221–2.

The earliest craft ordinances from the west midland towns are those of Bristol. Those of the fishmongers are from 1339, and those of the weavers, dyers, fullers and tailors are from 1346. They are said to contain rules observed *ab antiquo*, but there is no saying what was the degree of antiquity. Even at this late date, the ordinances do not constitute entirely satisfactory evidence of self-governing craftsmen's gilds. They are promulgated, not by the craftsmen, but by the mayor, recorder and town councillors. It was these municipal officers who appointed the craftsmen who were to see to the observance of the regulations. The bulk of the fines paid by breakers of the regulations went to the municipality, the whole amount in the case of the fullers and tailors, the greater part in the case of the weavers. The supervisory officials of the latter craftsmen were called 'aldermen'. They got some of the fines, yet only as individuals; but their name does suggest some existing form of organization. However, if there were organized gilds at this time, they seem to have been very much under the thumb of the merchant oligarchy.[50]

Rural Industry

The specialization by the towns and market centres, not merely in trading activities, but also in handicraft industry, was one of the most important economic developments between the eleventh and thirteenth centuries. It was a concentration which must have resulted in economies through a better organization of the purchase of raw material and the sale of the finished product than was possible in scattered handicrafts in the villages. These village handicrafts did not, however, disappear. There were those which were linked with the needs of agriculture, such as the smiths. Most villages had a smithy and, even in the thirteenth century, smiths often held land from the lord of the manor in return for services peculiar to their trade. The smith in Worcester Cathedral Priory's manor of Wolverley (North Worcestershire), for instance, had to provide the iron parts for one of the priory ploughs as rent for his land, though he got paid for the iron of another plough and for the iron work (*billa*) of the mill.[51] Spinning was a well-known rural occupation for women, and weaving and other processes in the manufacture of cloth cannot altogether have left the countryside.

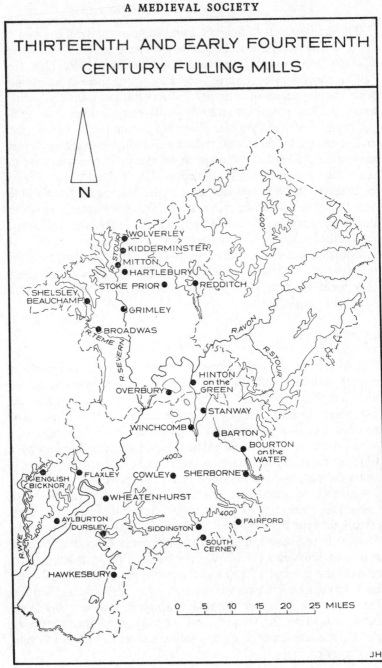

THIRTEENTH AND EARLY FOURTEENTH CENTURY FULLING MILLS

N

WOLVERLEY
KIDDERMINSTER
MITTON
HARTLEBURY
STOKE PRIOR
REDDITCH
SHELSLEY BEAUCHAMP
GRIMLEY
BROADWAS
R. TEME
R. SEVERN
R. AVON
R. STOUR
HINTON on the GREEN
OVERBURY
STANWAY
WINCHCOMB
BARTON
BOURTON on the WATER
ENGLISH BICKNOR
FLAXLEY
COWLEY
SHERBORNE
WHEATENHURST
AYLBURTON
DURSLEY
SIDDINGTON
FAIRFORD
SOUTH CERNEY
R. WYE
HAWKESBURY

400
400
400

0   5   10   15   20   25 MILES

JH

208

It was on the basis of a persisting domestic industry for local needs that the rural manufacture of cloth on a large scale expanded from the thirteenth century into modern times. Finally, there were industries such as the mining of coal and iron ore and the smelting of the ore which were necessarily rural because of the location of the mineral and the fuel for processing it.

The growth of the rural cloth industry is sometimes thought to have been primarily a feature of the late fourteenth and fifteenth centuries. It is true that the best evidence of the remarkable concentration of this industry in East Anglia, the west country and the Stroud valley comes from that period. But there seems to have been an earlier development in two separate zones in the west midlands well before the end of the thirteenth century. The evidence is mostly indirect, but unmistakable for all that. It consists principally of references to the existence of water mills for the fulling of cloth. When we find these in country villages, we can be fairly certain that they indicate the presence of a manufacture on a larger scale than would be necessary for purely local consumption. This process, by which the threads of woven woollen fabrics were closed together by pressing and kneading with the assistance of soap, was originally done by operatives who beat, kneaded or trod the pieces of cloths in a trough. The process was also called 'walking' and fullers were sometimes called 'walkers'. By the end of the twelfth century the process was being done by mechanical means, by water power. Water mills operated great wooden hammers which fell on to the cloth in the trough and fulfilled the tasks once performed by the walkers. Evidently, the expenditure involved in making one of these mills would only be undertaken where there was a considerable manufacture of woollens to make it worth while. Many of the mills were built by manorial lords, but the stringent methods they adopted to ensure that they retained a monopoly of mechanical fulling suggests that there were other entrepreneurs who also attempted to set up such mills. The evidence we have is naturally of the lords' mills, for it comes from the various documents (surveys, accounts and court rolls) which were a by-product of manorial administration.

The two main west midland concentrations of the rural cloth manufacture before the middle of the fourteenth century, as suggested by records of fulling mills, were the Cotswolds and north Worcestershire. The earliest mill of which we can be certain dates from about 1185. It is referred to in the great survey of the estates of the Knights Templar. The Knights had a group of estates in the north Cotswolds centring on the village of Temple Guiting, which the great baron Gilbert de Lacy had given them round about 1160. There was already a mill there at the time of his gift, probably a corn mill. The new owners then built (*fratres fecerunt*) two more mills in a hamlet of Temple Guiting, Barton, and sub-let them to a tenant called Wireth. One of these mills is described as a fulling mill (*molendinum fulerez*); the other is not, and was therefore probably a corn mill. The tenant paid 32s a year for the fulling mill, but only 12s for the corn mill, so the fulling mill must have been profitable. Another early Cotswold fulling mill was some miles south of Temple Guiting, at Sherborne, near Northleach. At a date which is difficult to establish, but was probably before 1200, the Abbot of Winchcombe, who was lord of Sherborne, transferred a mill on permanent lease to John of Hastings, a landowner in the neighbouring village of Farmington. In an acknowledgement of this transaction, John concedes that he will not make a fulling mill there without the permission of the abbey. The implication of this is that it would be in competition with an existing mill in the abbey's possession; and in fact, a late twelfth- or early thirteenth-century charter refers to an abbey fulling mill next to Westcroft in Sherborne. This abbey had built a fulling mill at about the same time in Enstone on the Oxfordshire side of the Cotswolds, together with a corn mill, for one of their tenants. How early they had a fulling mill in Winchcombe itself is not known, but the abbot renewed a lease of a fulling mill in Cotes by Winchcombe in 1309, which had already been running for twelve years and which the abbey had acquired before then from a local landowner, John of Wenland. Another Winchcombe charter by which this man announces his sale of property in the hamlet of Thropp to the not inconsiderable value of £100, to the abbey, includes in this property a fulling mill held by his tenants.

Another early fulling mill in the north Cotswolds belonged to the abbey of Evesham. It is mentioned in a list of rents allotted to the various obedientiaries drawn up during the prelacy of Abbot Randolf (1214–29). It was at Bourton-on-the-Water, and (together with a yardland attached) yielded an annual rent of three marks (£2) to the infirmarer. Evesham Abbey's near neighbour, the Benedictine house at Pershore also had, as we have seen, a certain amount of Cotswold property. In two of the principal Pershore Abbey Cotswold manors there were fulling mills. At Cowley, a few miles south of Cheltenham, the abbot leased a fulling mill (*molendinum fullotriticum*) to a fuller named William from the neighbouring village of Coberley. The mill had an arable holding of fourteen acres attached to it, and a piece of meadow by the mill pond. The fuller was also granted the 'suit of the men of Cowley', that is the monopoly of fulling the cloths woven by the abbot's tenants there. A similar monopoly was claimed by the abbey for its fulling mill in its manor of Hawkesbury, near Chipping Sodbury, for the enforcement of which we have court roll evidence.

The surviving evidence from the late thirteenth century emphasizes a group of mills in the south-east of the Cotswolds, towards the Thames valley. They were at Siddington (1274), South Cerney (1285), Fairford (1296) and Chedworth (1298), all lay estates, owned respectively by the St Amand, Langley, Clare and Beauchamp families. At the same period we have evidence of two groups of valley mills, mostly near the Cotswold scarp-foot. In the Avon valley mills Tewkesbury Abbey had a mill at Stanway (1291), between Broadway and Winchcombe, Gloucester Abbey had one at Hinton-on-the-Green (1266), and there were two at the foot of Bredon Hill, at Overbury and Kemerton. These belonged to Worcester Cathedral Priory (1240) and to the Mortimers (1297). In the Severn valley there were two mills at the foot of the scarp, one, as we have seen, in the Berkeley village of Cam (1322), the other at Dursley (*temp*. Henry III). On the Giffard manor of Wheatenhurst (Whitminster), near to the Severn's east bank, but probably driven by the river Frome, was another mill (1287). On the other side of the Severn, in or near the Forest of Dean, were the Cistercians' mill at Flaxley (1291), that of Lanthony Priory at Aylburton (1291), and that owned by the knightly family of Muscegros at English Bicknor (1301).

Now the Cotswold mills, particularly the cluster in the north, together with the Avon valley mills, suggest a localized industrial growth. In the same way the south Cotswolds group hints at an industrial development linked with Cirencester. It would, however, be unwise to overemphasize this, relying on a possible accidental survival of sources. But it is of some interest that there should as yet be so little evidence of the beginnings of a textile industry in the Stroud valley. As for the mills in the forest, they need not be taken as evidence of specialized industrial growth. They could have been fulling cloths for local consumption.

The surviving evidence for fulling mills in north Worcestershire comes mainly from documents of the estates of the church of Worcester. We must again be aware of constructing a local industry from accidental documentary survivals. However, it does fit in with later medieval evidence about the existence of a cloth industry in this district. There was, as we have seen, an industry of some importance at Kidderminster in the early fourteenth century, and there was a fulling mill there in 1293. Within a few miles, also in the Stour valley, there were mills at Wolverley (1240), Mitton (1250 c.), and Hartlebury (1299). Further away to the south-east were mills at Stoke Prior (1240) and Redditch (1339). Southwards to Worcester, on the river Severn at Grimley was another mill on the Cathedral Priory estate (1240). On the same estate, north-west of Worcester up the River Teme, was a mill at Broadwas (1240), and another further up the river at Shelsley Beauchamp (1302). The Broadwas fulling mill was leased out with the demesne in 1240; that at Wolverley was let out separately. Both were relet on a perpetual lease in 1253, implying some stability of cloth production to make the lessees' (or lessee's) investment worthwhile.[52]

Fulling mills were sometimes worked by the lord's servants, sometimes leased out to independent entrepreneurs. In either case, the preservation of the lord's monopoly, the veto on tenants taking their cloth to be fulled at any but the lord's mill was essential if the mill were to yield a profit. Offenders were presented in the manorial court, and these records are therefore invaluable evidence not only of the lords' economic exploitation of their jurisdictional power, but also of the importance of the local cloth industry. This is illustrated by the court records of the Abbot of Pershore's manor of Hawkesbury, where, as we have seen, there was a fulling mill in existence in the last quarter of the thirteenth century.

The Hawkesbury tenants lived in a number of scattered hamlets in the valleys between Wotton-under-Edge and Chipping Sodbury – Hawkesbury itself, Upton, Sturt, Hillsley, Tresham, Badminton, Killcot, Saddlewood and Chalkley. It is uncertain where the manorial fulling mill was situated, or whether indeed there was only one. An inquiry in 1315 by the whole homage of the manor states that the fulling mill at Killcot used to be rented for 20s a year, and was thereupon leased out for the same rent to a woman,

Hawisia la Walkere (that is, 'the fuller'). A statement in a reeve's account in 1331 refers to the expense of fulling 'bluett' cloths confiscated from a thief alongside another payment to a weaver who had made some white (that is, undyed) cloth for the lord. In other words, the lord was putting work out to independent craftsmen rather than operating his own equipment.[53]

The court records enable us to work back from 1315. Beginning in 1291, we have a series of prosecutions of tenants who had their cloth fulled at other mills than the lord's. These prosecutions came thick and fast between 1291 and 1295, when the first series of rolls finishes. The industry must have flourished during this period for there were even illegal immigrants, including one at Chalkley named as a 'stranger weaver'. Most of those prosecuted were women (twelve out of fourteen) and a fuller entry than most from a November court, 1292, illustrates the possible complexities in the interpretation of these records: 'Mathilda the widow of Henry, prosecuted in a case of not doing suit to the lord's fulling mill, says that she received a stone of "lokecif" (wool remnants) and had it spun and woven and after weaving gave it immediately to Alexander the chaplain as part payment of a debt.'

The phraseology suggests that this woman might not herself be a spinner or weaver, but put the raw material out for processing. But the actual organization of the manufacture is obscure. The offenders who are presented in the manor court are not normally charged in greater detail than that they took their cloths elsewhere than to the lord's mill.

The court cases recorded in the early 1290s have no immediate sequel. The next extant group of records begins in 1315 and continues for about ten years. Apart from the inquiry into the rent of the Killcot mill mentioned above, references to fulling have disappeared. It may be that the local cloth making industry collapsed, stricken perhaps by the difficulties of the years 1315-7. It is equally possible that the industry disappears from the record simply because, for some reason, prosecutions for non-attendance at the manorial mills were no longer made. An undated rental of Edward III's reign refers to regular payments by tenants for licences to full cloths in their own mills. If this licensing system became general, prosecutions would, of course, cease, and with them our evidence for cloth manufacture.[54]

The rural cloth industry is usually thought of as the most

characteristic of those industries which either escaped from or were never confined to the towns. But the mining of iron ore, of coal and of other minerals, as well as the smelting of the iron ore was necessarily done in a rural setting. Urban settlements were seldom associated with these industries in the middle ages. The search for the minerals by the miners tended to be concentrated in uncultivated areas, and, because of the primitive techniques employed, was a shifting search. The medieval iron forges or bloomeries too were for the most part temporary enterprises, though limited in the scope of their wanderings by the location of the raw material and the necessary fuel, that is, charcoal.

The west midland region, as we have seen, contained two important areas where mining and iron smelting was done, the Forest of Dean and the area around Dudley. As we have indicated, the proximity of the forest iron industry was reflected in Gloucester town's dues to the king in the eleventh century, though its earlier history, during the Roman occupation, is only known from archaeological evidence. The Forest of Dean was perhaps the most productive iron producing area in England in the twelfth and thirteenth centuries. The demand which it satisfied ranged from the king's constant requirements for arms and military stores to the needs of the textile industries in Coventry, Gloucester and Bristol. Probably the most sustained, though unmeasurable, demand was that of the smiths of countless villages working on plough and cart parts and other items of agricultural equipment. Nor must the building industry be forgotten. Every excavation of a medieval site, whether occupied by mainly stone or timber built structures, produces a considerable crop of iron nails, spikes, hasps, bolts, locks, hinges, knives and other products of the nailers, cutlers, lockyers and other workers in iron, most of whom were urban specialists, unlike the all-purpose rural smith.

The population of the Hundred or Liberty of St Briavels, which was almost co-terminous with the Forest of Dean, was very sparse compared with that of other districts in our region. It gives the impression of being more cut off and inaccessible than that of the Forest of Feckenham, partly because of the exclusive community of miners, suspicious of, and hostile to strangers, which was so important an element in the life of the forest. It is true, as we shall see later, that the local gentry, in particular the foresters-in-fee who controlled the bailiwicks into which the forest was divided, were socially predominant. But the miners must have constituted a strong element of freedom from lordly domination, for they had the right to sink pits for iron ore and coal wherever they chose, provided a fixed share was given to the king or to the local land-owner, and provided they paid a fee to the king's official, the Gaveller. Otherwise they seem to escape seigneurial control, for there is reason to think that the court they attended, for which the evidence is later than the thirteenth century, was in fact in exis-tence then. It was their own court, presided over, it is true, by the constable of St Briavels, but to which they alone owed suit, judge-ments being declared by juries of miners. There is, however, no evidence as to their numbers at the end of the thirteenth century, other than that from time to time the king demanded military service, as sappers, from anything between a dozen and forty of them.[55]

It is hardly possible to estimate the amount of production of iron ore and coal in the Forest of Dean. In 1280 the crown's profits from tolls on the movement of the minerals by land and river, together with the income from the lease of mining rights, amounted to a little under a third of the forest profits. The other items making up the forest profits included sales of timber, of pasture rights, profits of jurisdiction and rents paid by forge owners.[56] But these figures mean little. A better idea, still indirect, is to be gained from the probable annual production of the forest forges which were fed by the ore which the miners dug out. In 1282 there were about sixty forges. The annual average production of the medieval forge or bloomery has been estimated at two and a half to three tons of iron per forge. The total annual production at that date in the Forest of Dean would, therefore, have been 150 to 180 tons, between one-fifth and one-sixth of the country's annual output. The amount of ore needed would be at least five times (in weight) the amount of metal produced.[57]

The scale of production in mining was, of course, small. When the shafts from which the ore was dug were not horizontal, they were only small bell, or bee-hive, pits widening out below ground level from a small opening, and therefore limited in size by con-siderations of safety. They must, however, have been partly prop-ped, because one of the most important of the miners' common rights in the forest was a supply of structural timber.

The mining area, mainly on the western side of the forest where the biggest outcrop of carboniferous limestone was situated, with a lesser outcrop on the east from Mitcheldean, south to the Blackpool brook, did not only sustain the miners and the forge masters. Another essential element in the production of iron was the fuel used in the bloomeries. Coal was little used for this purpose, the smelters mainly relying on charcoal, made from both growing and fallen timber within the forest. In 1282 there were nine hundred charcoal burners' hearths in four only of the king's demesne woods. The number in the rest of the forest (including the private woods) must have been considerable. This resulted in a progressive destruction of the wooded cover, which the king attempted to limit by banning charcoal hearths. It has even been suggested that it was the decline of fuel supplies which led to a contraction of iron production long before the population collapse of the second half of the fourteenth century.[58]

Miners were free men, less controlled by lords than most men of the time. Charcoal burners were probably for the most part uncontrolled private entrepreneurs. The forges, however, were often owned and worked by lay and ecclesiastical landowners. The king had a great forge in the forest which, in the middle years of the thirteenth century, brought in between £25 and £50 a year. Flaxley and Tintern Abbeys had forges with the right to take timber for fuel, and gentry families with familiar names such as Cantilupe and Chaworth also had forges. In the other area of iron production in north Worcestershire, we find two 'great forges'. These are mentioned in the inquisition post mortem of Roger de Somery in 1281. This great magnate was lord of the borough of Dudley, and here he had a coal mine, a coal and iron mine and the two *grosse fabrice**. These large seigneurial enterprises were not the only forges however. A high proportion of the forges we know to have existed must have been smaller scale itinerant forges organized by craftsmen. Unfortunately, we know nothing of the labour force either of the large fixed forges or of the itinerant bloomeries at this date, nor of the currents of trade. Most of the town and country smiths must have got their supplies of iron from ironmongers, but the connections between forge masters, ironmongers and smiths in our region are so far completely obscure.[59]

---

* Could this have been a double hearth, bloomhearth and stringhearth, the one for the crude bloom, the other for reheating and beating ready for the blacksmith ?

CHAPTER 8

SOCIAL CONTROLS: JURISDICTION AND GOVERNMENT

No description of a society is complete which does not show the mechanism by which social relationships, social behaviour, economic and political obligations were enforced. The mechanism in this medieval society was complex and worked by the imposition of rules of custom, law and religion. To a considerable extent the rules were imposed by the sanction of force, but the fact that many of the rules by which people worked were customary implies that they were also accepted, at any rate by some. Once again we are limited by our source material in our attempt to grasp the essentials of the apparatus of social control. The evidence is unevenly distributed. The records of the sessions of the public, that is the royal courts, are quite abundant in the higher reaches. These higher courts were those presided over by justices appointed by the royal government and which held their sessions in the county towns. The records of the purely local courts, that is of county, hundred, borough and manor are far less abundant. Furthermore, the records of all these courts tell us about disputes, misdemeanours and felonies. They naturally emphasize the violence and frictions in society. The social conventions which exercise a less obvious influence on behaviour are hardly recorded, for the day of private papers and diaries, not to speak of interviews, is still far off. The influence of the moral code embodied in the teachings of the church is again largely recorded at the moment when church courts impose a punishment. We know, of course from penitentials, sermons and other religious writings what the church taught. But we have little means of knowing how far this was accepted.

If then our description of the controls which maintained the social hierarchy of the west midlands at the turn of the thirteenth

217

century seems to concentrate too much on the obvious mechanism and to say too little about influences which were not backed by the threat of force, this is because of the nature of the evidence. But it must not be forgotten either that this was a society which had by no means solved the problem of internal, day-to-day, violence, when the expectation of life was short and when death in all its forms was always present.

Probably the most important theme is the extent to which the exercise of power through law courts was still controlled by private persons, that is by the lords whom we have already attempted to depict. Constitutional and legal historians tend to stress the great extent of the public authority in thirteenth-century England, and in particular point to the relatively undeveloped character of private jurisdictions as compared with some parts of the continent. It must be remembered of course, that the comparisons are not altogether fair. The size of the political unit – the kingdom – is a factor of great importance when one considers the effectiveness of a central authority. The bulk of the English population, concentrated in the south-east of the country, could be reached with relative ease from the capital. Compare this with the problems of the French kings, with a population four times the size of England's, and immense distances between the capital and the major provinces. But in any case we must not be too impressed by the sophistication of England's central government machine. In spite of it, in spite of the great economic resources which the autocratic Edward I could mobilize, the British barons were in reality a very powerful group of men, much more so as a class than the French provincial nobility. And brutal as they now seem, they were, too, relatively politically sophisticated, as a class. They were not so much interested in political independence within their fiefs (except perhaps on the borders of Wales and Scotland), as in directly controlling the actions of the king through the council and through Parliament.

But what mattered for the style of life in provincial society was not so much whether the great lords were prepared to let the council and the king's justices look after political affairs and the major problems of peace-keeping for them. Peasants, burgesses, clerks, and artisans were mainly concerned with the day-to-day frictions of town and country life. Here the lord of the manor, the abbot, the bishop, the baron completely filled the social horizon.

They filled it, partly because the royal officials and judges were usually nominated from the ranks of the gentry and nobility. They also filled it because the local courts with which they were mainly concerned were practically all privately controlled. The fact that the law that was followed was the law of the land, and that it could be said that holders of rights of private jurisdiction were bound to apply it, under the king's correction, is not as important as it has seemed to some historians. What was important in an inevitably decentralized state was not so much what the law was, as who administered it, and in whose interests.

Government in the Boroughs

All courts were organs of government as well as courts of law. The courts which seem to modern eyes most like bodies of public rather than of private administration were those of the bigger boroughs, though even here the hand of the lay and ecclesiastical magnates was to be seen in public affairs. Details are rare before the fourteenth century, but the main pattern of borough development was shared by urban communities of very different types. Whether on the royal or on private demesne, burgesses wanted to exclude the king's or the lord's officials who presided over the borough court and collected the various revenues accruing to the lord, such as tolls, house and stall rents, profits of jurisdiction and so on. This was not achieved in a revolutionary way, as had sometimes happened on the continent, but by buying out the lord's rights. For example, the burgesses would acquire the right to commute the various revenues collected by the king's (or the lord's) officials for a lump sum paid, in the case of royal boroughs, to the exchequer annually. In 1189, Worcester acquired the farm of the borough (*firma burgi*) for £24 a year.[1] Gloucester's earliest charter referring to the farm is of 1194, but the charter itself refers to the farm of £55 as having been paid before the date of the charter itself.[2] The king took the opportunity of this confirmation to add a £10 increment. Bristol's revenues had been commuted to a lump sum by 1188, £145 a year, but this was not paid by the burgesses as a community, but by a midlands magnate, Hugh Bardolf. The burgesses themselves did not control the farm until 1227 and even then the right was not *in perpetuum* as with other towns, but renewable, and so liable to suspension.[3] Bristol in fact was too rich, strategically placed and turbulent to be given the privileges to which its status entitled it.

Warwick never acquired borough autonomy, financially or otherwise. As late as the end of the fifteenth century, the borough revenues were being collected by officials of the earl.[4] Coventry's burgesses, rich and powerful though they were, did not get the farm of the borough until 1345, a consequence of the dual seigneurial control to which we have referred. Cirencester, Evesham, Pershore, Stratford, and Kidderminster, flourishing towns, but under the hand of lay and ecclesiastical lords, naturally had even less chance of this simple but basic autonomy, the right to exclude the rent and toll collectors sent from outside. Of the smaller towns only Droitwich, because of its complex industrial administration, obtained the farm of its revenues, by a charter of King John in 1215.[5] But Winchcombe, also on the royal demesne like Droitwich, had been a borough of some importance in the eleventh century, yet never achieved any borough privileges subsequently. As an administrative unit it was combined with the surrounding rural hundreds of Holford, Greston and Kiftsgate; its revenues were either collected by the sheriff or farmed to the abbot of Winchcombe. So although this ancient abbey was not lord of the town, as in the case of the abbey at Cirencester, it performed in practice a similarly dominating role.[6]

Those boroughs whose leading inhabitants were allowed to run their own affairs did so in the thirteenth century through two institutions, the borough court and the gild merchant. The borough court, probably in earlier days with the jurisdiction of a hundred court, would have as its suitors certain persons, whose rights would be dependent on their tenure of burgages. The grant of successive privileges to borough communities extended the scope of the courts. Bristol, Gloucester and Worcester all got charters in the thirteenth century which guaranteed that their burgesses would not have to plead in any except the borough court for matters which concerned them in the borough itself. Most borough courts by this time had evolved a special form of borough custom concerning property, debts, trespass and the like. At Bristol, special sessions of the court were held in the market for commercial cases and another mercantile court, the Tolsey court, made its appearance. The control of this customary law was placed in the hands of the burgesses by provisions which excluded royal officials, such as the sheriff, from interference.[7] In the Gloucester charter of 1200, the presidents of the court were to be two reeves, watched by four coroners. These officials were all chosen from the leading men of the town at Gloucester, as we have seen. The reeves had the responsibility for the rendering of the town's farm to the exchequer and the coroners had to keep the pleas of the crown until the king's justices should appear to try them. In this sense they were still crown officials, but their primary allegiance would be to the town. Even where a mayor makes his appearance (as at Bristol) as the burgess community's rather than the king's man, the reeves or (as they were called at Bristol) stewards, were municipal rather than royal officials, many of them subsequently becoming mayor. Reeves or bailiffs were, however, more common as the presidents of the borough courts than the mayor, who was by no means universal as the chief official of the medieval borough. In bigger towns like Worcester and Gloucester, as in seigneurial boroughs like Stratford-on-Avon or Kidderminster, bailiffs were the chief officials of the towns, until the end of the middle ages.*

The gild merchant was originally an unofficial organization of the merchants and richer craftsmen of a town. It was primarily designed to ensure control by the local men of the town market. According to Worcester's 1227 charter, for instance, no one outside the gild was to make any merchandise within the city or suburbs without the citizens' consent.[8]

These gilds gained official sanction in early charters in so far as the king or lord gave their existence official recognition, and authorized them to collect dues (sometimes also known as 'gild' or 'hanse') from their members. Bristol's gild merchant existed in the thirteenth century but was not officially recognized, no doubt because of the royal suspicion of the burgesses. But Gloucester's gild merchant was recognized in the charter of 1200 as the already existing though hitherto unofficial form of burgess corporate organization. An abortive attempt to create one for the prior's men in Coventry in 1267 was not revived until 1340. But the essence of the gild merchant was control over the commercial life of the borough, and thus could assume other forms. The controlling families in the borough court were normally the same who exercised control in the gild, so much so that the two institutions often,

---

* Thomas Payn is described as mayor of Warwick in 1280, but the office seems to have had no future. *PRO*, E.164, vol. xv, f. 1ᵛ.

as at Worcester, became utterly confused. Alternatively, where the lord's presence inhibited burgess action in the official borough court, gilds might assume the form of a shadow government behind the scenes. Shadow governments, however, do not leave records of their deliberations, so it must remain a matter for guesswork whether, for example, the gild of the Kalendars at Bristol, or the gilds of Holy Cross, St Mary and St John at Stratford-on-Avon fulfilled this function, as the Holy Cross at Stratford and the Holy Trinity Gild at Coventry certainly did by the fifteenth century.[9]

Burgesses, even those who seem to have achieved a large measure of urban autonomy, had to look carefully to powerful private interests, as well as to the apparently fickle conduct of the king and the officials, if they were to steer their town on an even course through local and national politics. The more important the town, the more hazardous its political history, as the history of London in the second half of the thirteenth century shows. Bristol burgesses by no means had full control of their borough. It was not simply that much town property was owned by landowners from outside. In 1285, for instance, twenty-three of those with obligations of suit to the borough court by reason of their tenements were named.[10] Eight of them were heads of religious houses, most of the rest of them being lay magnates. Only one is named as a burgess. More important was that many of these magnates claimed privileges of varying profitability. One such privilege was the Abbot of Glastonbury's freedom for his abbey and his tenants from borough tolls. Another was the right, given to the Dominican and Franciscan friars by the king, to appropriate fish from the catch brought in by water. Others got exemption from the royal levy on ale brewed in the city, which the burgesses had to pay under the name of the *Tyna Castri*. The prior of St James (a daughter house of Tewkesbury Abbey) had the right, not only to all the profits of the Whitsuntide fair, but to all the profits normally going from the town to the crown during the same period. Most serious of the private claims was that of the Berkeley family, old enemies and neighbours of the burgesses. They claimed the jurisdiction of a hundred court as well as all royal rights (*jura regalia*) over their tenants in the urbanized quarter, south of the Avon, centred on Redcliffe Street and Temple Street. This area largely inhabited by weavers and fullers was already within the walls, and the burgesses wanted to ensure that it was under their own jurisdiction. There were, however, to be many bloody incidents before the Berkeleys relaxed their grip in 1331. Bristol burgesses whose suit of court was demanded by the Berkeleys were beaten up in the streets by their agents for refusing it. The mayor of Bristol himself was attacked at Doundrey Fair and Bristol men were harassed in the surrounding market towns by Berkeley retainers.[11] They made illegal distraints on ships on the river Avon. The Bristol jury's claim in 1285 that the town was 'royal and free of itself' was, in view of all these lordly privileges, somewhat of an exaggeration, a programme for the future rather than a description of facts.[12]

Coventry, as we have seen, was divided between two lords, of which one represented that type most oppressive of urban communities, a Benedictine monastery, the cathedral priory. This religious house not only held jurisdiction over the northern part of the town but was lessee of the earl's half, and a considerable owner of urban property as well. The frustrated burgesses, before achieving a proper settlement in 1355, were even reduced in 1323 to attempting to get rid of all their overlords by witchcraft.[13] Worcester and Gloucester were not faced with such problems as either Bristol or Coventry. It seems probable that there was an enclave in the south-west of the city around Worcester cathedral where the prior had jurisdiction over the townspeople dwelling there. At any rate this area was omitted from the earliest extant (1498) perambulation of the city bounds.[14] The cathedral priory was a considerable property owner in the city, and the bishop was lord of the suburbs of Northwick. But there seems to have been little friction between the city, the cathedral and the bishop. The same, perhaps, was true of Gloucester. The major presence here which might have seemed incompatible with a burgess community was that of the Abbey of St Peter. This abbey's chronicle, while recording its disputes on the most trivial matters with other landowners, secular and ecclesiastical, says nothing of its relations, good or bad, with the townspeople. This in spite of its considerable property holdings which (like other abbeys, such as Lanthony) it had in the town. Perhaps it maintained a lofty and aristocratic reserve. The chronicler writes of a feast that was held in the great hall of the abbey in 1305 in honour of the assize justices who were on tour. There were seventy guests, including thirty knights, the priors of Lanthony and St Oswald, other ecclesiastical personalities and the most honourable persons of the county. No burgesses are mentioned. This aloofness did not exclude some interest on the part of the monks. They recorded in their cartulary the burgesses' justifications of their liberties before the justices of Quo Warranto in 1287, as well as the earlier (1272) inquiry into their own claim to be exempt when the king tallaged the town, an exemption that was supported by a jury from the borough and its suburbs.[15]

We have suggested that the nearest approach to what we would regard as a public authority were these governments of the larger towns where burgess communities had been more or less enfranchised.⸱ Some historians on the other hand equate urban particularism vis-à-vis the royal authority with the particularism of the nobles. It is a matter of perspective. We tend to regard the crown, being the fountain of the power and legitimacy of the central government, as being the public authority in embryo. But in a thirteenth-century context, urban governments, striving against the particularisms within their walls of the abbots, bishops and barons, must have thought of the direct representatives of the royal authority as equally unwelcome intruders. In Bristol, Worcester and Gloucester the royal castle stood outside borough jurisdiction like a private franchise. The lord of the castle, theoretically the king's representative, whether constable in Bristol or sheriff in Worcester and Gloucester, was often a local magnate acting in his own as well as (or more than) in the king's interests. In Worcester the castle was always in the hands of a hereditary sheriff, the greatest local magnate, the reigning member of the Beauchamp family. The actual work of sheriff was done by a member of the local gentry, appointed by the reigning Beauchamp. In Coventry, a curious situation arose in that a royal person succeeded a private magnate in a similar enclave within an already divided borough. When he leased the earl's half of the borough to the cathedral priory in 1249, Roger of Mold reserved to himself the earl's manor of Cheylesmore, situated within the suburbs.[16] In 1327 it passed into the hands of Queen Isabella and to the Prince of Wales, and its court may even, during a period of dispute with the prior, have become the place of judicial resort for all the men in the earl's half.[17]

The history of Gloucester during the troubled times of the Barons' Wars illustrates the ambiguous position of the sheriff and his castle. The details come mainly from the metrical chronicle of

Robert of Gloucester. In 1260, the sheriff of Gloucester and constable of the castle was a Frenchman, Sir Matthew de Besile. The
local magnates decided to replace him with 'a knizt of the contreie,
Sir William Traci'. Sir Matthew made his return in force when Sir
William was holding the shire court, captured and imprisoned him.
But the Gloucestershire baron, Sir John Giffard of Brimpsfield
and the Marcher lord, Sir Roger Clifford, captured the castle.
When political allegiances changed Clifford went over to the king
and garrisoned Gloucester Castle, Giffard (still a baronial partisan)
doing the same at Brimpsfield. After a year and a half of siege,
counter-siege and skirmish around the city, Giffard and another
knight disguised themselves as merchants in Welsh cloaks. Riding
on wool packs, as if from Wales, they presented themselves at the
west gate of the city and obtained entry as a couple of woolmongers.
Once in, they let in other Montfort supporters, and were apparently welcomed by the burgesses. When the Lord Edward (the
future king Edward I) came to besiege the town in his turn, he was
supported by Clifford from the castle, and eventually managed to
get into the castle from the river. After a prolonged stalemate
between the castle garrison and the baronial forces in the town,
Edward promised peace to the burgesses, and the barons left.
Characteristically his rage overcame his honour and instead he
treated the burgesses as thieves and traitors, extorting great ran-
soms from them.[18] Such were the relations between borough and
castle.

Of these events in Gloucester, the St Peter's Abbey chronicler
says nothing. Bristol's relations with the constables of the castle
were no happier. The constable was not in the same position as a
sheriff of a county. The sheriff in his fortified enclave within the
county town was by this time a busy administrator and keeper of
public order for his whole county. The Bristol constable had nar-
rower functions, which affected the town much more closely than
did the sheriff of Gloucestershire those of Gloucester, or even the
hereditary sheriff of Worcestershire those of Worcester. The
Bristol constable looked after the castle and the king's interests in
this second most important port in the kingdom, this vital link with
Wales, Ireland and the Atlantic coast of Europe. All the same, the
king's rights, exercised through the constable, give much more the
impression of the rights of a great private lord than of the holder of
the public authority. This is, of course, an aspect of the ambiguous

character of the medieval king, part sovereign and part feudal over-lord. Historians who examine his role in central government natur-ally incline to emphasize his public, sovereign capacity. Locally, his role as feudal prince appears more strongly. And each role could be used to strengthen the other.

The constable was first of all a castellan and spent money on the maintenance of his castle's fabric. So Nicholas Fermbaud, who was constable in 1295, had to account for expenses he had to make repairing and building up wall and battlements. It is of some inter-est that the estimate of the dimensions of the wall, on which would depend the auditors' acceptance of the amounts spent on labour and materials, was made by view of the two town bailiffs, Thomas de la Grave and the better known William Randolf: authorities whose estimate would be accepted by the exchequer auditors in the capital.[19] But he was a good deal more than simply a castellan. He acted as bailiff of the king's rural tenants in Stapleton, Mangots-field and Easton and of the king's demesne in his 'barton', just outside the town. He tendered accounts for those properties like any manorial official. He also had to supervise the maintenance of the king's corn mills. Other elements of the constable's accounts show him as the agent of a feudal overlord rather than the public authority, syphoning off part of the profits from commercial activity. The king retained a number of local tolls on such com-modities as herrings, onions, teazles, leek seed and the like. He had customs payments, not part of the national customs system, on wool, hide, cloth, butter, iron, tallow, grease and other vendible commodities brought into the town. He derived a similar customs payment from wine imports (again not part of the national system). He also received customary payments from certain trades, in effect licence fees to pursue their calling. These were, weavers, cobblers, bakers and what we would call greengrocers (known then as re-grators of beans, peas, apples, etc.). He had the toll of beer brewed in the borough, known as the *Tyna Castri*. And naturally there was some income from house property, including the houses of Jews who had been hanged in the course of the antisemitic campaign leading up to the expulsion of 1290.[20]

When the liberties of the city were suspended, as was not infre-quent in the reigns of Edward I and Edward II, it was the constable who took over as governor. These bad relations between crown and borough culminated in the famous Bristol rebellion of 1312–6,

when the constable was a great magnate, Bartholomew of Badles-
mere. The king had given the constable the custody of the town
which meant that it was he who accounted to the exchequer, not
only for the normal receipts of the castle and the king's barton, but
for the revenues of the borough as well. The story is complicated.
The 'popular' party led by John le Taverner (mayor 1312-3) to
which we have referred, seems to have led the opposition to the
constable. But that was complicated by an internal struggle between Taverner's party and another party, possibly the former
ruling oligarchy, led by a previous mayor, William Randolf, who
was friendly to the constable. The trouble was made worse by the
crown's imposition of the tallage of a fifteenth on goods and a tenth
on rents, which was naturally opposed, particularly since the king
had arrested Taverner and others of his party. Feeling was further
inflamed by the tactless despatch to the town of a royal commission, headed by none other than the burgesses' major enemy
Thomas of Berkeley.[21]

Private Jurisdiction in the Countryside

This discussion about the west midland towns was intended to
show how forms of medieval government where private authority
could be expected to be at its minimum, were nevertheless, partly
undermined by the privileges of lay and ecclesiastical potentates.
These private rights were of course much more prominent in the
countryside, none of whose inhabitants had acquired chartered
privileges comparable to those of the burgesses. As we have already
emphasized, the scope of royal action, judicial and administrative,
was considerable, particularly when compared with the limitations
on royal authority in other contemporary European kingdoms. But
from the point of view of the villager, the lord's power must have
loomed very large.

The point at which the lord's power was excercised most con-
tinuously over the villager was the manor court, to whose activities
we have already made many references, and from whose records so
much of our evidence has come. It was considered at this time to
be the natural right of any lord to hold a court for his tenants. It
was not simply that the tenant–lord relationship had much wider
implications than in modern times, but that many lords had, in
addition to jurisdictional rights over their tenants with respect to

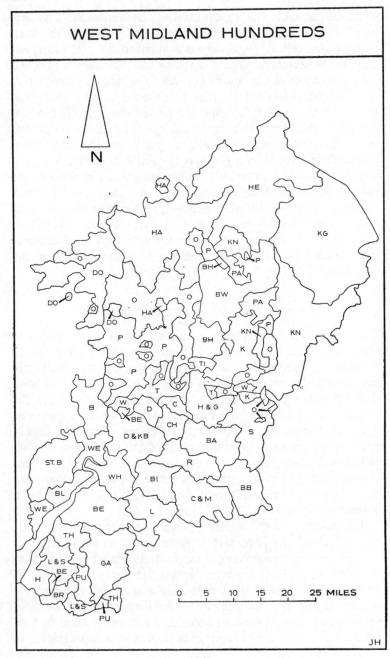

WEST MIDLAND HUNDREDS

N

0   5   10   15   20   25 MILES

JH

228

Boundaries of hundreds in the medieval west midlands

Even this complicated map embodies some simplification. Note the outlying parts of Worcestershire in the other counties. Most of these are parts of Oswaldslow Hundred, based on the estates of the church of Worcester.

Key to the west midland hundreds

Warwickshire

BW – Barlichway
HE – Hemlingford
KN – Kineton
KG – Knightlow
PA – Pathlow

Worcestershire

BH – Blackenhurst or Fishborough
DO – Doddingtree
HA – Halfshire
O – Oswaldslow
P – Pershore

Gloucestershire

BR – Barton Regis
BE – Berkeley
BI – Bisley
B – Botloe
BL – Bledisloe
BA – Bradley
BB – Brightwells Barrow
CH – Cheltenham
C – Cleeve
C & M – Crowthorne and Minety
D – Deerhurst
D & KB – Dudstone and Kings Barton
GA – Grumbalds Ash
H – Henbury

H & G – Holford and Greston
K – Kiftsgate
L & S – Langley and Swineshead
L – Longtree
PU – Pucklechurch
R – Rapsgate
St B – St Briavels
S – Slaughter
T – Tewkesbury
TH – Thornbury
TI – Tibblestone
WE – Westbury
W – Westminster
WH – Whitstone

the holdings and the services due from them, a number of other rights and privileges. These other rights and privileges were often of doubtful origin, or, from the point of view of the crown, legality. But they buttressed the lord's powers considerably, and jurisdictional rights and claims of different character tended to become blended together in a body of customary practices in the manor court. Cases appropriate to the court baron (the court held by a lord for his tenants because of their tenure), were held at the same session as cases appropriate to the view of frankpledge (an inspection of tithings and receipt of their presentments properly held by the sheriff in the hundred court).[22] Additional control could be imposed if the lord had the view of the assize of bread and ale; and the whole range of jurisdictional rights could be legitimated by the claim for the judicial privileges of pre-conquest origin expressed in the obscure phrase 'sake and soke, toll and team and infang-thef'.[23] 'Infangthef', as we have seen, was the right to hang thieves caught with the goods on them. It meant in fact, the right to have a private gallows, and the chattels of the hanged thief. Let it not be supposed that the private gallows was only a status symbol. In a society without a competent system for the detection of crime and criminals, many thefts would in fact be proved by finding the stolen goods on the thief.

The west midlands was well supplied with private gallows at the end of the thirteenth century. Judging by the claims made during the Quo Warranto proceedings,* there were about a hundred in the counties of Gloucester and Warwick. The Worcester proceedings are missing but there was probably a substantial number there as well.[24]

An example of the confusion of jurisdiction is to be found in the articles under which enquiries had to be made of tithingmen at the Abbot of Stoneleigh's private view of frankpledge for the inhabitants of the large manor of Stoneleigh.[25] The manor itself (composed of several hamlets as well as Stoneleigh village) was sometimes known as the 'soke', a term implying an area of jurisdiction. There are fifty-five heads altogether under which enquiry was to be made, as compared with the thirty heads listed in the apocryphal Statute of Frankpledge.[26] Many of the heads deal with the matters of public order which were proper in the view of frankpledge, and when not alienated by the crown would be dealt with at the sheriff's view of the tithings at his tourn in the hundred courts.[27] An example is 'Concerning housebreakers who are awake at night and sleep during the day and who frequent the tavern and about whom nobody knows how they get a living, for they do no work'. But others relate to the assize of ale which was a separate franchise from that of the view of frankpledge, and which is considerably elaborated in this list. For example, not only is there to be a general inquiry into breakers of the assize of ale, and presentment of those who sell ale which the ale tasters have not tasted, or made in unsealed vessels, but 'those who sell red unhealthy ale, and those

* For these, see below, p. 234.

who, having put up the sign for sale, sell either before the sign is put up or after it is taken down'.

Other items are those one would expect rather in the court baron, such as those which attempted to prevent tenants from dealing in land other than through machinery of the lord's court. Heads of enquiry of this type are entitled 'Concerning tenements alienated by charter or without the lord's permission', 'Concerning tenements leased by the lord for life or at farm, the heir to hold by hereditary right or letting them in fee to other persons to the lord's prejudice'. Others concern such largely seigneurial problems as 'whether any serf has flown and withdrawn from the lordship' or 'concerning boundary and other such marks which have been pulled up, ploughed in or taken away' or 'concerning diminution or concealment of the lord's rights by the bailiffs or other tenants of the lord'.

This Stoneleigh list was drawn up after the middle of the fourteenth century, but the actual records of various manor courts at the end of the thirteenth century show that this mixture of public and seigneurial jurisdiction, derived, as we have seen, from several sources, was enjoyed by many lords of manors. The most voluminous series of thirteenth-century court records such as those of Halesowen, Hawkesbury and Tardebigge have been frequently quoted in earlier chapters, and hardly need further words about them here. But it is worth noting that the Abbot of Bordesley's court at Tardebigge, an ordinary manorial court with view of frankpledge, was sometimes referred to as the 'Hundred of Tardebigge'.[28]

As we have mentioned briefly the petty police jurisdiction implied in the right to hold the view of frankpledge was originally and properly located in the court of the hundred, that subdivision of the shire which emerged in the course of the administrative reorganization of the tenth and eleventh centuries, in the period of recovery from the Scandinavian invasions. It was supposed to be held once or twice a year when the sheriff made his tour, or 'tourn', of the hundred courts. But the appropriation by private persons of this important franchise was not simply a matter of subtraction from the public jurisdiction of the hundred court, although this clearly often happened. In some areas the hundred court itself was held by a private person, or rather by his bailiff, who was the substitute for the royal bailiff appointed by the sheriff. The rights of private lords were very varied and could run from virtually complete control of all normally public administrative and judicial activities, including the view of frankpledge, to a mere share, with the crown, in the financial profits of the hundred.

The west midlands was an old stronghold of private hundredal jurisdiction, especially in the Severn and Avon valleys and the Cotswolds. It is indeed possible that the concession by the old English kings of at least one area of private jurisdiction preceded the formation of the hundred system. This was the triple hundred of Oswaldslow, a franchise granted in the tenth century to the cathedral church of Worcester, and exercised jointly in the thirteenth century by the bishop and the cathedral priory. It included a substantial proportion of central and southern Worcestershire with parts of what has since become northern Gloucestershire. It was not all in one continuous piece, being based on the scattered landed property of the bishop and the priory.[29] In addition, the bishop alone had two other areas of hundredal jurisdiction, the liberty of Pathlow in southern Warwickshire, based on his manor and borough of Stratford-on-Avon and the hundred of Henbury near Bristol, based on the manor of the same name. Although the bishop could not deal with felonies in his hundred courts – these had to be reserved for the itinerant justices – he had in Oswaldslow, Pathlow and Henbury the right to exclude all royal officials, his own bailiff executing all writs sent from Westminster ('return of writs').

The other major ecclesiastical estates in Worcestershire had also formed the basis of private hundreds. The abbots of Westminster and Pershore shared the hundred of Pershore (itself based on the old Pershore estates) in the proportion of two-thirds to one-third of the profits. The hundred of Fishborough or Blackenhurst in the south-east of the county was based on the core of the estate of the abbots of Evesham and coincided too with the ecclesiastical deanery of the Vale, over which, as we have seen, a monastic obedientiary presided as Dean of Christianity. The abbot's jurisdictional rights in this hundred were already well entrenched at the beginning of the twelfth century.[30] The king's officials were excluded from the liberty and the abbot enjoyed that range of baronial jurisdictional rights still described by the vague phrase 'sake and soke, toll and team and infangthef'.

A substantial proportion of Worcestershire, then, was included in the liberties of the great ecclesiastical landlords of the county. The two northern hundreds, Doddingtree to the west of the Severn, and Halfshire in the north-east, were theoretically royal hundreds. However, the jurors of whom the inquisitions of 1274–5 made their enquiries, stated that the two hundreds were in the hands of William de Beauchamp of Elmley.[31] They were a bit out of date, since this William had died some years earlier; but the point was that he and his son as holders of the hereditary shrievalty of the county were therefore entitled to appoint the hundred bailiffs. One could say that the Beauchamps were royal officials and that their nominees were also. But from the local point of view it must have seemed that in both hundreds there was as over-powering a combination of feudal landed power and control of the public authority as was to be found in an old established franchise like Oswaldslow.

The private hundredal franchises stretched in a broad band into Gloucestershire. Straddling the North Cotswolds and Avon valley were the three hundreds of Kiftsgate, Holford and Greston, formally in the king's hands, in practice, as we have seen, farmed out to the Abbot of Winchcombe. A little further west was the Earl of Gloucester's hundred of Tewkesbury. To the south of this was the hundred of Deerhurst, shared by the Abbot of West-minster and the Prior of Deerhurst. To the east was the Abbot of Fécamp's hundred of Cheltenham which he had acquired from the king, together with the Cotswold hundred of Slaughter (near Salmonsbury), some years previously in exchange for Rye and Winchelsea in Sussex. Here he claimed not only the return of writs and other high, but not abnormal franchises, but the right to appoint his own justices to hear pleas normally held by the itiner-ant justices,* a franchise much complained about by the jurors of neighbouring hundreds.[32]

The biggest hundredal franchise in the Cotswolds, however, was that of the Abbot of Cirencester who was lord of the hundreds of Cirencester, Longtree, Bradley, Rapsgate and Brightwellsbarrow. This was not an ancient private franchise but a grouping of hundreds round a royal manor. It was not given to the abbey until 1189[33] and since these hundreds already contained the

---

* Cheltenham and Slaughter presentments are not to be found in the Assize Rolls of this period.

well-entrenched estates and private interests of other powerful land-owners, the abbots of Cirencester had to concede jurisdictional exemptions to them, concessions which were probably a recognition of *faits accomplis*. Further south-west, not far from the Somerset boundary, was the Bishop of Bath's private hundred of Pucklechurch.

The private hundreds so far listed were predominantly under ecclesiastical control. There were one or two hundreds in the hands of lay magnates such as Bisley in the Cotswolds, Thornbury, on the east bank of the Severn, and Westbury, and Bledisloe on the west bank. This control, or rather the profits, by the end of the thirteenth century, had become divided by inheritance. One private hundred in lay hands deserves special mention, however, for being essentially based on a private estate, it had a coherence which gave its lord considerably more influence than in hundreds (such as those of Cirencester) where the lord of the hundred was faced with other potentates. This was the hundred of Berkeley, essentially coincident with the landed estate of the Berkeley lords. The estate was itself known in the twelfth century as 'Berkeley harness' and this term was derived from an old English word 'herness', meaning 'obedience', 'jurisdiction'. It is a late example of the way in which the organization of hundreds was often based on pre-existing property or settlement units.[34]

In Gloucestershire then, twenty hundreds out of thirty were in private hands, counting the large royal hundreds leased to Winchcombe Abbey. The whole of Worcestershire, as far as jurisdiction of the lesser type was concerned, was controlled by the local magnates since according to the county jurors the Beauchamps clearly behaved as lords of the hundreds of Doddingtree and Halfshire. In Warwickshire, however, the hundreds (apart from the Bishop of Worcester's liberty of Pathlow) were in royal hands and private franchises were limited to the manorial level. The small scale of the Warwickshire franchises is obviously related to the small scale and late development of ecclesiastical and baronial estates in the county.

The view of frankpledge in private hands could be the consequence of the lord of the manor's instructions to his tenants, or indeed to all the inhabitants of his village whether tenants or not, to make their presentments of misdemeanours through their tithingmen at a view of frankpledge held in the manor courts.[35]

Alternatively if the lord of an estate was the private lord of a hundred, all men in the hundred, unless attending another lord's private view, would be made to attend the view at the traditional place of meeting of the hundred court. The actual records of these courts would, of course, provide the best evidence for this type of jurisdiction, but since few of these have survived the best overall evidence comes from the royal inquiries into private franchises which were carried out in the reign of Edward I. An enquiry was made by royal justices in 1274–5, mainly in order to investigate cases of usurpation and oppression that had occurred during the recent civil war. The results of the enquiry were enrolled on what have come to be known as the Hundred Rolls. The king subsequently despatched successive judicial commissions round the counties with instructions to enquire by what warrant (*quo warranto*) various privileges, mainly of judicial character, were held by private persons. The Warwickshire (1285) and Gloucestershire (1287) returns are very detailed, but unfortunately no return for Worcestershire has yet been found.[36] The king's intention was probably to challenge and resume as many franchises as he could, but by 1290 objections by the barons prevented him from doing this except in a minority of cases.[37] The claims which landowners made serve as a fair indication therefore of what was the actual situation with regard to their local powers.

The landowners claimed many other privileges than that of the right to hold their own view of frankpledge. These included, among others, the right to deal with pleas of distraint (*vee de naam*), to punish those who broke the assize of bread and ale, to have markets and fairs, to have the exclusive right to hunt such small animals as rabbits, hares and foxes (the freedom of the warren). We shall here, however, concentrate on the private view of frankpledge because it was this right which gave an extra degree of social control to private landowners over their tenants and subjects. It should be noted in any case that lords who managed to get the right to the private view of frankpledge usually enjoyed most of the other common franchises as well. Most of them enjoyed the freedom of the warren on their demesnes, most of them had one or two markets or fairs in the villages of their estate, most of them had supervision of the assize of ale, if not of bread.

Confining our attention, then, to the private view of frankpledge, we find that in 1285 about fifty Warwickshire lords put in claims with respect to tenants and suitors to courts in some one hundred and fifty villages. In Gloucestershire there were some sixty claimants for about the same number of villages. We cannot say what numbers would have been returned for Worcestershire, but it would hardly be rash to suggest that something like one hundred and fifty lords in the west midland counties had established private views covering all or some inhabitants of four hundred or more villages and hamlets. Some of the claims were backed by the production of royal charters, but most were justified by prescription, that is because the claimant and his ancestors had enjoyed them beyond the memory of man. This probably means that these lords had been strengthening their control over their tenants by this means over the past century. This is, of course, just the period that saw the deterioration in the legal position of the customary tenants in England and the culmination of the period of growth of local private jurisdiction in western Europe as a whole.

The distribution of private views of frankpledge follows the pattern of the distribution of landed property. Well endowed lay and ecclesiastical lords tried to assert this right over all the tenants on their estates. Those who had lordship over hundreds were able to do this relatively easily. The villagers' representatives, that is either the reeve and four men or the heads of the tithings (chief pledges or tithingmen), would expect to come to the normal place where the hundred court met. The Earl of Gloucester as lord of Tewkesbury and Thornbury hundreds, held a view of frankpledge in both hundreds for all the inhabitants (*de omnibus commorantibus*), with the exception of the abbot of Tewkesbury's tenants who went to the view at the abbot's manor courts. Then the earl had three other views for his own tenants, one at Fairford, attended also by men from Eastleach and Arlington-by-Bibury; one at Rendcombe attended by the men of Over Rendcombe, Woodmancote, Calmsden, Aylworth and Harford (both in Naunton), Trewsbury and Coates; and one at Shorncote attended by men of Siddington and Northcote. Tewkesbury, Thornbury and Fairford views were each equipped with engines of punishment: gallows, tumbrel and pillory.

The Bishop of Worcester's policy with regard to the view of frankpledge is not clear, owing to shortage of evidence. What there is suggests that the tendency was for jurisdictional activity to be drawn to the manorial and away from the hundred courts. In the bishop's 1299 survey, references to attendance by his tenants at views of frankpledge as part of their tenurial obligation are made without any indication that the view was held at Oswaldslow, outside Worcester, rather than in the manor court.[38] One would have thought that it would have been more convenient for tenants to attend the view locally rather than at the hundred centre. However in 1274 tenants of the bishop, both free and unfree, were complaining that his bailiffs were amercing them for breaches of the assize of ale at each session of the manor courts instead of twice a year in the Oswaldslow hundred court. This admittedly is not a reference to the view of frankpledge, but it seems possible that the view was similarly being transferred from hundred to manor, even though the lord was the same person in both tribunals. Similarly suitors to the Wimburntree hundred (a sort of Cotswold branch court of Oswaldslow), when pleading absence ('essoin) from the hundred court session, had to present themselves to guarantee their plea of absence ('warranting their essoin') not at the Wimburntree hundred court, but at the Blockley manorial court.[39] The conflict seems to have been not so much over the place where suit of court was done, but over frequency, for manorial courts certainly met more often than the great biennial session of the hundred.

That lord of many Cotswold hundreds, the Abbot of Cirencester, having (as we have mentioned) arrived rather late on the scene, compared with the Bishop of Worcester, found that he was by no means in full control of the frankpledge jurisdiction in these hundreds. The abbey's cartulary contains a rather late (probably fifteenth century) calendar of the views of frankpledge in the so-called seven hundreds, but which must certainly reflect a much earlier situation.[40] The calendar lists views in fifty-seven villages in Crowthorn, Rapsgate, Bradley, Brightwellsbarrow and Longtree hundreds. In thirty-nine cases the normal procedure was followed, that is, the tithingman with the men of his tithing came, after reasonable summons, to the hundred court twice a year, at Martinmas and Hockday. There he presented all things pertaining to the view before the bailiffs of the lord of the liberty (that is the abbot). On the other hand there were eighteen villages where the local lord had established some degree of control over the view, though in no case involving complete usurpation.

There had indeed been attempts at such usurpation, but in the middle decade of the thirteenth century the abbots of Cirencester had re-asserted some degree of control. For instance, the prior of the small alien monastery at Horsley had, since the end of John's reign, managed to exclude the Abbot of Cirencester's bailiffs from Horsley manor and had held his own view. Then in 1256 the Abbot of Horsley Priory's parent house at Troarn, Normandy, agreed that the Cirencester bailiffs should have access, though the view was still to be held in Horsley manor rather than at the Longtree hundred court at Chavenage (a hamlet in Horsley parish), and the Abbey of Troarn was to have the profits, less a mark a year paid to Cirencester.[41] Another case of usurpation was at Lechlade. Isabella, widow of Roger Mortimer of Wigmore, was lady of Lechlade and owned a market there. She made an agreement with the Abbot of Cirencester by which she was able to have a view of frankpledge in the market itself with a tumbrel and pillory to punish offenders. The inhabitants and users of the market would make their presentments in Lechlade before the bailiffs of the abbot who would make a biennial tourn. Other burgesses of Lechlade would have to go to Brightwellsbarrow hundred court in Hatherop as before. This agreement was made some time (perhaps twenty years) before 1250. But Lechlade in 1252 was given to the powerful Richard, Earl of Cornwall, the king's brother, and he seized the whole view there, not restoring it until 1258.[42] Even so, the view continued to be held in the manor (or borough), though presided over by the abbot's bailiffs. The same situation obtained at Chedworth (a manor of the earls of Warwick), at Brimpsfield, Birdlip and Cranham (Giffard), Northleach (Abbot of St Peter's, Gloucester), Shipton Pelye (Robert Pulye), Yanworth (Abbot of Winchcombe), Kempsford (Chaworth), Hatherop (Abbess of Laycock) Minchinhampton (Abbess of Holy Trinity, Caen), Woodchester (Maltravers) and Shipton Moyne (Moigne).[43]

Sometimes the lord of the manor took all the profits, sometimes he shared it with the abbot. Other arrangements also obtained, all involving concessions to the manorial lords. At Siddington Musard (now Lower Siddington) the lord (of the Musard family) held the view and took all the profits, but the Siddington bailiff or reeve had to attend the Crowthorn hundred court twice a year to ask for this right from the abbot's bailiffs, who then had the right to a meal at Siddington at the expense of the lord of the manor. The tithing-man and four tenants from the manor of Pinbury (near Duntisbourne Rous) had to attend the same hundred court and pay nine-pence each time, though without making any presentments, which would have to be made in the manor. At Marsden, a grange and manor of the Oxfordshire Cistercian Abbey of Bruern in Rend-comb parish, the steward of Cirencester Abbey held a view for the Abbot of Bruern's servants after the Rapsgate hundred view had been held, and after being entertained to dinner.[44]

The Abbot of Cirencester had to give way to powerful local pressure, even though he was himself a powerful local lord.[45] It was natural that more effective encroachments should be made on hundreds in crown hands, for however powerfully the king could at times act, he was, most of the time, no stronger than his local agents. The most effective pressure of course, came from the few lay and ecclesiastical magnates with really big territorial holdings though, as we have seen, in some cases these private views derived from the private possession of hundreds rather than from appro-priation from the royal, or public, hundred courts. However, these massive private views of frankpledge with participants from widely scattered parts of a lord's estate by no means predominated, even in Gloucestershire, and featured even less in Warwickshire.

Another important Gloucestershire landowner, who possessed no private hundred, nevertheless claimed (and therefore probably exercised) view of frankpledge in a number of his manor courts. This was the Augustinian prior of Lanthony by Gloucester. He held the view in six courts. At Brockworth it was held for twelve priory tenants, at South Cerney for two-thirds of the inhabitants of the village, at Barrington for the whole village* and at Turkdean for the inhabitants of Lower Turkdean. His court at Alvington (on the west bank of the Severn) was held for all the villagers and for two priory tenants at Harn Hill in Aylburton. The view at Hemp-stead, near Gloucester, was held for all the men of that village, for the whole village of Quedgely, for six tenants at Nibley and two from Elmore. The view was held twice a year, no royal officials attended and no payment was made to the crown by the prior from the profits of the view. For lack of court rolls we cannot say who attended in order to make presentments for small groups of ten-ants in outlying villages. In cases like this the system of mutual pledge may have broken down. However, the reality of the prior's power was expressed by three gallows, one at Hempstead, one

* Probably both Great and Little Barrington.

at South Cerney and one at Alvington; and by tumbrels at Brockworth and South Cerney.

In Warwickshire the principal claimants for private views were ecclesiastics, the most prominent being the abbots of Combe, Pipewell, Evesham and the priors of Kenilworth and Coventry. The Earl of Warwick made surprisingly modest claims, though he had a view and a gallows at Sutton. His jurisdictional powers were probably greater in Worcestershire where the Beauchamps had been longer entrenched. Otherwise the principal lay claimants were John of Hastings, lord of Allesley and Roger de Somery of Dudley. These greater lords claimed the private view of frankpledge for their tenants in between eight and a dozen manors each. Some of them were surprisingly well equipped too with private gallows: the Prior of Coventry had eleven. But for the most part, the other claimants concerned themselves with one or two private views only, even where their actual manorial holdings were wider.

It is not easy to sum up this aspect of social control in the west midland countryside. Purely manorial justice was ubiquitous, but it was not everywhere reinforced by the additional control given by the manorial lord's possession of the private view of frankpledge. And although we have enumerated the claimants to private views, as well as the places in which they had tenants or others who attended them, it would be impossible to give comparative figures of the peasants and others who attended or who were represented at the private manorial views, as compared with those covered by the hundred courts still in royal hands. We can say with some confidence, however, that the right to hold a private view of frankpledge was not widely distributed socially. A third of the claimants in Gloucestershire and Warwickshire were ecclesiastics; more than a third were from baronial or upper gentry families. Very few of the rest were not from established knightly families. Yet when this is said, when all the visible and legitimate forms of private jurisdiction in the west midlands at the end of the thirteenth century are added together, they clearly constituted, from the point of view of the majority of the population, a formidable element of control. For however short of continental *haute justice* might be the powers of the bishop, the abbots, the earls, the barons and the knights, we must remember that they reinforced a much more solid and powerful economic position as lords of tenants than was enjoyed by most landowners in other parts of western Europe. We must remember, in addition, that apart from private jurisdiction as already described, the local landowners in the west midlands, as well as in any other region, were normally the class from which the crown's agents and judges were drawn.

Law and Disorder in the Forest

In this connection it is of considerable interest to see how the areas under royal forest law were governed during this period. In theory the forests were places where above all one would expect the royal will to be untrammelled by local interests. As we have seen, the chief areas under forest law were the royal forests of Dean in Gloucestershire and Feckenham in Worcestershire. Within the forest boundaries, a hierarchy of officials, backed up by periodic visitations of forest justices, were expected to protect the venison, which the king and his friends hunted for pleasure and for meat, and the vert, which was the woodland cover where the game lived and bred until it was time for it to be killed. The venison was protected by reserving the hunting of it to the king and to those having his express licence to do so. Anyone found in the forest armed with bows and arrows, or carrying dead game, or accompanied by hunting dogs whose feet had not been 'lawed' (crippled by cutting off toes) was liable to the penalties of the forest law. Those who cut down or harmed the timber for any purpose, such as for building, for firewood, or for the extension of cultivation were equally liable to punishment unless they were exercising carefully defined rights of common.[46]

Forest law applied to the whole area of the forest, whether it was royal demesne or the land of individual lords. It was by no means as stringently applied in the thirteenth as it had been in the previous century, and as we shall see, it is doubtful whether the king got as much profit or enjoyment from the forests as did various local potentates. The crown continued its attempts in the thirteenth, as in the twelfth century, to expand the areas under forest law, though the question of the exact bounds of the forest is much confused by dubious claims and counter-claims by crown agents on the one hand and local landowners on the other. It seems that the Gloucestershire forest area had considerably increased between the middle of the twelfth century and 1228. According to a perambulation of that year it had doubled.[47] By the end of Edward I's

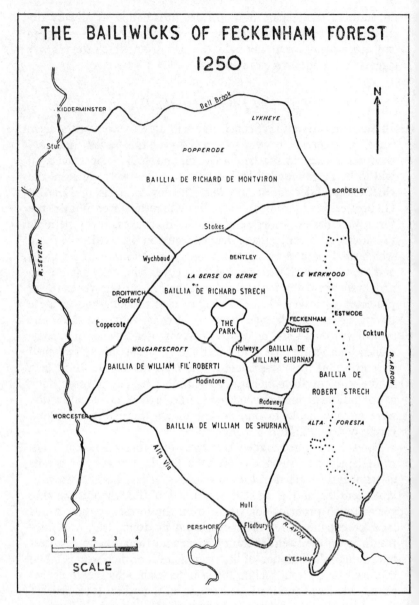

THE BAILIWICKS OF FECKENHAM FOREST
1250

reign, the local Worcestershire landowners claimed that Feckenham forest had been enlarged sixfold since the mid-twelfth century, but there seem to be good grounds for doubting this. For one
thing there had been important disafforestations, of Ombersley
north of Worcester and Horewell in the south of the county. These
had come into operation by about 1230. For another, the jurors
who made the perambulations of the forest in 1300 were apparently
grossly minimizing the extent of the forest in the twelfth century.
This misrepresentation was, of course, part of a general campaign
to reduce systematically the area under the forest law. The campaign had been mounted against Edward I much to his resentment,
but it achieved success (in spite of Edward's promises) only by the
1330s. It seems certain that in fact the area in Worcestershire under
forest law, as early as Domesday, stretched from the Herefordshire to the Warwickshire boundaries and from the river Avon to
Staffordshire. These areas, admittedly, were not all in the Forest
of Feckenham only, but were also included in Wyre, Ombersley,
Horewell and Malvern Forests, the last three of which, by the
mid-twelfth century were either disafforested, or (Malvern)
converted into a private chase.[48]

These disputes between the crown and the local landowners,
focused at the time of the perambulations on the disputed bounds,
give a false impression of the real situation. The position of the
crown had become by no means so absolute as the local landowners, whose interests are reflected by the perambulations,
attempted to claim. In reality, the royal forests in the thirteenth
century were riddled with private exemptions and the men who
were supposed to be looking after the king's interests were largely
concerned with their own private profit.

It is true that, apart from the jurisdictions of the manorial courts,
there were no exceptional private jurisdictions in the forest.
Nevertheless, hereditary feudal rights which limited the crown's
range of action were strongly entrenched, and their holders tended
to corrupt the crown's appointed agents rather than being
controlled by them.

The two big forests with which we are concerned were each
placed under the custody of a warden, who was usually a landed
magnate influential at court. These men seldom did duties in person, and consequently appointed a deputy or deputies. The
thirteenth-century wardens of Dean, who were normally also

constables of the royal castle of St Briavels in the heart of the forest, included such potent names as Clare, Beauchamp, Giffard and Botetourt. The wardens of Feckenham, although occasionally drawn from such families as Clifford or Mortimer of Richard's Castle, were usually drawn from a lower social group than those of Dean, particularly from the 1270s. This was perhaps because King Edward I, correctly regarding Feckenham as less important and profitable than Dean, had virtually made it over as an endowment to the queens of England, as (with some vicissitudes) it continued to the end of the middle ages. The appointed wardens had little influence on the king's behalf in the forest, and in so far as they were active at all were often revealed at the sessions of the itinerant justices as the chief offenders against the forest law.

Wardens and appointed deputies came and went, often having made their pile, particularly from the illegal sale of timber. For example, the damages to the king's woods for which keepers of Dean, John Giffard and Thomas de Clare, were responsible in a period of at the most seven years (1263–70) was estimated in 1270 at £2,378. Adam le Bolde, steward of Feckenham 1272–80 was fined 100 marks in 1280 for 'making and permitting waste', a phrase which implies illegal exploitation of the timber resources. The day-to-day enforcement of the law of the forest,[49] was more effectively in the hands of the families who held by hereditary right the bailiwicks into which the forests were divided. The tenure of these bailiwicks was normally attached to a landed holding in the forest and the duties of the 'foresters-in-fee', as they were called, were in theory performed in return for the land. In practice, of course, the performance of the duty brought a profit, a more substantial reward than the land itself. Dean was divided into ten bailiwicks by 1280 and Feckenham into five, and a park. These feudal offices probably originated in the twelfth century, but it is not until the middle of the thirteenth century that the evidence permits us to see who were these entrenched hereditary foresters.

The hereditary foresters were not of baronial status, and for the most part not even from knightly families. Nevertheless, they seem to have established a sort of feudal power which even the itinerant justices of the powerful Edward I found impossible to diminish. Although they were supposed to attach offenders against the forest law and present them to the swanimotes (the first rung in the ladder of the forest courts), the records of forest proceedings show

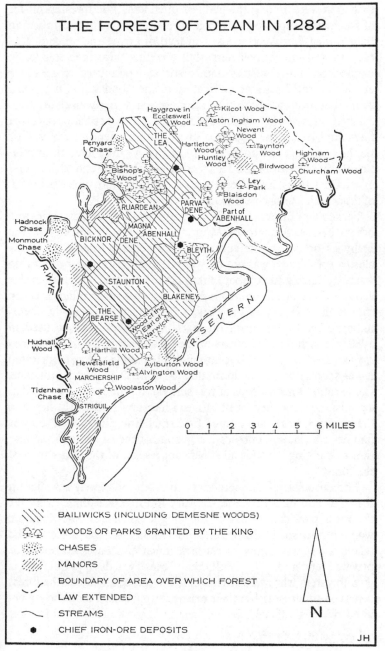

THE FOREST OF DEAN IN 1282

Haygrove in Eccles; well Wood
Kilcot Wood
Aston Ingham Wood
Newent Wood
Penyard Chase
THE LEA
Hartleton Wood
Taynton Wood
Highnam Wood
Huntley Wood
Birdwood
Churcham Wood
Bishop's Wood
Ley Park
Blaisdon Wood
RUARDEAN
PARVA DENE
Part of ABENHALL
Hadnock Chase
MAGNA DENE
ABENHALL
Monmouth Chase
BICKNOR
BLEYTH
R. WYE
STAUNTON
BLAKENEY
R. SEVERN
THE BEARSE
Wood of the Earl of Warwick
Hudnall Wood
Harthill Wood
Aylburton Wood
Hewelsfield Wood
Alvington Wood
MARCHERSHIP
Tidenham Chase
OF
Woolaston Wood
STRIGUIL

0 1 2 3 4 5 6 MILES

BAILIWICKS (INCLUDING DEMESNE WOODS)
WOODS OR PARKS GRANTED BY THE KING
CHASES
MANORS
BOUNDARY OF AREA OVER WHICH FOREST
LAW EXTENDED
STREAMS
CHIEF IRON-ORE DEPOSITS

N

JH

that they were among the greatest offenders. The foresters-in-fee of Dean were supposed to appoint under-foresters to assist them in their duties, but were accused instead of giving the office of forester to well-known poachers, thus enabling these men to operate unchecked. The foresters both made and permitted to be made encroachments of arable cultivation in the woodland. They felled timber, appropriated the king's demesne lands to themselves, overstocked the common pastures with their beasts and embezzled the fines imposed by the regular courts on other offenders which they themselves were supposed to collect. They must have been relatively uninterested in the deer themselves, for only one of the worst of the Dean foresters-in-fee, Ralph of Abenhall, lord of the bailiwick of Abenhall, was accused of this.[50]

Feckenham foresters-in-fee were convicted of similar crimes and others beside. Richard of Montviron, hereditary forester of the bailiwick of Popperode and the king's demesne 'hay' (forest enclosure) of Lickey, was not only found in 1270 to have been laying waste by cutting the timber, but to have associated with him in this activity three of his under-foresters and two other officials called 'tunwards'.* Henry of the Park, a hereditary forester who seems to have been a retainer of the Earl of Warwick, was accused in 1280 of poaching with others of the earl's retainers (*aliis de familia comitis de Warewyk*).[51] But although his bailiwick was confiscated it was soon restored, no doubt due to the earl's powerful influence. Confiscation for misdeeds of this sort was not uncommonly used as a punishment for the Forest of Dean foresters-in-fee. But here too the bailiwick was soon restored for a small fine, and the old forester families continued in possession in spite of their systematic spoliation of the king's woods and their oppression of the lesser men of the forest.

The misdeeds of the hereditary foresters, so clearly revealed in the mid- and late thirteenth-century forest proceedings, were for the most part committed at the king's expense in the demesne woods of the crown. But we must remember, too, that although the whole forest was under forest law, much of its area consisted of private woodland. The landlords of these woods appointed their own foresters who were responsible for presentments to the forest courts of offences within their masters' woods, and could be supervised by royal officials. By Edward I's reign there were thirty-six

---

* 'Tun' means township.

private chases, parks, groves and woods in the Forest of Dean and well over fifty in Feckenham.* These were largely in the hands of the greater landowners of the region, including the ecclesiastics. In the Forest of Dean, for example, the Abbot of St Peter's, Gloucester and the Bishop of Hereford had private woods, as had the Earl of Lancaster, the Earl Marshal, the Earl of Warwick, the baron Richard Talbot, not to speak of lesser lay and ecclesiastical lords. In Feckenham there was an even wider distribution of private woodland among the county aristocracy, headed on the ecclesiastical side by the Bishop and Prior of Worcester and on the secular by the earls of Warwick and Pembroke. The knightly families of Worcestershire and western Warwickshire are also both represented by such familiar names as Abetot, Pauncefot (Grimbald Pauncefot was also for a time royal keeper of Dean), Sudeley, Lucy, Corbucion and others.[52]

Some of the most influential of these lords were granted immunity in their private woods from the regards and views of the forest. In effect, this meant the exclusion of the official verderers and regarders, and *carte blanche* at least for the cutting of timber and the making of assarts. The Bishop of Worcester was one of the earliest to get such privileges, as early as the end of the twelfth century, but the abbots of Bordesley and Evesham and the priors of Worcester also got considerable exemptions.[53] Private deer parks such as that of the abbots of Westminster at Pershore were not uncommon. Many lords had rights of free warren, that is exclusive rights to hunt the smaller game (hare, rabbit, fox). And from these private strongholds, poachers of the king's game were encouraged and given shelter. The private officials were not, and could hardly be expected to be more conscientious than the royal officials, and by the hereditary foresters-in-fee they were set the worst possible example.

In the royal forest, then, where aristocratic privilege might have been expected to be at a minimum, the reverse was in practice the case. The parallel with the jurisdictional privileges of the landowners in the hundred and manorial courts does not, of course, hold good in this sphere, for we do not see in the forest the local magnate interposed between the public authority and the peasantry.

* The private woods of Feckenham are named in enquiries of 1262, 1272, and 1280, and are located in fifty-three named places. Eighty-seven owners are mentioned but there were certain changes in ownership between 1262 and 1280.

It is true that the powerful men of the forest, whether landowners or officials, oppressed the poorer forest inhabitants by exacting illegal hospitality, by overcharging the commons and by the unequal application of forest justice. But the chief victim of the depredations of these men was the king. This potentially most profitable crown resource was systematically pillaged for both meat and timber, not only by the humble outlawed poacher of legend, but by the nobility and gentry, not forgetting the ecclesiastics. Even the regular, though small, cash income due to the exchequer seldom reached its proper destination. It has been calculated that between 1155 and 1307 only sixty per cent of the Forest of Dean profit ever reached Westminster.[54]

Honest Felons and Well-born Bandits

The social conditions in the forests at the end of the thirteenth century arose from the failure of the crown, in an area where its jurisdiction and administration should have been more effective than in the open country, to control the social forces at work in regional society. In the forest, the wilfulness of the local potentates stands out clearly in opposition to the interests of the crown. The result, as we have seen, was disorder and systematic pillage. This contrasts with the situation in the villages and hamlets, at any rate as we see it through the records of the manor court. It is true that within the villages there was no lack of friction between lord and tenant, between the employers of labour and the workers, and over a whole range of matters from disputes about pasture to village quarrels arising (for instance) from the sharp tongue of the village shrew. But these matters were settled in the manor court. The accused normally faced their accusers and paid their amercement or fine if they were found guilty by the court. Flight from the manor was not yet a commonplace of peasant life, as it was to be a century later.

The matters dealt with by the manor court were, though serious to the villager in his everyday life, not issues of life or death. Manorial jurisdiction had no cognizance (unless the lord had the right of infangthef) of any crimes punishable by hanging. Felonies were pleas of the crown and had to be presented before the king's justices by juries of indictment. The records of these royal courts tell us to what extent with regard to those more serious matters the king's peace was kept, that is, whether men and women could sleep in their beds, go out into the fields, or travel to market without fear of being pillaged or murdered.

The assize rolls of the early years of Edward I contain many cases which were a hangover from the period of the rebellion. Violence, and the usurpation of individual and crown rights by royal and seigneurial officials are a commonplace in these court records of the 1270s. The courts were attempting to deal with much the same sort of problems as were presented to the royal commissioners who went round the counties in 1274 and 1275 to ask questions about the state of the peace and about oppressions and usurpations. These Hundred Rolls are particularly full for Gloucestershire and give a remarkable series of nearly two hundred major and minor oppressions and usurpations, many of them during the civil war. They range from the Earl of Cornwall's illegal prison and gallows at Lechlade to the malicious impounding by the Earl of Gloucester's bailiff at Thornbury of the cattle and sheep of a local freeholder, William de Veym.[55] The overall picture, as one would expect during a period of civil war, is of the intensification of the normal oppression of the weak by the strong. The weak probably hoped that the new king's vigorous inquiries and his legislation would result in a better life for them in the future.

In this, however, they were probably disappointed. Lawful habits, resulting from the certainty of the detection and punishment of crime, could not be expected straight away after a period of turmoil. But one would have thought that several decades of the rule of a king who has the reputation of defending other men's rights as well as his own would have resulted in a tolerable peace in the countryside. The west midlands evidence hardly shows that this was the case, even after twenty or thirty years of Edwardian justice. It must be admitted that the evidence from the sessions of the justices of assize is not easy to interpret. In the first place, one naturally gets an unrelieved picture of continuous crime from the courts of criminal law whose function was to receive a succession of indictments for felony from the hundred, borough and township juries. Next, one wonders to what extent the malice of the presenting juries makes the picture seem even blacker than it was, since the second juries which were summoned to pronounce on the guilt of the indicted persons very frequently declared them guiltless. There are some figures however which seem difficult to explain away. At the Worcester gaol delivery of 1304, thirty-six persons had been indicted for felony, but only five were punished, that is, hanged, although eighteen of the felonies were cases of murder. Seventeen of the felons produced royal pardons, sixteen were acquitted by the juries, two showed they had been acquitted at a previous trial and one successfully claimed benefit of clergy. Two of those exonerated had already prejudiced their cases by disappearing, and were subsequently outlawed.[56] But after all, these were escapes from prison of men who had already been caught. At the Warwick assizes of 1306 when the juries received indictments of persons accused of felony who had not yet been imprisoned, it was reported that ninety-one who were accused of murder and thirty-four of other killings had fled rather than submit to trial.[57] The judges instructed the sheriff to have them all outlawed, but only a minority would be brought to book, and most of these would get off.

Juries of presentment might with reason be suspected of unjust accusations, as is suggested in the contemporary *Outlaw's Song of Trailbaston*.[58] Details of assault and robbery could be invented or exaggerated. But death by violence is self-evident, and if jurors were acting rightly to declare so many accused of murder to be innocent, this simply meant that there were as many undiscovered murderers at large. One cannot escape the conclusion that when it came to the point, fear or pity persuaded the juries to declare guilty men innocent. Since the king was issuing pardons to murderers who had happened to have served in his armies, local juries may perhaps be forgiven for their attitude to civilian felons. These royal pardons seem to have been sought by killers who had fled after their crime. William le Welle of Bretford in Warwickshire killed a fellow villager in January 1303, and then fled. He was indicted before the king's justices at Warwick three years later but produced a charter of pardon for services with the king's army in Scotland, dated at Dunfermline the November after the killing.[59] Another Warwickshire murderer, Henry the son of Hugh le Keu of Tachbrook had killed Simon Clay of Radford in 1298. Having obtained sanctuary in Radford Church he was allowed to abjure the realm, but reappeared with a charter dated at Westminster in April 1298, that is not long after the murder, granted to him because he had been in the king's army in Flanders.[60] A Herefordshire knight, Miles Pichard, operating in a gang with a former vicar of Leamington and three others unnamed, robbed the rector of Great Wolford and another man, Richard of Caus, and (presumably during the course of the robbery) killed John Barectour of Wolford. The gang then fled, but Miles appeared before the juries at Warwick in 1306 armed with two royal pardons for all felonies and outlawries because of his service in Scotland. One was dated at Stirling in July 1304, the other at Lanercost in October 1304.[61]

Hence, although we cannot believe everything in the indictments when we attempt to assess the peacefulness or otherwise of life in the west midlands in the late thirteenth and early fourteenth centuries, we must be equally sceptical about the declarations of juries who pronounced the innocence of men who had been accused of crimes which are described with remarkably circumstantial detail. All these factors' taken into consideration, the impression we get is of quick recourse to violence, especially about disputed rights. This violence however was, so to speak, often rational; it was in pursuit of rational aims and could be absorbed by the rural communities without proliferating into a sequence of senseless acts of violence. Such was a Warwickshire case presented in 1306. Adam of Clattercote, hayward of the village of Claverdon, found John of Sutton with his animals feeding on the grain growing in the village fields. He asked him for a pledge (*vadium*) that he would pay for the damage, John's reply to this was to draw a knife and chase the hayward until they reached the edge of a deep river. Adam could not escape and hit John with a pole axe, killing him. The jury thought that Adam acted in self-defence and was not guilty, so the justices sent him to prison to wait for the king's grace.[62] Conflicts over pasture were common causes of village fracas. A case in Worcestershire in 1275 looks, in the indictment, like the activities of a gang of bandits, for Mathilda of Walecot near Pershore accused twenty-nine locals, by name, of coming to her house, insulting her and stealing two hundred pigs from her park. She did not put in an appearance at the sessions, but the accused were represented. The case could have gone by default. However the justices, for the sake of observing the king's peace, about which everybody was concerned at this period, ordered the jurors to enquire. The jury said that Mathilda had been impounding the men's pigs for small offences (*parvo delicto*) – probably trespass – and that they could not be treated as robbers in their recovery of their own animals.[63]

251

These disputes certainly sometimes had far from trivial results. The jurors of Knightlow Hundred reported to the justices at Warwick in 1285 that John, a monk of the Cistercian Abbey of Stoneleigh, who was the monastic granger, went to the house of Henry of St Maur in the neighbouring village of Cubbington to recover some draught animals which had been impounded there, presumably having strayed on to Henry's corn or grass. Henry and the monk quarrelled, so Henry cut John's throat. At which, Ermegarde, Henry's wife, ran up and finished the monk off by breaking his head open with a stone. As one would expect, the guilty couple, together with Geoffrey of Hunningham who had joined in on their side, fled. The incident happened at least two years before the court session. Henry and Ermegarde abandoned a considerable estate and £33 worth of chattels, and clearly did not intend to return to face the justices.[64]

This seemingly excessive violence was characteristic of the epoch. The justices at Worcester in 1306 were told that four years earlier Joan, the aggrieved wife of Edmund Sneed of Hampton Lovet, scratched out the eyes of Christina, her husband's mistress, and blinded her. But after that, husband and wife had found sustenance for Christina, and one of the issues of the case was how secure was Christina in this sustenance.[65] Even more horrific was a case in Warwickshire in 1298 in which popular justice and private passion seem strangely mingled. A man from Ilmington, Richard the son of Geoffrey Simound, was accused of robbery, by whom it was not stated. His father's wife, Joan (presumably Richard's step-mother), together with four other villagers took him and handed him over for custody to the tithingmen. They then removed him from the custody of the tithingmen and dragged him in front of the house of Geoffrey, his father, where one of the four, Ralph Bithebrok, with agreement of the others, killed him with a stick. They then cut off his head, and later buried him, strangely enough with the knowledge of the coroner.[66]

There were, however, disturbances to the peace which can hardly be seen, like those we have quoted, as the consequence, in a violent age, of the natural conflicts of society. These other disturbances were the consequences rather of deliberately antisocial activity by bandits. Robbery and violence by gangs was all too common, and was quite different in character from the hot-blooded action of individuals in defence of their rights. And all too often gang leaders were drawn from those social classes, the gentry and the clergy, whom one might have expected to have been the protectors of the social order from which they gained their livelihood.

The records of the justices of the King's Bench sitting at Westminster in 1280 to try cases from the counties illustrate the gang element in robbery at the time. The parson of Mancetter (Warwickshire) was robbed by a group of ten parishioners and others of horses, a cart, food and clothing; Henry Bagot, a landowner at Ullenhall (Warwickshire), was robbed of £10 worth of grain by a gang of ten led by Ralph the Barber. James Clinton, a member of the gentry, with twenty-four followers including some of his relations, and supported by a cleric, Master John Burgyson, who had his own following of nine, broke into a house at Baddesley Clinton (Warwickshire) and took £2 worth of goods.[67] A few years later (January 1285) the assize justices at Warwick were presented with an even more astounding tale of gangsterdom. Joan of Cruddeshale was on her way home and was passing through Preston Bagot when (according to her story) she was set on by a gang of twenty persons, whom she named. One of them was a chaplain, another was the clerk of the rector of Preston Bagot, and two others were the rector's servants. They took her to the Montfort castle at Henley-in-Arden, where they kept her from Monday to Thursday before releasing her and after taking away her purse and more valuable clothes, such as a buckle, a belt and a silk veil. She accused the rector of organizing the whole episode. This man, Peter of Leicester, a notorious pluralist, had been clerk, and steward to the Bishop of Worcester but was shortly to lose the bishop's favour. His involvement in an unsavoury episode does not seem out of character, though he may also have made unscrupulous enemies. Her accusation failed because of a technicality – she did not mention the year of the incident, and a local jury in any case exonerated all the accused. But as we have seen, this need not mean that they were innocent.[68]

The favourite targets of the more professional bandits were merchants travelling with money and goods. Merchants going to or from Worcester seem to have been particularly unlucky. Four of them in 1280 impleaded John,* a scion of the Beauchamp family,

---

* The place of the incident is not mentioned, but it could very well have been at Holt, a village on the Severn north of Worcester. It was a Beauchamp manor and became the seat of a famous collateral branch. See above, p. 44.

for robbing them of £5 of merchandise which they were taking up the river Severn to Shrewsbury.[69] According to Worcester indictments in 1305, Trimpley pass, on the edge of the Wyre Forest, three miles north-west of Kidderminster, was infested by a gang who robbed foreign merchants on their way through. One of the robbers, William of Nonnechurch, was captured and declared guilty by the jury. He saved his life by successfully pleading his clergy. Another indictment at the same time was against Felicia la Nywemannes from Kingsford, some two or three miles north-east of Trimpley, who apparently kept the gang supplied with food and drink.[70] Another haunt of bandits who specialized in robbing merchants was Lynholtwood in Feckenham Forest where in 1307 some Worcester merchants, John Lumbard (evidently an Italian by origin), Richard of Evesham, Roger le Spicer and others were robbed of money. The ringleader seems to have been a man called William of Barnedale, a well-known malefactor. This affair was sufficiently notorious to have been presented by jurors from both Blackenhurst and Oswaldslow hundreds as well as from Droitwich town.[71]

Members of the gentry families appear with such considerable frequency, in proportion to their total numbers, that disorder appears almost to be a by-occupation of the class. Some prospered in this activity, others did not. Sir Thomas of Hopton (probably in Shropshire), knight, was accused in 1275 by a Worcestershire gentleman, William le Poer, of a robbery which he (Hopton), together with his brother, another man from Hopton and three Welshmen had committed against William's father. They were all outlawed and the sad sequel appears in the presentments made by jurors from the town of Dudley. In this place, at the house of Thomas of Saltley, probably an inn, there came the constable of Bridgnorth Castle, Walter of Wynterton, together with Sir Thomas of Hopton, his esquire, Mathew of Kaunt and his page, Richard of Stapleton. Sir Thomas stabbed himself during the night and died, and at first the esquire and the page were held on suspicion, but a judgement of suicide (*felo de se*) was given. When it was realized that the suicide was the outlaw, it was asked of the constable of Bridgnorth why he was in such company. The reply was that he had merely met him on the Bridgnorth road two leagues from Dudley.[72] But if Sir Thomas's misdeeds and subsequent outlawry were what weighed on his mind there were other gentlemen criminals who showed no such fine feelings. Of these Malcolm Musard is an excellent example.

Malcolm Musard was a member of a family established in Gloucestershire at the time of the conquest. The main branch was situated at Miserden, a village named after the family. Malcolm however was lord of Saintbury (Gloucestershire), a village on the northern slope of the Cotswolds looking towards the Vale of Evesham. He also had land in the Abbots Morton (Worcestershire), a manor of Evesham Abbey and possibly in Aston Somerville (Gloucestershire), another village of the valley.*[73] His career seems to be one of wickedness rewarded, for following the events to be described below, he became chief forester of Feckenham (before 1315) and in 1321, constable of Hanley Castle.[74]

One of Musard's least reprehensible activities, shared with country men of all classes, was poaching in the preserves of the great magnates. The Worcester county indictment of 1305 shows him surrounded by a gang of supporters. These included his brothers Ralph and William, Geoffrey, the rector of Abbots Morton, and others from the same and other nearby villages. They first broke into the Abbot of Westminster's park at Tiddesley just outside Pershore, killing and taking away the game. They also invaded the Earl of Warwick's park at Beoley, a favourite target for poachers, and took game from there as well. There were however much more unpleasant aspects of Musard's activities. He, the parson of Abbots Morton and two other members of the gang broke into a house at Kenswick and stole a falcon. Members of the gang, on Musard's instructions, beat up Richard of Oddingley in Droitwich. Musard also led his gang in person to Blockley fair where they beat up Thomas of Chetynton, not as a result of a spontaneous brawl, but by malice aforethought. Musard's page (*garcio*), John Baldwyn, also indicted as a murderer, broke into a woman's house, and raped her. Others of the gang, led by Richard of Winchcombe, a warrener at Martley in west Worcestershire, beat up the bailiff of Sir John de Botetourt at Shelsley Walsh. This may have arisen from some sexual rivalry, for the beating was done in the house of Juliana Young (*la Jeovene*). At the same time Musard himself was active in

* In the *Registrum Sede Vacante* (Worcester Historical Society), p. 68, Malcolm is described as lord of Morton and patron of the church, 1302. It is suggested in *VCH* Worcs., II, p. 350, that he was merely the lessee of Evesham Abbey.

this same district, forcing Peter Fyllol, the rector of Martley, to give him ten quarters of wheat for the sake of peace. At the same time, Musard and his gang were inevitably coming into conflict with landowners in the more immediate vicinity of Abbots Morton. Musard and the others put their beasts to pasture on Thomas of Lench's grain in Meadowcroft in Rous Lench, and Musard's ally, the parson of Abbots Morton, came with others from the same gang, armed, and cut down two hundred oak trees in Thomas of Lench's wood.

Next year the sheriff of Worcestershire was instructed to arrest Musard and twenty-eight of his associates. None was to be found, and only one was so careless as to leave goods within the sheriff's bailwick for distraint.[75]

Musard's activities are not all easily explicable from the evidence. We do not know what personal rivalries were involved in the beatings up of individuals, though competition for pastures and thefts of timber were commonplace enough crimes. However a curious case reported in the Gloucestershire indictments throws an even more unpleasant light on Musard's life than the cases already quoted. This case is already hinted at in the Worcestershire indictments in a part of the manuscript which is only partly legible.[76] We are told that Musard and Elias Lyvet were in the habit of going to take seizin, together with their following, for a reward (*pro munere*) and that they had gone at the instance of Godfrey, rector of Weston-sub-Edge church, but for what reason the jury of presentment did not know. Godfrey the rector was also indicted for bringing Musard and Lyvet along. Now Weston-sub-Edge was, as we have already mentioned above, a manor of a collateral branch of the Giffard family. Its recent lord had been Godfrey Giffard, Bishop of Worcester, who had died in 1301. The bishop had presented and instituted Godfrey of Crombe to the rectory of the village in 1297 while he was only a minor and in sub-deacon's orders, for which he was criticized by the prior and the monks of the cathedral monastery. The bishop apparently had promised this living to the young man on account of the nobility of his birth* and had agreed to hold it for him and to appoint a keeper meanwhile.[77]

When the bishop died he was succeeded as lord of Weston-sub-Edge by a relative, Sir John Giffard. According to an entry in the

---

* His father was lord of Earls Croome, then known as Croome Adam or Croome Simon.

register of Bishop Giffard's successor, William of Geynesburgh, Sir John presented a priest, Thomas of Weston, as rector, and he was instituted under instructions from the bishop on 13 June 1304. Now a Thomas of Weston, bishop's clerk, had been given premises in Weston by Bishop Giffard in 1299 and it seems possible that he may have been the keeper whom the bishop promised to appoint during Godfrey of Crombe's minority. Perhaps Sir John Giffard thought he was preferable to the young man, and indeed, in view of Godfrey of Crombe's recorded behaviour, it would seem that Sir John was right.[78]

Godfrey of Crombe is indicted as leader of a gang which came to Chipping Campden on Hockday (7 April) 1304. This gang beat up a man from Weston, William Lovekyn, and the next day went to Weston itself where they broke into William's house, maltreated him and then ran around the village doing damage. Besides Godfrey of Crombe, at the head of the list of names of the gangsters were two others from Crombe, Adam and Alexander, said to be emissaries of Lord Simon of Crombe. This suggests that Godfrey's relatives were taking a hand in this apparently revengeful behaviour. The others however are described as common malefactors, disturbers of the peace and on hire for any evil-doing (*locabiles ad omnia mala facienda*).[79]

It seems to have been after the institution of Thomas of Weston to the benefice that Malcolm Musard put himself and his gang at the disposal of the evicted rector. At the beginning of August a gang provided by Musard but under the leadership of Godfrey of Crombe came to Weston, broke into the rector's house and stole his grain and goods. They then shot up the manor house and the lord of the manor's servants with their bows and arrows. Then at the beginning of September a raid was mounted with Malcolm Musard in person, and a number of rather more prominent persons than before. These included Geoffrey of Saintbury, rector of Abbots Morton, who had been presented to that living by Musard in 1302;[80] Ralph and William Musard, Malcolm's brothers; and a certain Hugh of Wardington who seems to have been the organizer of this particular raid (it was done *per procuracionem Hugonis de Wardyngton*). It was certainly organized on a grand scale for the party came on horseback, armed with pennons (*cum equis, armis et pencellis*). They repeated the previous month's performance, breaking up the rector's house and his fishponds.

Malcolm Musard hardly suffered any punishment for these exploits, although in 1305 the juries of every hundred and several towns in Worcestershire had made presentments about his crimes. In January 1306, having eventually surrendered to the Gloucestershire justices, he was fined for his part in the Weston raids. The next year he was put in prison at Worcester, but faced no more serious indictment at the gaol delivery than that of having received John Baldewyn, his page, who had been indicted for murder, and who had been outlawed. Musard, together with a group of other obviously hardened criminals, was declared innocent. His career was by no means finished. As chief forester of Feckenham for some years before 1318 he had scope for a series of similar misdeeds, associated as before with clerics of similar disposition, such as William, the rector of Aston Somerville and Geoffrey, rector of Abbots Morton.[81] But his career is in fact quite monotonous and to pursue it further takes us too far on from the last years of Edward I.

The figures of indictments and convictions, the references to successful careers of crime suggest that at the turn of the thirteenth century the sanctions of the common law were ineffective in curbing violence. The same appears to be the case with regard to corruption and oppression by royal and private officials. The long list of complaints which we find in the Hundred Rolls of 1274–5 mostly record the perpetual small change of local life rather than (as has often been thought) the overflowing bitterness of men oppressed by both sides during the wars between the royal and baronial partisans. Sometimes oppression was the expression of a will to power. The agents of great lords, such as the earls of Gloucester and Warwick or the lords of Berkeley frequently asserted unlawful rights for their masters. For example, the Earl of Warwick's bailiff in Wickhamford usurped the view of frankpledge due at the hundred court of Holford and Greston, held it in the earl's manor and forced a man living in the jurisdiction of the parish church of Wickhamford to abjure the village. Maurice of Berkeley forced another lord, Anselm of Gurnay, to take measures for use at his markets under his (Berkeley's) private seal, rather than the king's officially sealed measures. Nor were the bailiffs of ecclesiastical lords any more tender in their treatment of their lords' subjects. Complaint was made that in the Bishop of Worcester's hundred of Henbury (near Bristol), rich and poor, powerful and weak were all amerced by the will of the bailiffs, not according to the offence, nor by the judgement of neighbours nor according to Magna Carta.[82]

Although the officials of private lords were accused, perhaps most frequently, of attempting to extend the private jurisdictions of which they had charge, the most common fault of royal officials was taking bribes. Walter of Bockinges, under-sheriff of Gloucester, appears frequently in the 1274–5 Hundred Rolls as an active collector of payments from miserable men in his power. Sometimes he released the guilty, as when he took 20s from Adam Freke of Beckford who had been hiding his son, a murderer, and who therefore might himself have been indicted for the felony of concealment. At other times he imprisoned the innocent, as when he kept Richard and John of the Wood for three weeks in Gloucester castle until they paid him 90s. Together with other officials, he took considerable sums from wool merchants to help them on their way during the period of the royal ban on wool exports to Flanders after 1270.[83] Walter must have made well over £100 from bribes from wool merchants alone, and other opportunist officials joined in the same game, though perhaps not with such great profit. He had his counterparts elsewhere, of course. William of Morteyn, sheriff of Warwickshire, also took substantial bribes, five marks for instance from Richard of Marston, an imprisoned felon, for his liberty and the pretence that he was dead.[84]

Oppression by officials and their corruption, closely linked traits, are characteristics of a primitive, yet partially commercialized society where the officials of administration and justice are without adequate, regular, fixed pay, themselves insecure, yet in temporary possession of considerable unchecked power over other men. Consequently the features of west midland social order which appear in the 1260s and 1270s are to be found regularly in similar forms twenty, thirty or more years later, and especially well illustrated whenever the king invited his subjects to complain about his servants. Such an opportunity occurred when the king's justices were given a commission of inquiry into the misdeeds of royal officials in the county of Worcester in 1324, an inquiry during which the activities of these officials as far back as the later years of Edward I were investigated. The presentments that were made against William Roculf, senior, a bailiff of the city of Worcester in the reigns of both Edward I and Edward II, describe events which are a fitting pendant to the earlier misdeeds of Walter of Bockinges, and a suitable accompaniment in an urban setting to the activities in open country of Malcolm Musard, Roculf's contemporary.[85]

The elder Roculf, apart from being accused of collusion with Roger d'Amory, husband of one of the Clare heiresses,* and enemy of the king, a charge of which he was (rightly or wrongly) acquitted, seems to have misused the influence he had in the borough court, as bailiff and therefore president, to gain money. In fact, like many other men in the indictments of this period, he took bribes from both parties with the promise of favouring their suit. For example, Edith of Bishampton and her son John impleaded the prior of the Cathedral monastery and another person by a writ of novel disseisin concerning some tenements in Worcester. The plaintiffs seem to have approached Roculf for his favour in the suit and this he promised (*pro essendo de consiliis ipsorum Edithe et Johannis*) in return for a mark. However, shortly afterwards, the prior got at him and gave him an annual pension of 20s for life. Roculf therefore advised Edith and John not to prosecute the writ any further.

The retaining fee of 20s a year may have been intended to cover other requirements of the prior as far as the city administration was concerned. Some will argue that this sort of pension was a normal means by which the wheels of justice were greased at the time. This is undoubtedly true, but another case shows Roculf positively exacting an annual pension from a man in a much less powerful position than the Prior of Worcester. This person was William of Throckmorton, a tanner of the city against whom Roculf pursued something of a vendetta. He procured an indictment against William by which he was accused of forestalling (cornering goods outside the control of the market), and in different ways, both inside and outside the city, Roculf harassed William until he granted him an annual pension for life of 40d. Other forms of harassment included demanding one of William's horses which he (Roculf), who must have had agricultural land outside the city walls, wanted to use for harrowing. William refused, so Roculf had the horse confiscated as if for government purposes (*ad opus regis*). A final ploy against the unfortunate William was that Roculf made representations to the Earl of Warwick that William was the earl's villein. This gave the earl the opportunity to seize £40 worth of William's goods. This was not an uncommon action by landowners when they

---

* He fell foul of Hugh Dispenser, his brother-in-law, and therefore of the king. T. F. Tout, *The Place of Edward II in English History*, p. 140.

found well-to-do townsmen whom they could squeeze on the pretext of their own, or their father's villeinage.

William of Throckmorton was not the only victim of Roculf's form of blackmail, but an exceptionally complicated case shows another means by which Roculf, as an official of the city, could make money illegally. The events described in this accusation probably took place in the early years of Edward II's reign. Walter Pukerel of Clun in Shropshire, a tenant of the Earl of Arundel, seems to have been a dealer in cattle. Thieves stole four of his oxen at Clun and drove them to Worcester market where they were bought by three city butchers. Walter Pukerel was so close on the trail however, that the thieves, who would have been hanged if they were caught, disappeared before they got their price (four marks). The oxen were slaughtered, but Pukerel recognized their hides in the butchers' shops, so he went to Roculf, as city bailiff, to complain. Roculf must have put him off for a time, for he then sent for the butchers, advised them to conceal the hides, without the evidence of which Pukerel would have no case, and relieved them of the four marks, which they would have paid the thieves. Pukerel, unable to make a case, went back to Clun, in great anger, no doubt. At any rate, the next time Worcester merchants went to Clun fair and bought stock, they were attacked by the Earl of Arundel's bailiffs and not allowed to go back to Worcester until Pukerel was compensated for his four oxen.

Social Morality and the Church

The administration of justice by the king's judges in the royal courts, and by the officials of the landowner in the courts of hundred and manor did not comprise the whole apparatus of social control. There was also a hierarchy of ecclesiastical courts, of more limited competence perhaps than the secular courts, but still of considerable scope. Since the shortcomings of the secular courts in discouraging violence, oppression and corruption are made plain in the very records of those courts, an examination of what are called the spiritual courts is important, since the failure of the secular apparatus must to some extent be due to the refusal of important social groups to accept what (it was hoped) were the norms of social behaviour. These norms, in a society dominated by the organized Christian church, were inculcated by that church in so far as it formed opinions through education and precept. They were also supposed to be enforced by the penitential system and through the church courts at various levels.

These courts are regarded by historians as being of the first importance. Writing about the bishops, A. H. Thompson, a foremost authority on the medieval English church, describes them in the following terms: 'the highest officers of the church exercised powers which were pre-eminently judicial: their pastoral care was discharged, not in evangelical exhortation and pious encouragement but in bringing their subjects to book for defaults against the spiritual code.'[86] The bishop was the *judex ordinarius* in the diocese, and could exercise his judicial powers in person in his consistory court, or delegate to a vicar-general in his absence, or to his official as the permanent head of the court, or (when bishop's orders were needed) to a suffragan. In theory, the local delegation of his jurisdictional powers was done through his archdeacons. There were two of these in the Worcester diocese, one for Worcestershire (including western Warwickshire), the other for Gloucestershire. But archdeacons were notoriously more prone to accept money (that is procurations) instead of making visitations. At local level therefore, the effective exercise of ecclesiastical jurisdiction was done by rural deans. These were usually beneficed clergy whose benefice was in the area of which they were dean. When the bishop ordered an excommunication or wanted to summon a delinquent to his consistory court he did this through the rural deans, who also held periodic courts, called chapters, at various churches in their deanery.

Unfortunately there are no medieval consistory court records for Worcester diocese, and the records of the bishop's jurisdiction are only indirectly reflected in his register, which records, in more or less detail, his acts and his instructions. There is however a record of the acts of the chapter of the rural dean of Droitwich in 1300, the earliest record of a ruridecanal court in the country.[87] We are bound to presume that its proceedings are typical.

The bishop and his officials were concerned for the greater part of the time with the affairs of the clergy rather than of the laity. Apart from ordinations of persons into the various grades of holy orders, the institution of clerks into benefices and the settling of innumerable disputes connected with ecclesiastical property and rights, they also had jurisdiction in the ordinary sense of the word over the members of the clerical order. To give an example, in

1275, William of the Chapel, an acolyte (the lowest of the holy orders), had been indicted before the king's justices for the murder of John Gogun of Pershore. He claimed his right as a cleric to be judged only in the spiritual courts and was cited before the bishop's commissary. Here he cleared himself of the accusation of murder by the archaic method of compurgation, still used in ecclesiastical courts, though long since abandoned in most lay courts. In this case, four priests, two sub-deans and six acolytes swore to his innocence, and he was released. The alternative would have been imprisonment, for ecclesiastical judges were forbidden by canon law to shed blood.[88]

As far as the laity was concerned, the main sphere in their affairs with which the ecclesiastical courts were concerned was the proof of wills, cases connected with the swearing of oaths, matrimonial cases and the correction and punishment of offences against morals. Offences against the moral code were also supposed to be dealt with by the imposition of penance by confessors, but all we can know about this is the tariff of penances for various offences and the advice given to parish priests in the statutes of diocesan synods and in literary productions such as John Mirk's *Instructions for Parish Priests*.[89] There is no means of knowing what was the effectiveness of the confessional system in controlling behaviour. Breaches of the ten commandments and commission of the seven deadly sins, could, one supposes, have been more numerous than was the case in the period with which we are dealing, but since we know neither the full extent of crime and sin nor what it might have been without the admonitions of the clergy, speculation is vain.

Something can, however, be said about the main target of the church courts as far as the regulation of morals of the laity is con-concerned. Their first concern, of course, was the protection of the church and its liberties. It was in order to do this that excommunications were most abundantly distributed. The liberties of the church could be great or small. In 1275 the rural dean of Droitwich had to discover who had burnt down the Abbot of Bordesley's hedges, summon them, and if they did not appear, excommunicate them. In the same year he was instructed to threaten the same penalty against certain laymen who had taken some animals from the pasture of the rector of Hampton Lovet. One of the *causes célèbres* in the diocese of Worcester concerned the bishop's right to visit Great Malvern Priory, a cell of Westminster Abbey. In pursuit of this right, Bishop Giffard had deposed the prior, William of Ledbury, for (amongst other things) illicit relationships with twenty-one women, and felt obliged to excommunicate a considerable number of laymen who continued to have relationships with the excommunicated William. He even went so far as to put all villages and towns subject to the Abbot of Westminster (who contested his claim to visitation) under an interdict. [90]

A liberty of the church which was most ardently defended was the right of sanctuary for those pursued by lay officials for real or supposed crimes. Several cases occurred during Giffard's prelacy, of which the most striking, especially in its unexpected results, was at Bristol in 1279. [91] There a man who had taken sanctuary in the yard of the church of SS. Philip and James, was dragged out and beheaded by the order of the constable of the castle, Peter de la Mare. Those responsible were excommunicated and condemned to various forms of penance, such as exhuming the body of the beheaded man and reburying him, erecting a stone cross, feeding a hundred poor, proceeding on a crusade, and so on. But the feeling aroused took forms which the bishop deplored. William of Lay, the dead man, began to be venerated as a saint and martyr and songs were written about him, so the bishop next had to fulminate against the persons responsible. In spite of all this, however, breaches of sanctuary continued as before, as did both major and minor encroachments on church property. There was hardly a point at which ecclesiastical and secular interests did not make contact, so incursions by the one into the sphere of influence, interest or jurisdiction of the other were inevitable.

It could be said however that ideas and feelings which affected social behaviour were rather peculiarly the concern of the church, and it is of some interest to see how both laymen and churchmen approached the problems connected with the moral sanctions in social life. If we leave aside the effects of the penitential system which are intangible and concentrate on what we can discover about actual ecclesiastical jurisdiction, we find the action of the church courts curiously limited. So long as her material interests and her recognized jurisdictional and other rights were left intact, the church's main concern, as far as the morals of the laity could be influenced by punishment rather than by exhortation, was with sexual behaviour. It is true that we have a reference in Giffard's Register under the year 1283 to some men in Hillborough who ate meat during a period of fast, against the warning of the parish priest,[92] but otherwise the relations of the sexes seem completely to fill the horizon of the church's social morality.

The record of the corrections ordered by the Droitwich rural deanery chapters in 1300, to which we have referred, may be fragmentary. Ruridecanal chapters are recorded as being held in the churches of Dodderhill (near Droitwich), Salwarpe, St Andrew's, Droitwich and Northfield. A hundred and seven persons from fifteen different parishes in the deanery were cited. One case concerns wife beating, the rest are all fornication and adultery, many of them, so we are told, not for the first time. Sometimes a process of compurgation is recorded, but the entries most frequently simply state the offence and the punishment. The usual punishment was beating, but a few accused persons were declared contumacious, presumably because they refused to accept the jurisdiction of the court. These were excommunicated. Most were brought to heel by this punishment. At Dodderhill, for instance, Henry the cooper of Birmingham was said to have fornicated several times with Ysabella, daughter of Richard the potter. Both of them gave in and were beaten, once for contumacy, and once for fornication, in the usual way (*in forma commune*).

There are not a few references to sexual cases, which must have been dealt with in the higher courts of the diocese, in the bishops' registers. While the persons beaten for fornication at the order of the rural deans were apparently peasants and artisans, the higher courts deal with the departures from the sexual morality of the church committed by the higher classes. These do not seem to lead to beating which (unless the offence was particularly offensive to lay as well as to ecclesiastical society) would not have been accepted by the accused. One man however seems to have been imprisoned (Walter of Lodington in 1275). Another was excommunicated but does not seem to have been deterred thereby. This was Henry Fown or Fohun who abducted Agnes, the wife of a knight, James of Ebryington. He detained her publicly in adultery for five years and would not dismiss her. In fact, 'she died in his unlawful embraces'. Fown was excommunicated and this fact was announced in 1278 by Bishop Giffard in letters to the king's justices and to the Bishop of Coventry and Lichfield.

In 1283, according to the bishop's register a prominent Worcestershire knight, William le Poer, committed adultery with Isabella de Percy. Nothing seems to have happened to him, other than that the alimony was fixed for his wife in 1291 by the bishop. The bishop clearly disapproved as much of departures from the code of sexual morality by the nobility as by the peasants, but was not able to do much about it. When Edmund, Earl of Cornwall, abjured his wife, the Archbishop of Canterbury took a hand in the matter and instructed the bishops of Hereford and Rochester to take him to task. When their admonitions failed he then enlisted the help of the bishops of Winchester, Worcester and St David's. These were delicate matters. Whether in the villages or in the manor-houses and castles, the information about people's personal lives must have come to ecclesiastical ears by means of gossip, not always reliable. The bishop was informed in 1289 that William de Montchesney was living with Amy, widow of the knight John of Hulle, as his concubine, and cited him to appear before him. Amy, however, had recently died in childbirth, and the parish priest of Hill Croome (Worcestershire) came forward to testify that he had married the pair in his church as long ago as 1279.[93]

Felonies and misdemeanours were dealt with in lay courts, and as we have seen, without noticeable deterrent effect. The same might be said about the church's attempt to enforce its code of sexual morality which it appears to have regarded then as later as being the most important aspect of moral behaviour. In view of the high regard which the church had for celibacy, the failings not merely of the laity but of the clergy as well in this respect must have been a great disappointment. This must have been so not only because of the fear of sex which pervaded the official attitude of the church, but because of the complications of matrimonial regulations, wills and therefore decisions about rightful heirs which were the province of the church courts.

The fact that laity and clergy at the end of the thirteenth century were violent, lawless and immoral means that not only common law and canon law had failed to mould social behaviour, but that the moral code embodied in the ten commandments and the precepts which parish priests were supposed to teach their parishioners were more disregarded in practice than obeyed. In view of the frequent licensed absences of incumbents, not to speak of pluralism and the pursuit of pleasure or profit, the code of social behaviour that was in fact inculcated must have been of lay, local, popular origin rather than inspired by the clergy. The pressure to conform to the ancient routines of the village community, based on the rhythm of the seasons, were (in spite of evidence of occasional outbreaks of violence) more effective than teaching from outside. This does not mean, however, that the church meant nothing to the people. What filters through the inadequate records, is not that the church was effective as a guide to behaviour, but that what really counted was its rituals, the part played by its sacraments in making men and women fear Hell less, and have better hopes in Heaven than life on earth gave to most of them. In 1269 the men of Norton by Kempsey complained that the vicar of Kempsey would no longer baptize, marry and purify in Norton chapel.[94] The bishop supported them, and added the right to mass every Sunday and feast day. The wish for the sacraments is behind many a petition for chapels in outlying hamlets and oratories in manor houses, at a time when we can be sure that the distributors of these sacraments either would not care to tell their parishioners how to behave, or if they did, would have little effect. The church's influence on the mentality of the people was at its most effective where it was least rational.

The description of west midland society at the turn of the thirteenth century which we have attempted to present has a number of obvious gaps.

The products of the society's creative imagination have been left on one side. The reason for this, in the case of literary creation (apart from the author's incompetence in this field), is that very little even of the literature in the west midland speech can be localized with any certainty to our region. In the case of the plastic arts and of architecture, much could be said by those competent in the field, and perhaps the evidence about the various social groups in the region which we have presented might be of some interest to specialists in the history of art and architecture.

However, there are conclusions about this society which we have drawn in the course of our analysis which would probably not be fundamentally modified by the study of this other evidence. Most important, of course, is the great influence over all other social strata exercised by a few great lay and ecclesiastical magnates, all of them deriving this influence primarily from their landed possessions. The local social and political influence of the landed classes was, of course, to last for many centuries, but at this period it was openly institutionalized in the various forms of private jurisdiction, and hardly less openly exercised in the effective control of royal, or public, institutions, offices and jurisdictions by these same landowners. As contrasted with some parts of the continent the exercise of private jurisdictions was limited (as far as the justiciable were concerned) to customary or servile tenants: but these, in fact, were probably a majority, at any rate of the rural population. Nor could lords of manors freely hang delinquents within their area of jurisdiction, as some continental *seigneurs* were entitled to do. But, as we have seen, the king's justices themselves did not have all that much success in hanging all those who should have had this penalty imposed on them if the law were rigorously enforced.

A particular feature of the region, or at any rate of the greater part of the counties of Worcester and Gloucester, was the importance of monastic landowners, especially of the old established Benedictine houses founded before the Norman conquest. The total number of monks was quite small; there is no evidence that they influenced in any way the conduct of other men in conformity to the code of behaviour for which the church, and especially this former spiritual leadership of the church, stood. Their social role was primarily as the preservers of the 'classical' type of medieval landlordism, based on the tenacious, consistent and no doubt (within limits) competent management of servile labour and subordinated tenants. The considerable development of relationships expressed in monetary terms did not, in the period with which we have been concerned, fundamentally alter the old social structure although it undoubtedly caused considerable strains as well as bringing new opportunities.

The peasant economy, while retaining its fundamentally subsistence character, was also subjected to strains as a result of cash demands by lords, by government agents and by merchants and artisans. These difficulties coincided with others which were the direct consequence of the pressure of an increasing population on resources. Since the techniques at the disposal even of landlords, let alone peasants, were not noticeably improving productivity, the demands for extra sustenance were met by expanding arable at the expense of pasture. The average holding tended to become smaller and the competition for pasture necessarily increased social tensions. Peasant society was even more differentiated socially than it had been at the time of the Domesday survey in 1086. All the same, and in spite of some blurring of social distinctions between the prosperous freeholders and the lesser gentry, the peasantry remained a distinct class with its own way of life.

The development of urban institutions, of the mercantile and industrial classes, is often thought to have made the old social forms disintegrate. Eventually this happened. But at this period, although commercial and industrial elements in the economy, both in town and country were rapidly developing, the social as well as the political predominance of the lay and ecclesiastical aristocracy was, if not unchallenged, unshaken. When the challenge came, from peasants or from burgesses, the bishops, monks and barons found that the crown, with whom they might quarrel on other matters, in the long run supported them; and that the county gentry hardly thought of themselves as a separate interest, so closely were they bound to the magnates by ties of tenure, loyalty, money and marriage.

We have already admitted that this description of west midland society possibly errs in being too static. We have attempted to catch the essentials at one period of time – even though the evidence used may sometimes have been regrettably dispersed chronologically. Our excuse is that this description is to serve as a starting point for an examination of social and economic movement in the following two centuries. Some economic historians have characterized the later middle ages as an era of stagnation. But it also saw some appalling upheavals, beginning with the great famine of 1315–7 and continuing with a series of epidemics which caused a serious demographic collapse in the second half of the fourteenth century. The social consequences were by no means negligible. The balance of forces between the main social classes was noticeably altered in favour of tenants as against landlords, though this did not go so far as to shake the political control of the aristocracy. In our region changes in the internal composition and modes of behaviour of the landowning classes are, however, easily discernible. Estate management and land use underwent an important process of evolution which affected the pattern of settlement, of industry and of trade. The social upheavals of 1381 had their counterpart here, as did the Lollard heresy, essentially plebeian after 1414. The period was by no means uneventful, and it is to be hoped that this book will have helped to lay a firm basis for understanding what happened next.

LIST OF ABBREVIATIONS

Ann. Mon.   *Annales Monastici,* edited by H.R.Luard, *RS,* 1864–9.

Ann. Wig.   *Annales Wigornienses,* being volume IV of *Annales Monastici.*

Antiquities   *The Antiquities of Warwickshire,* by Sir William Dugdale, 1656; and (edited by W.Thomas), 1730.

ASE   *Anglo-Saxon England,* by F.M.Stenton, 1947.

Beauch. Cart.   Beauchamp Cartulary, *BM* Additional MS. 28024.

BM   British Museum.

BRS   Bristol Record Society.

CS   Camden Society.

CCR   Calendar of Close Rolls preserved in *PRO.*

CChR   Calendar of Charter Rolls in *PRO.*

CPR   Calendar of Patent Rolls in *PRO.*

Ciren. Cart.   The Cartulary of Cirencester Abbey, edited by C.D.Ross, 1964.

Cov. Reg.   Register of Coventry Cathedral Priory, *PRO* E.164, vol. 21.

Dug. Soc.   Dugdale Society.

Ec. HR   Economic History Review.

EHR   English Historical Review.

Ev. Cart. I.   Evesham Abbey Cartulary, *BM* Cotton MS. Vespasian B xxiv.

Ev. Cart. II.   Evesham Abbey Cartulary, *BM* Harleian MS. 3763.

Ev. Chron.   *Chronicon Abbatiae de Evesham,* edited by W.D.Macray, *RS,* 1863.

Geynesborough   The Register of William de Geynesborough, Bishop of Worcester, 1302–7, edited by J.W.Willis Bund and R.A.Wilson, *WHS,* 1907–29.

Giffard   Episcopal Registers, diocese of Worcester, register of Bishop Godfrey Giffard 1268–1301, edited by J.W.Willis Bund, 1898–1902.

Glouc. Cart.   *Historia et Cartularium Monasterii Gloucestriae,* I III, edited by W.H.Hart, *RS,* 1863–7.

Glouc. Rec.   Records of the Corporation of Gloucester, edited by W.H. Stevenson, 1893.

Glouc. Subs. 1327   Gloucestershire Subsidy Roll, 1 Edward III, 1327, *Typis Medio-montanis,* n.d.

GRB   The Great Red Book of Bristol, I–IV, edited by E.W.W.Veale, 1931–53 (*BRS*).

Halesowen A & B   Court Rolls of the Manor of Hales, 1270–1307, edited by John Amphlett and S.G.Hamilton, 1910–12 (*A*) and 1933 (*B*) (*WHS*).

Landboc   *Landboc sive Registrum Monasterii de Winchelcumba,* I and II, edited by D.Royce, 1892 and 1903.

Lanth. Reg.   Registers of Lanthony Priory, *PRO,* C.115 A. 1, 2, 6, 9, 13.

Lib. Alb. (WHS)   The *Liber Albus* of the Priory of Worcester, edited by J.M.Wilson, *WHS,* 1919.

Lib. Alb. (Bishop)   The *Liber Albus,* a cartulary of the bishopric of Worcester, *WCRO.*

Life   *Life in an Old English Town,* by M.D.Harris (1898).

LRB   The Little Red Book of Bristol, I and II, edited by F.B.Bicklet, 1900.

Persh. Cart.   Cartulary of Pershore Abbey, *PRO,* E.135, vol. 61.

PN Worcs, War, Glouc.   *The Place Names of Worcestershire,* edited by A.Mawer, F.M.Stenton and F.T.S.Houghton, 1927 (English Place Name Society).

The Place Names of Warwickshire, edited by J.E.B.Gover, A.Mawer, F.M. Stenton and F.T.S.Houghton, 1936 (*ibid.*).

The Place Names of Gloucestershire, edited by A.H.Smith, 1964–5 (*ibid.*).

P & P   Past and Present.

PQW   *Placita de Quo Warranto*, edited by W.Illingworth, *RC*, 1818.

PRO   Public Record Office.

RBW   The Red Book of Worcester, I–IV, edited by Marjorie Hollings, *WHS*, 1934–50.

Reynolds   The Register of Walter Reynolds, Bishop of Worcester, 1308–13, edited by R.A.Wilson, *Dug. Soc.*, 1928.

RC   Record Commission.

Robt. of Glouc.   The Metrical Chronicle of Robert of Gloucester, edited by W.A.Wright, I and II, *RS*, 1887.

RH   Rotuli Hundredorum temp. Hen. III *et Edw.* I *in turr' Lond' et in curia receptae scaccarii West. asservati*, I and II, edited by W.Illingworth, *RC*, 1812–8.

RH (*War.*)   Unprinted hundred rolls for Kineton and Stoneleigh hundreds, Warwickshire, *PRO* E.164, vol. 15.

RH (*Cov.*)   Unprinted hundred rolls for Coventry in the Leigh Collection, Shakespeare's Birthplace, Stratford-on-Avon.

Rot. Parl.   Rotuli Parliamentorum; ut et petitiones et placita in Parliamento, I–VI (1783), VII (1832), *RC*.

RS   Rolls Series (Chronicles and Memorials of Great Britain and Ireland during the Middle Ages).

Smyth I, II, III   The Berkeley MSS. I and II, Lives of the Berkeleys; III, The Hundred of Berkeley, by John Smyth of Nibley, edited by J.Maclean, 1883–5.

SLB   The Stoneleigh Leger Book, edited by R.H.Hilton, *Dug. Soc.*, 1960.

Tax. 1291   Taxatio Ecclesiastica Angliae et Walliae auctoritate P. Nicholai IV circa AD *1291*, edited by T.Astle, S.Ayscough and J.Caley, *RC*, 1802.

TBAS   Transactions of the Birmingham and Midland Archaeological Society.

TBGAS   Transactions of the Bristol and Gloucester Archeological Society.

Templars' Inquest   Records of the Templars in England in the Twelfth Century, The Inquest of 1185, edited by B.A.Lees, British Academy, 1935.

TRHS   Transactions of the Royal Historical Society.

UBHJ   University of Birmingham Historical Journal.

VCH   Victoria History of the Counties of England.

War. subs. 1327, Transactions of the Midland Record Society, 1899–1902.

War. Subs. 1332   The Lay Subsidy Roll for Warwickshire of 6 Edward III, 1332, edited by W.F.Carter, *Dug. Soc.*, 1926.

Wenlok   Walter de Wenlok, Abbot of Westminster, edited by Barbara Harvey, *CS*, 4th Ser., II, 1965.

Westminster   Westminster Abbey muniments.

WCRO   Worcester County Record Office.

Worc. D & C   Muniments of the Dean and Chapter of Worcester Cathedral.

WHS   Worcester Historical Society.

Worc. Inqs. p.m.   The *inquisitiones post mortem* for the county of Worcester, I and II, edited by J.W.Willis Bund, *WHS*, 1894, 1909.

Worc. Reg. I   Register of Worcester Cathedral Priory, *Worc. D & C*, Reg. I (A.4).

Worc. Reg. II   Registrum sive liber irrotularius et consuetudinarius prioratus prioratus deatae Mariae Wignorniensis, edited by W.H.Hale, *CS*, 1865.

Worc. Subs. 1275   Lay Subsidy Roll for the County of Worcester, *c.* 1280, edited by J.W.Willis Bund and J.Amphlett, *WHS*, 1893.

NOTES

INTRODUCTION

1 For example G. Fourquin, *Les Campagnes de la Région Parisienne à la Fin du Moyen Âge*, 1964.
2 J.E.T. Rogers, *A History of Agriculture and Prices*, I, 1866, pp. 217–8. He divides high prices from low prices at 6s a quarter. The figure of 7s a quarter as an indication of difficult harvest conditions for the rural poor is suggested by M.M. Postan and J.Z. Titow in 'Heriots and Prices on Winchester Manors', *Ec. HR*, 2nd Ser., XI, 1959, p. 404.

CHAPTER 1

1 *PN War.*, p. xvi.
2 *Glouc. Rec.*, p. 4; *PRO*, KB 27/621, m.17. The first reference giving free passage to Gloucester men by the river Severn for wood, coal and other merchandise is a royal charter, 1163–74; the second is a suit in 1416 against the Prior of Wenlok who was accused of obstructing the river with weirs, whereas by rights the Severn's course was free from 'Inberdyspole' in Shrewsbury to the sea for goods such as wine, oil, fruit, pitch, tar and other goods, on trows and boats (*in trowys et batellis*).
3 G. Webster and B. Hobley, 'Aerial Reconnaissance over the Warwickshire Avon', *Archeological Journal*, CXXI, 1964.
4 W.T. Whitley, 'Saltways of the Droitwich District', *TBAS*, vol. 49, 1926.
5 Conrad Gill, *History of Birmingham*, I, 1952, pp. 18–9; *VCH, War.*, VII, p. 76.
6 See below, p. 241, for forest boundaries.
7 G.B. Grundy, 'The Ancient Woodland of Gloucestershire', *TBGAS*, 1936.

8 *Rolls of the Justice in eyre, being the rolls of pleas and assizes for Lincolnshire, 1218–9, and Worcestershire, 1221,* ed. D.M.Stenton, Seldon Society, 1934, p. 448. It concerns land in Yardley (Worcestershire).

9 See the discussion of this question in the introduction of *PN, War.*

10 *Beauch. Cart.,* f. 105ᵛ ff.

11 This is illustrated by charters in the Combe Abbey cartulary *BM,* Cotton MS. Vitellius A.1, for example on ff. 70ᵛ, 84, 89ᵛ, 95, 106, 106ᵛ, 112, 115, 121.

12 See the argument in C.S. and C.S.Orwin, *The Open Fields,* 1954, part I; Joan Thirsk, 'The Common Fields', *P &P,* No. 29.

13 G.C.Homans, 'The Partible Inheritance of Villagers' Holdings', *Ec. HR,* VIII, 1938. I suspect that there were relics of partible inheritance at Erdington (Warwickshire) in the fourteenth century. There are groups of heirs rendering homage together; in one case a man and his sister. *Birmingham Reference Library MSS.* Nos. 347851, 2, 4.

14 Details in *RH (War.),* for which see below p. 90.

15 Smyth, I, p. 113. He is referring to the time of Thomas I, lord of Berkeley, 1220–43.

16 *Worc. Reg. I,* f. 58ᵛ.

17 *Ev. Cart. I,* f. 66. *Daniel tenet i virgam terre de feld acris et masuagium summ super ii cotlandas.* For 'londes' at Kingshill near Stoneleigh, see below, p. 117.

18 *Worc. Reg. I,* f. 37ᵛ.

19 *WCRO,* 1188/12; T.Madox, *Formulare Anglicanum,* 1702, pp. 156–7. The Feckenham map referred to is reproduced in *WHS* Miscellany, I, 1960.

20 *SLB,* p. 102; Stratford-on-Avon Record Office, Leigh Collection, Early Deeds, A.89.

21 *Cov. Reg.,* ff. 213–5ᵛ.

22 *RBW,* pp. 61–86. See C. Dyer, *Lords and Peasants in a Changing Society,* 1980, p. 3, for dating.

CHAPTER 2

1 *Smyth I,* p. 166.

2 *Giffard,* p. 551.

3 R.A.L.Smith, *Canterbury Cathedral Priory,* 1943, p. 44.

4 *Valor Ecclesiasticus temp. Henr. VIII auctoritate regia institutus,* six vols., edited by J.Caley and J.Hunter, Record Commission, 1810–34; for *Tax. 1291,* see list of abbreviations. The best description of the Valor is still that of Alexander Savine, *English Monasteries on the Eve of the Dissolution,* Oxford Studies in Social and Legal

History, I, 1909. There have been a number of studies of the 1291 taxation, including W.H.Lunt, the *Valuation of Norwich*, 1926; R.H.Snape, *English Monastic Finances in the Later Middle Ages*, 1926; R.Graham, *English Ecclesiastical Studies*, 1929. The most useful general reference work for English monastic foundations is that of D.Knowles, *The Monastic Order in England*, 1940. The first volume (1948) of his *The Religious Orders in England* deals with the thirteenth and early fourteenth centuries.

5 *Tax. 1291*, pp. 217, 227, 220b.

6 *Ev. Chron.*; *Ann. Wig.*; first volume of *Glouc. Cart.*; Tewkesbury annals are in volume I of *Annales Monastici*, edited by H.R.Luard (*RS*), 1864.

7 The extent of the Worcester properties is quickly discovered from *Worc. Reg. II* and *RBW*.

8 For Gloucester and Winchcombe properties, see *Glouc. Cart.*, especially volume III; *Landboc*; R.H.Hilton, 'Winchcombe Abbey and the manor of Sherborne' in *Gloucestershire Studies*, edited by H.P.R.Finberg, 1957; and *idem*, 'Gloucester Abbey Leases of the Late Thirteenth Century', *UBHJ*, IV, 1953–4.

9 The extent of Evesham Abbey properties can be deduced from *Ev. Chron.* and *Ev. Cart. I* and *II*; for Pershore Abbey, see R.A.L. Smith, *The Estates of Pershore Abbey*, unpublished London M.A. thesis, 1939, and *Persh. Cart.* (arranged topographically). Apart from information in *Tax. 1291*, in manuscript at Westminster and elsewhere, and in *VCH, Worc.* and *Glouc.* (under appropriate parishes), the most useful insight into Westminster's west midland estates is in *Wenlok*.

10 The alleged immoralities of Prior William of Ledbury occupy much space in *Giffard*. See below, p. 264.

11 *Cov. Reg.* contains rentals and surveys of the Cathedral manors drawn up in 1411; but the demesne extents included in them seem to be copies of documents drawn up in Edward I's reign.

12 Editions of the *Carta Caritatis* and other Cistercian documents are discussed by D.Knowles in *The Monastic Order in England*, p. 208 n.

13 *SLB*, p. 15. *Et primitus quidem in loco vbi nunc est grangia de Crulefeld manserunt translatis hominibus qui ibi habitauerant* [sic] *ad villam que nunc dicitur Hurst*. The story that Over and Nether Smite were depopulated by the Combe Abbey Cistercians is told by M.W.Beresford in 'The Deserted Villages of Warwickshire', *TBAS*, lxvi, 1945–6, p. 95, and in *The Lost Villages of England*, 1954, p. 152, and repeated by W.G.Hoskins in *Medieval England*, ed. A.L.Poole, 1958, p. 20. It derives from *Antiquities*, 1656, p. 143b. Dugdale says

that the depopulation of the Smites 'hath been very antient, it seems, for the *vestigia* of the towns are scarce now to be discerned'. He makes no suggestion that the monks were responsible.

14 For Combe Abbey's cartulary, see note 11 to chapter 1; *The Cartulary of Flaxley Abbey*, 1887, is edited by A. W. Crawley-Boevey.

15 *PRO*, S.C.12, 18/22; but see C. D. Ross in *Ciren. Cart.*, I, xxv, where it is argued that Cirencester's spiritual income was less than that of other Augustinian abbeys.

16 *Lanth. Reg.*, I, section IX.

17 These remarks about St Augustine's, Bristol, have to be based on general evidence, as in *Tax. 1291* and the *Valor Ecclesiasticus*, and on later material, such as 'Two Compotus Rolls of St Augustine's Abbey, Bristol', and 'Some Manorial Accounts of St Augustine's Abbey', edited by G. Beachcroft and A. Sabin, *BRS*, IX and XXII, 1938 and 1960. The Cartulary of St Augustine's in the hands of the Trustees of the Berkeley Estates, is inaccessible.

18 See below, p. 159. The most striking evidence of this abbey is in *Halesowen*. In addition to the court rolls, there are late medieval accounts in the Birmingham City Reference Library.

19 *Templars Inquest*, pp. 47, 50.

20 For Clare and Mortimer, see G. A. Holmes, *The Estates of the Higher Nobility in Fourteenth Century England*, 1957. This admirable book also contains material on other Marcher families and on the Beauchamps. The principal known facts about the lives of the nobility can be found in *The Complete Peerage* by G.E.C., 1910–59.

21 *CPR*, 1307–13, p. 369.

22 Apart from G.E.C. *op. cit.*, see also *Antiquities*, 1956, p. 312 ff. The main source for the history of the Beauchamp family in the thirteenth century is *Beauch. Cart.* Estate documents are later in date and are scattered. For the castle at Elmley, see *VCH Worc.*, III, pp. 339–40 and R. H. Hilton, 'Building accounts of Elmley Castle, Worcs., 1345–6', *UBHJ*, 1966.

23 *Worcs. Inqs. p.m.* I, p. 59 ff.

24 *Antiquities*, 1656, pp. 312, 314, 315. The editor of *Giffard* gives details of William Beauchamp of Elmley's will (p. 8) but not of his son's.

25 For the Berkeleys, see *Smyth I* and *II*. Until historians can gain adequate access to the Berkeley muniments, this great work of the early seventeenth century must remain the chief source of our knowledge of this family and its estates.

26 See for example. *Glouc. Cart.*, I, pp. 27, 147.

27 J. N. Langston, 'The Giffards of Brimpsfield', *TBGAS*, lxv, 1944, an article which unfortunately lacks proper references. See also W. Dugdale, *Baronage*, 1676, pp. 499–501.

28 F. M. Powicke, *King Henry III and the Lord Edward*, 1947, pp. 495–6.

29 The editor of *Giffard* writes about the bishop, and other matters in his introduction. The edition, like other early *WHS* editions, is by no means impeccable. For the properties of Archbishop Walter and Bishop Godfrey, see *Calendar of Inquisitions*, II, 183, and IV, 101.

30 *Glouc. Cart.*, I, p. 32, a laconic entry in the abbey chronicle demonstrating little scholarly enthusiasm.

31 *CChR*, II, p. 252.

32 *PRO*, C.135./5 (2).

33 *PRO*, C.133./76 (4).

34 The estates of Theobald de Verdon who died early in Edward II's reign are summarized in *Calendar of Inquisitions*, V, 187.

35 F. M. Stenton. *The First Century of English Feudalism*, 1932, p. 132 ff.

36 This subject needs to be understood in a European rather than in a merely English context. See G. Duby, 'La noblesse dans la France médiévale', *Revue Historique*, CCXXVI, 1961.

37 These financial problems are dealt with, from differing standpoints, in J. C. Holt, *The Northerners*, 1961, and H. G. Richardson, *The English Jewry under the Angevin Kings*, 1960.

38 *Worc. Reg. I*, pp. 14^v–17, 37, 37^v. A similar case in *Persh. Cart.*, f. 22.

39 *Landboc*, II, pp. 233–53; I, p. 122.

40 *Beauch. Cart.*, ff. 154^v–5.

41 The cost of being a knight has been frequently emphasized by (among others) N. Denholm-Young, *History and Heraldry, 1254–1310*, p. 20; M. Powicke, *Military Obligation in Medieval England*, 1962, p. 68.

42 F. M. Powicke, *The Thirteenth Century*, p. 539 ff. and elsewhere for the knights' activities.

43 N. Denholm-Young, 'Feudal Society in the thirteenth century: the knights' in *Collected Papers*, 1946. See also *PRO*, JI.1, 1028, *passim* and JI.1, 965, m. 15^v.

44 *RC*, edited by F. Palgrave, volume I, pp. 418–9.

45 *War. Subs. 1332*; *Glouc. Subs. 1327*; *Worc. Subs. 1275*.

46 The editor of this lay subsidy dates it 'circa 1280'. There was no subsidy at that date. After hesitating between 1275 and 1283 I have decided for the earlier date. There is an interesting entry on the 'mode of taxing the thirtieth of all moveable goods' in 1283 in *Giffard*, p. 196.

47 *Smyth, I*, p. 147, one of the earliest historians to quote this episode.

48 These are county lists in *Calendar of Inquisitions Miscellaneous*, I, 1916, of landowners whose lands were confiscated because of their support of the king's enemies.

49 F.M.Powicke, *King Henry III and the Lord Edward*, p. 493.
50 *Lib. Alb. (Bishop)*, f. lxxv; *Warwickshire Feet of Fines*, I, edited by F.C.Wellstood and F.T.S.Houghton, *Dug. Soc.*, 1932.
51 *Giffard*, ciii.
52 *ibid.*, p. 396 ff.
53 *ibid.*, Appendix IV, where ordinations are summarized.
54 W.A.Pantin, 'Medieval priests' houses in south-west England', *Medieval Archaeology*, I, 1957.
55 *Glouc. Subs. 1327*, pp. 29, 50.
56 G.G.Coulton, *The Medieval Village*, 1925, p. 293.
57 J.West, *The Administration and Economy of the Forest of Feckenham in the Early Middle Ages* (Birmingham unpublished M.A. thesis, 1964), p. 164 and Appendix VIII.

CHAPTER 3

1 R.H.Hilton, 'The Content and Sources of English Agrarian History before 1500', *Agricultural History Review*, III, 1955.
2 M. Chibnall (ed.), *Charters and Custumals of the Abbey of Holy Trinity, Caen*, 1982; *WCRO*, 705; 11 BA 1488; *RBW*; *Ev. Cart. I; Templars Inquest*.
3 *Worc. Reg. II*; *RBW*; *Glouc. Cart.*, III.
4 'A Transcript of the Red Book' (of Hereford), edited by A.T. Bannister, Camden Miscellany, XV, 1929; *PRO*, S.C.12, Portf. 18/22; *ibid.*, SC.12, 36/11.
5 H.Hall, *The Pipe Roll of the Bishop of Winchester, 1208–9*, 1924; N.R.Holt, *The Pipe Roll of the Bishopric of Winchester, 1210–11*, 1964.
6 The accounting system is discussed by N.Denholm-Young, *Seignorial Administration in England*, 1937; R.H.Hilton, 'Ministers' Accounts of the Warwickshire Estates of the Duke of Clarence', *Dug. Soc.*, 1952.
7 *Wenlok*, p. 55.
8 *Westminster*, 25900.
9 References to accounts will be given individually as cited.
10 *Ev. Chron.*, pp. 205–21. Although the *cellerarius generalis* is not in this list, which details the rents due to each obedience, his duties with regard to the feeding of the monks are laid down.
11 R.A.L.Smith, 'The *Regimen Scaccarii* in English Monasteries', *TRHS*, 4th Ser., xxiv, 1942; *Early Compotus Rolls of the Priory of Worcester*, edited by J.M.Wilson and C.Gordon, *WHS*, 1908; *Ciren. Cart.*, I, xx, No. 327/186; *Glouc. Cart.*, III, p. 105.
12 *WHS, op. cit.*; *PRO*, S.C.6., 1123/5.

13 The reference to court rolls will be given as cited individually. The later court rolls which will not be cited include Bromsgrove *Court Rolls of the Manor of Bromsgrove and Kings Norton*, 1494–1504, edited by A.F.C.Baber, *WHS*, 1963; Feckenham, *WCRO*; BA.118–705:59; Bisley, *PRO*, S.C.2., 175/7; Pershore, *Westminster*, 21943.

14 *Cambridge Economic History of Europe*, II, 1952, p. 166.

15 N.Denholm-Young, *op. cit.*, pp. 22–3.

16 *Smyth I*, p. 306; *RBW*, p. 547.

17 These accounts are printed by *WHS*, see note 13 above.

18 R.H.Hilton, *The Economic Development of Some Leicestershire Estates*, 1947, p. 25 ff; M.Morgan, *English Lands of the Abbey of Bec*, 1946, p. 45 ff.

19 *Westminster*, 8424; 8423, 27693, 27699; 25906, 25921. *PRO*, S.C.6, 856/15, 17, 18, 19. The last account (856/9) is incorrectly listed in a PRO list as 14–15 Edward I.

20 *Ann. Wig.*, pp. 391, 394, 369, 423, etc; *Worc. Reg. II.*

21 *PRO*, S.C.6, 851/4, 5, 6.

22 *Westminster*, 25901, 27693, 8424.

23 F.B.Pegolotti, *La Pratica della Mercatura*, 1936, ed. Allan Evans pp. 258–69; A.Sapori, 'La Compagnia dei Frescobaldi in Inghilterra', in *Studi di Storia Economica Medioevale*, 1946, pp. 581–2 (long footnote).

24 *Westminster*, 25900, 1; 8232; 27693, 9; 8424; 22092. *VCH Glouc.*, VI, p. 245, 1890.

24a *Glouc. Cart.*, I, p. 39.

25 *Walter of Henley's Husbandry*, 1890, edited by Elizabeth Lamond; *Glouc. Cart.*, III, pp. 105–8, 213–21; R.H.Hilton, 'Rent and Capital Formation in Feudal Society', *Second International Conference of Economic History, 1962*, 1965.

26 *Reynolds*, p. 34.

CHAPTER 4

1 *R.H. (War.)*.

2 T.Sharp, *The Anatomy of the Village*, 1946, p. 3.

3 F.W.Maitland, *Domesday Book and Beyond*, 1897, p. 437; J.C. Russell, *British Medieval Population*, 1948; J. Krause, 'The Medieval Household: Large or Small?' *Ec. HR*, 2nd ser., IX, 1957; H.E.Hallam, 'Some Thirteenth Century Censuses', *ibid.*, X, 1958, 'Population Density in the Medieval Fenland', *ibid.*, XIV, 1961.

4 *PN, Glouc.*, II, p. 45.

5 W.G.Hoskins, 'The Rebuilding of Rural England' *P & P*, 4, 1953.

6 The reports on excavations at Wharram Percy, Yorkshire, in *Medieval Archaeology*, 1957–, under the sections entitled 'Medieval Britain', make this point clear.

7 Gloucester County Record Office, Sherborne muniments.

8 *BM*, Cotton MS. Nero C.VII.

9 *BM*, Additional Charters 49157.

10 In areas influenced by Scandinavian languages, the house plot was called the toft.

11 For crofts *pede cultis*, see *Geynesborough*, p. 2, referring to land in Wickhamford (Gloucestershire). William Dugdale, in *Antiquities*, 1730, p. 300, quote a similar phrase from Northburgh's register, vol. II, f. 109a, referring to Cubbington (Warwickshire).

12 Many books have been written about timber-framed construction but see especially F. W. B. Charles, *Mediaeval Cruck Building and its Derivatives*, 1966, based mainly on Worcestershire evidence.

13 These conclusions are mainly based on excavations at Upton, near Blockley, see 'Upton, Gloucestershire, 1959–1964', by R. H. Hilton and P. A. Rahtz, *TBGAS*, 1966.

14 R. K. Field, 'Worcestershire Peasant Buildings, Household Goods and Farming Equipment in the Later Middle Ages; *Medieval Archaeology*, IX.

15 *Westminster*, 22092; T. H. Lloyd, *Some Aspects of the Building Industry in Medieval Stratford-upon-Avon*. Dug. Soc. Occasional Paper No. 14.

16 *PRO*, JI.1/966, m. 5d; *Halesowen*, p. 167.

17 See elevation and plan of Noakes Court by F. W. B. and Mary Charles.

18 *WCRO*, 92007. This evidence is in the earliest surviving manorial account of Blockley, 1383–4, and is therefore a little late for this argument. The sheepcote that was being built in this year was roofed with Snowshill slates.

19 *PRO*, S.C.2, 210/25, m. 12.

20 R. K. Field, *op. cit.*, appendix B, table IV.

21 *BM*, Harleian MS. 3763, ff. 186–7.

22 *ibid.*, f. 187.

23 E. Powell, *A Suffolk Hundred in the Year 1283*, 1910; A. T. Gaydon, 'The Taxation of 1297', *Bedfordshire Historical Record Society*, XXXIX, 1959.
M. M. Postan, 'Village Livestock in the Thirteenth Century', *Ec. HR*, 2nd Ser., XV, 1962; *TBGAS*, XIX, 1894–5, pp. 196–8.

24 *Halesowen*, pp. 31–2.

25 *PRO*, SC.12, Portf. 18/22.

26 *Landboc*, II, p. 308.

27 *PRO*, SC.2, 175/80, m. 3.

28 *Worc. D. & C.*, Court Rolls. I owe this reference to Mr E. K. Vose.

29 G. C. Homans, *English Villagers of the Thirteenth Century*, 1942, p. 424 (citing inquiries into the lands of Robert Walerand in *PRO*, E.142).

30 Postan, *art. cit.* in note 23 above.

31 Figures for Minety calculated from a tallage return, printed by E. A. Fuller in *TBGAS*, *art. cit.* in note 23.

32 *PRO*, SC.2, 175/79.

33 *Smyth III*, p. 324.

34 *PRO*, E.372, No. 179, m. 35d. I owe this reference to Mrs D. Styles.

35 *Worc. D & C*, E.6.

36 Postan, *art. cit.*, p. 237.

37 *PRO*, SC.2, 175/82, m. 2; *Worc. D & C*, E.13.

38 *PRO*, SC.2, 175/41, m. 4.

39 *ibid.*, E. 146, 3/2 m. 2.

40 *ibid.*, S.C.2, 175/85, m. 2.

41 R. H. Hilton, 'Notes and Comments', *P & P*, No. 23, 1962.

42 *Worc. Reg. I*, p. 7.

43 *Landboc*, I, pp. 329, 279, 222; *Lib. Alb.* (*WHS*), xlix, Nos. 355 and 742.

44 M. M. Postan and J. Z. Titow, 'Heriots and Prices on Winchester Manors', *Ec. HR*, 2nd Ser., XI, 1959.

45 M. Hollings, 'The Survival of the Five Hide Unit in the West Midlands', *EHR*, 1948; *Ev. Cart. II*, f. 168ᵛ; *Beauch. Cart.*, f. 93.

46 *Worc. Reg. II*, p. 256; *Smyth II*, p. 13 and III, p. 2.

47 *Ciren. Cart.*, No. 383.

48 Stratford Record Office, Gregory Deeds, No. 101.

49 *PRO*, SC.12, 36/11.

50 A. Clark, *The English Register of Godstow Nunnery*, I, Early English Text Society, 1905, No. 182.

51 *Gloucester Cathedral*, Dean and Chapter MSS., Deeds and Seals, VI, 6.

52 *Glouc. Cart.*, II, p. 285; C. E. Hart, *Commoners of the Forest of Dean*, 1951, pp. 3–10; T. Madox, *Formulare Anglicanum*, 1702, pp. 55, 245, 254.

53 *SLB*, p. 113.

54 *Glouc. Cart.*, III, p. 215.

55 Elizabeth Lamond (ed.), *Walter of Henley's Husbandry*, 1890, p. 13; R. Trow-Smith, *A History of British Livestock Husbandry to 1700*, 1957, p. 116.

56 *Westminster*, 27699.

57 *RBW*, I, p. 61 ff., especially p. 66; *Lib. Alb.* (*Bishop*), f. xliiᵛ.

CHAPTER 5

1 The problems of the relation of the manor to the village and of manorial structure at the end of the thirteenth century are exhaustively discussed by E.A. Kosminsky, *Studies in the Agrarian History of England in the Thirteenth Century*, 1956.

2 *Inquisitions and Assessments relating to feudal aids* . . . in the *Public Record Office*, 1899–1920, V, p. 174 ff., II, p. 263 ff.

3 *RH (War.)*, ff. 52–3^v, 28^v.

4 For what follows, see R.H. Hilton, 'Freedom and Villeinage in England', *P & P*, No. 31, 1965.

5 The use of the word *peisaunt*, peasant, is uncommon, but see an early fourteenth-century example in *Glouc. Cart.*, I, pp. 147–9 (in French).

6 *RBW*, pp. 146, 167, 186, 257, 431, 440, 441; F.W. Maitland, *Domesday Book and Beyond*, 1897, p. 305 f.; F. Liebermann, *Die Gesetze der Angelsachsen*, 1903–16, I, p. 73, II, p. 59; *Worc. Reg. II*, pp. 44a, 44b; *Glouc. Cart.*, I, p. 223.

7 *Glouc. Cart.* III, pp. 185, 187.

8 R.H. Hilton, *The Social Structure of Rural Warwickshire in the Middle Ages*, Dug. Soc. Occasional Paper No. 9; *RBW*, pp. 61–79.

9 *Glouc. Cart.*, I, p. 31; *Ann. Mon.*, I, p. 146.

10 *Glouc. Cart.*, III, pp. 61–4.

11 *Beauch. Cart.*, f. 138.

12 *Worc. Reg. II*, p. 15a.

13 E.K. Vose, *The Estates of Worcester Cathedral*, chapter I (an unpublished work based on *Worc. D & C*).

14 *Westminster*, 22092, 9; 27693; 2799; 8232; 25906; 8232; 8423; 8424.

15 R.H. Hilton, 'Gloucester Abbey leases of the Late Thirteenth Century'. See note 8 to Chapter 2.

16 See the surveys already cited for Evesham, the Templars and Worcester; for Winchcombe see R.H. Hilton in *Gloucestershire Studies*, p. 105. See note 8 to Chapter 2.

17 *Worc. Inqs. p.m.*, I, p. 59 ff.; *RH (War,)* f. 73; *Gloucestershire Inquisitions Post Mortem*, edited by W.P. Phillimore, G.S. Fry and E.A. Fry, Index Library, 1893, contain Gilbert of Clare's i.p.m.s.

18 See R.H. Hilton, 'Elmley Castle Building Accounts', *UBHJ*, X 1966.

19 The charters connected with the Gloucester Abbey almoner's endowments in Frocester Register (B) in the muniments of Gloucester Cathedral show this.

20 *Worc. Inqs. p.m.*, I, pp. 5–7.

21 *PQW*, p. 778; *PRO*, S.C.6, 859/33; see also note 19 to Chapter 1.

22 *SLB*, introduction.
23 *P & P*, No. 31, p. 12.
24 *Worc. Reg. II*, p. 15a; Minchinhampton court rolls containing the data quoted are *PRO*, S.C.2, 175/79–86.
25 Minchampton accounts are *PRO*, S.C.6, 856/15–22.
26 *Westminster*, 25921, 8232, 8424, 27699, 22099.
27 *PRO*, S.C.6, 850/1–6. Dr Cyril Hart has demonstrated, in a paper to be published, that this was not Allaston in Lydney. The figures from the Berkeley manors are from account rolls photographed by permission of the Trustees of the Berkeley Estates and deposited in the Cambridge University Library.

CHAPTER 6

1 *Halesowen*, p. 147.
2 *ibid.*, pp. 162, 126; *PRO*, S.C.2, 175/83, 85.
3 *WCRO*, 899: 95; *Halesowen*, pp. (A). 419, 423, 431, 432, 466, (B) 129; *Lib. Alb. (Bishop)*, f. xlii^v.
4 Above, p. 79.
5 *Worc. Reg. II*, pp. 88a, 10a, 41b, 47b.
6 *Beauch. Cart.*, f. 10^v.
7 *PRO*, S.C.2, 175/41, m. 2.
8 *ibid.*, S.C.2, 175/41–44; *Worc. D & C*, E.193 and E.13; *CCR*, 1323–7, p. 265; see *SLB* pp. 83–4. This book contains many previous cases of conflict.
9 *Ciren. Cart.*, No. 358.
10 *ibid.*, Nos. 20, 75.
11 *ibid.*, Nos. 267, 216.
12 *Halesowen A.* pp. 119–20.
13 *RH*, II, p. 98 for the Shropshire jurors. See also G.C. Homans, *English Villagers of the Thirteenth Century*, pp. 276–84 and R.H. Hilton, 'Peasant Movements before 1381' in *Essays in Economic History*, *II*, 1962, edited by E. Carus-Wilson.
14 *Halesowen A.*, pp. 19, 147, 165; *Worc. D & C*, E, 193, 196; E.6 & E.7; *PRO*, S.C.2, 175/80, m. 4.
15 *Worc. D & C*, E.195; *Glouc. Cart.*, III, p. 217; *SLB*, p. 105.
16 *Worc. D & C*, E.193; *PRO*, JI.1, 1028, m. 16.
17 *SLB*, p. 30 ff.
18 *PRO*, S.C.2, 175/79, m. 5.

CHAPTER 7

1 There have been many calculations of medieval town populations. J.C. Russell's comprehensive work, *British Medieval Population*, 1948, has been modified by such writers as G. Williams, *Medieval London, from Commune to Capital*, 1963, and E. Miller in *VCH*

Yorks, The City of York, 1961, p. 40. The subject is by no means closed.

2 H.P.R.Finberg's 'The Genesis of the Gloucestershire Towns' in *Gloucestershire Studies*, 1957, should be mentioned as an interesting attempt to deal with a group of towns as a whole. Detail without synthesis can be found in the volumes of *VCH*.

3 The assessments of 1334 have not been printed for our three counties and must be found among the lay subsidies in *PRO*. The 1327 subsidy returns are all available in print (see below pp. 199–200), as is *War. Subs. 1332*. The 1334 assessment is referred to here and elsewhere because it was intended to correct earlier ones, and remained unchanged throughout the middle ages, except for some fifteenth century reductions for towns and villages pleading poverty.

4 £25 as against £54 1s 6d *PRO*, E.179 113/29.

5 Finberg, *op. cit.*, pp. 43–5.

6 Relatively high population density in the Avon valley is already apparent in 1086. See *The Domesday Geography of Midland England*, 1954, edited by H. C. Darby and I. B. Terrett, p. 240.

7 *The Overseas Trade of Bristol in the Later Middle Ages*, edited by E.Carus-Wilson, *BRS*, 1937.

8 *CPR*, 1272–81, p. 68. Evidence of this property is in the Warwick entry in *RH (War.)* f 1ᵛ. For Warwick in general see H. A. Cronne, *The Borough of Warwick in the Middle Ages*, Dug. Soc. Occasional Paper No. 10, 1951.

9 *War. Subs. 1332*, pp. 3–5; *PRO*, E.179/192/7.

10 The main indication of iron-working in Birmingham and district is in the occupational designations contained in charters in the Birmingham Reference Library's large collection of original deeds.

11 *VHC,Worcs.*, III; 'The Borough of Droitwich and its Salt Industry', by E.K.Berry, *UBHJ*, VI, 1957; A.R.Bridbury, *England and the Salt Trade in the Later Middle Ages*, 1955; W.T.Whitley, 'Saltways of the Droitwich District', *TBAS*, XLIX, 1924.

12 Market charters are normally found in the Calendar of Charter Rolls. There is a Gloucestershire list printed in *Gloucestershire Studies*, pp. 86–8 and in R.C.Gaut, *A History of Worcestershire Agriculture and Rural Evolution*, 1939, pp. 39–41. There is no similar Warwickshire list.

13 See note 18 to Chapter 5.

14 Carrying services are described for sixteen manors in *Worc. Reg. II* and for nine manors in *RBW*, 1291.

15 F.M.Powicke, *The Thirteenth Century*, 1953, pp. 621–2; *RH*, I, pp. 180, 176. For Tintern Wool production, see *Tax. 1291*, p. 284b; *CPR*, 1272–81, pp. 13–36.

16 *RH*, I, p. 177 and pp. 166–81, *passim*. For Southampton wool exports in the 1270s, see A.A.Ruddock, *Italian Merchants and Shipping in Southampton 1270–1600*, chapter I.

17 *Wenlok*, I, Nos. 306, 46; G.Williams, *Medieval London*, p. 112; *Lib. Alb.* (*WHS*), No 656.

18 *PRO*, JI.1, 286, m. 4.; Williams, *op. cit.*, pp. 112, 116, 151; *Ciren. Cart.*, Nos. 134, 350; *Lanth. Reg.* (A.9), f. clxiiii^v; *Lib. Alb.* (*WHS*), No 551.

19 *RH*, I, p. 181; *PRO*, JI.1, 1028, m. 6^v.; *ibid.*, JI.1, 286, m. 1^v. For Ferrers see G.E.C. *Complete Peerage*.

20 *PRO*, JI.1, 1027, m. 6^v.; *PN Glouc.*, III, p. 128; JI.1, 966, m. 6.

21 *Wenlok*, I, Nos. 1, 336, 300.

22 JI.1, 1028, m. 7; *RH* (*Cov.*), ff. 1, 12, 14, 16; *Calendar of Inquisitions*, III, No. 247.

23 *SLB*, p. 127. Cf. W.H. Stevenson's remarks in *Glouc. Records*, pp. x, xiii–xix.

24 The returns are: *Worc. Subs. 1275; RH* (*Cov.*), *Glouc. Subs. 1327; War. Subs. 1332*; and the Bristol tallage printed by E.A.Fuller in 'The Tallage of 6 Edward II and the Bristol Rebellion', *TBGAS*, XIX, 1894–5.

25 *RH* (*Cov.*), ff. 10^v–11.

26 C.D.Ross discusses Bristol topography in the introduction to *The Cartulary of St Marks Hospital, Bristol* (*BRS*, 1959); L.E.W.O. Fullbrook-Legate, *Anglo-Saxon and Medieval Gloucester*, 1952; *Cov. Reg.* contains much material about Coventry's suburban hamlets, much however from the fourteenth century; likewise *Lanth. Reg.* for Gloucester's southern suburbs.

27 Bristol's development is concisely summarized by H.A.Cronne in his introduction to *Bristol Charters 1378–1499* (*BRS*, 1946). See also the introduction to *Historic Towns; Bristol*, by M. D. Lobel and E. M. Carus-Wilson, 1975. The complex dispute about the two lordships of medieval Coventry is summarized in *Medieval Coventry – A City Divided?*, ed. Trevor John (Coventry Branch of the Historical Association).

28 *Gloucestershire Inquisitions Post Mortem IV* (Index Library), p. 89; V, pp. 78, 81.

29 *RBW*, p. 260 ff.

30 Copy of charter, *WCRO*, BA 2636.009.1. No. 43696, f. 93.

31 *RBW*, p. 471 ff. E. M. Carus-Wilson, *EcHR*, 1965.

32 *VCH Glouc.*, VI, p. 240; *Glouc. Subs. 1327*, p. 40.

33 *RH* (*War.*), f. 11^v; *Antiquities* (1956), p. 30.

34 *Persh. Cart.*, f. 12^v; *PRO*, S.C.2, 210/25.

35 H.A.Cronne, *op. cit.*, pp. 27, 62–3; J.W.Sherborne, *The Port of*

Bristol in the Middle Ages, 1965; M.K.James, 'The Fluctuations of the Anglo-Gascon Wine Trade during the Fourteenth Century,' *Essays in Economic History*, II, edited by E.Carus-Wilson, 1962, p. 130; E.A.Fuller, *loc. cit.* For woad, see the references in *Bristol Charters 1155–1373*, edited by N.Dermott Harding (*BRS*, 1930). Export figures in general are in *England's Export Trade 1275–1547*, 1963, by E.Carus-Wilson and O.Coleman.

36 Milling and toll figures are in the constables' accounts *PRO*, S.C.6, 851/1–6; *LRB*, II, p. 64 refers to restriction in grain purchases (no date).

37 *Bristol Charters 1135–73* (1216 and 1317 paras.).

38 An estimate tentatively based on *RH* (*Cov.*).

39 R.A.Pelham, 'The Early Wool Trade in Warwickshire and the Rise of the Merchant Middle Class', *TBAS*, LXIII, 1944.

40 C.E.Hart, *The Miners*, 1953, p. 159; *Domesday Book*, I, p. 162; *VCH Glouc.*, II, p. 202; J.T.Rogers *Six Centuries of Work and Wages*, 1903, p. 105; *Glouc. Rec.*, *passim*; Fullbrook-Legatt, *op. cit.*

41 F.M.Stenton 'The City of Worcester' in *VCH Worcs.*, IV; *Original Charters relating to the City of Worcester*, edited by J.H. Bloom (*WHS*, 1909); J.R.Burton, *A History of Kidderminster*, 1890; Stratford-on-Avon MSS. XII, 199 at Shakespeare's Birthplace.

42 *Beauch. Cart.*, f. 8^v; *RH* (*War.*), ff. 1–5^v, For Edward I's anti-semitic campaign, see H.G.Richardson, *The English Jewry under the Angevin Kings*, 1960.

43 *PRO*, JI.1, 1036.

44 The list of mayors in Ricart's *The Maire of Bristowe is Kalendar*, edited by L.Toulmin-Smith (C.S., 1872), is corrected by C.D. Ross, *op. cit.* Appendix II; *Rot. Parl.*, I, p. 327.

45 Pelham, *op. cit.*; *Parliamentary Writs*, I, p. 100; *RH* (*Cov.*), f. 12^v.

46 *Cov. Reg.*, f. lxxxvii et seq.; *RH* (*Cov.*), ff. 2^v, 5, 6, 7.

47 *Glouc. Rec.*, *Gloucester Abbey Deeds; St. Peter's Abbey Cartulary B* (all in Gloucester Cathedral Library), *passim* for the bailiffs; tallage of 1304 is *PRO*, E. 179, 113/3.

48 See note 41 above for Worcester city deeds.

49 Stratford-on-Avon deeds, XII, Nos. 1, 202; *Landboc*, I, p. 232; *CChR*, III, p. 378; *Worc. Inqs. p.m.*, II, p. 73.

50 *LRB*, II. *passim*.

51 *Worc. Reg. II*, p. 93a.

52 *Templars' Inquest*, pp. cxxiv, 50; *Landboc*, I, p. 185, 195, II, 155, 273; *Ev. Chron.*, p. 212; *Persh. Cart.*, f. 23; *Tax. 1291*, pp. 171, 172, 236; *Glouc. Cart.*, III, p. 60; *Worc. Reg. II*, p. 74a; *Gloucestershire Inqs. IV*, pp. 86, 138, 179, 189, 199, 231; I.Jeayes, *Catalogue of the MSS. in Berkeley Castle*, 1892, p. 102. *PRO*, S.C.11, 245; above p.

67 (Cam); *Worc. Inqs. p.m.*, I, p. 43, and II, p. 7; *Worc. Reg. II*, pp. 32a, 41a, 92b, 99b; *Ann. Wig.*, p. 442; *RBW*, p. 191; J. R. Burton, *op. cit.*, p. 21. J. Tann discovered hitherto unknown evidence of a number of Gloucestershire mills, *Aspects of the Development of the Gloucestershire Woollen Industry* (University of Leicester Ph.D. thesis, 1964). For the whole subject, see the pioneer article by E. Carus-Wilson, 'An Industrial Revolution of the Thirteenth Century', *Essays in Economic History*, I, pp. 41–60.

53 *PRO*, S.C.2, 175/42; S.C.6, 854/10.

54 *Ibid.*, S.C.2, 175/41. There seems to be some disagreement about the dating of these rolls. Professor Carus-Wilson thinks they are from the reign of Edward II (*op. cit.*, p. 50), I from that of Edward I; *ibid.*, S.C.11, 230.

55 C. E. Hart, *op. cit.*, pp. 1–24.

56 M. L. Bazeley, 'The Forest of Dean in its relations with the Crown during the twelfth and thirteenth centuries', *TBGAS*, XXXIII, 1960, p. 236.

57 *History of the British Iron and Steel Industry*, by H. R. Schubert, 1957, pp. 100, 109, 139 n3.

58 Bazeley, *op. cit.*, p. 266; Schubert, *op. cit.*, p. 112.

59 *VCH Glouc.*, II; *Worc. Inqs. p.m.*, I, p. 35.

CHAPTER 8

1 *VCH Worcs.*, IV, p. 380.

2 *Glouc. Rec.*, pp. 4–5.

3 H. A. Cronne, *BRS*, 1946, pp. 44–6.

4 *The Borough of Warwick in the Middle Ages*, by H. A. Cronne, Dug. Soc. Occasional Paper No. 10, p. 19; 'Ministers' Accounts of the Warwickshire Estates of the Duke of Clarence', ed. R. H. Hilton (*Dug. Soc.*, 1952), pp. 1–26.

5 *VCH Worcs.*, IV, p. 384.

6 *Landboc*, I, p. xix ff.

7 *GRB*, III, introduction, and *Cartulary of St Mark's Hospital, Bristol*, ed. C. D. Ross, *BRS*, 1959, p. xli.

8 *VCH Worcs.*, III, p. 74.

9 *The Maire of Bristowe is Kalendar*, ed. L. Toulmin-Smith, *CS*, 1872, pp. v–vii; *LRB*, I, pp. xxvi, 202; The *Borough Town of Stratford-on-Avon*, 1953, by L. Fox, pp. 87–95; *The Register of the Holy Trinity Guild, Coventry*, ed. M. Dormer Harris (*Dug. Soc.*, 1935), pp. xvii–xix.

10 *GRB*, I, p. 97 ff.

11 *Rot. Parl.*, I, p. 168 a, b.

12 *GRB*, I, p. 111.

13 *Life*, pp. 66–7.

14 *VCH Worcs.*, IV, p. 384.

15 *Glouc. Cart.*, I, pp. 38, 320; III, p. 252.

16 *Warwickshire Feet of Fines*, I, No. 689 (*Dug. Soc.*, 1932).

17 *Life*, p. 70.

18 *Robt. of Glouc.*, 11, 11,061 ff.

19 *PRO*, S.C.6. 851/5.

20 *Ibid.*, S.C.6, 851/1–6.

21 E. A. Fuller, *TBGAS*, 1894–5.

22 See N. Denholm-Young's comments in *Seignorial Administration in England*, 1937, p. 95.

23 *ASE*, p. 487 ff. Sidney Painter, *Studies in the History of the English Feudal Barony*, 1943, Chap. IV.

24 *PQW*, pp. 241–65, 777–85.

25 *SLB*, pp. 98–100.

26 *Statutes of the Realm*, I; of *Ciren. Cart.*, No. 651.

27 The view of the Crown Lawyers at the time was expressed by W. Inge with respect to a Gloucestershire plea by William Beauchamp: '. . . *ille qui habet visum franciplegii talem habet libertatem quod omnes illi qui etate duodecim annorum compleverunt semel vel bis per annum comparere debent in curia sua pro conservacione pacis et in eadem curia fere omnia capitula que liberari solent in itinere justiciorum liberari debant et ad illa responderi unde disicut predicta libertas est quedam justiciaria que mere spectat ad dignitatem regis . . .*'

28 For example in the court of the Thursday after St Edmund the Archbishop (16 November), 24 Edward I, *WCRO*, 1188/12.

29 For Oswaldslow Hundred, see F. W. Maitland, *op. cit.*, pp. 267–9, H. M. Cam, *The Hundred and the Hundred Rolls*, 1930, p. 147, and *passim* for other hundreds; Sir Frank Stenton, *op. cit.*, p. 409; Eric John, *Land Tenure in Early England*, 1960, Chapters V, VI, VII.

30 For Blackenhurst Hundred, see *VCH Worcs.*, II, p. 348.

31 *RH*, II, p. 282. They may, of course, have meant to refer to his son William, but if so, it is odd that they should not give him his title, Earl of Warwick.

32 *RH*, I, pp. 171, 173.

33 *Ciren. Cart.*, I, No. 32.

34 For 'harness' see *PN*, *Glouc.*, II, p. 207. For the Hundred of Berkeley see *Smyth III*.

35 Complaints were, however, made before the itinerant justices. Walter Beauchamp of Powick and William de Valence were accused in 1275 of taking men away from the sheriff's biennial tourn of the hundred and making them do suit to private views of frankpledge. *PRO*, JI.1/1028, m. 2ᵛ, 11.

36 *PQW*, *loc. cit.* Where not otherwise stated, information about private hundreds and news of frankpledge in the following pages comes from this source.
37 For the whole question, see D. Sutherland, *Quo Warranto Proceedings in the Reign of Edward I*, 1963.
38 *RBW*, *passim*; see index *sv*.
39 *RH*, II, p. 283.
40 *Ciren. Cart.*, II, No. 739.
41 *ibid.*, I, No. 353.
42 *ibid.*, I, No. 231, II, No. 650.
43 *ibid.*, I, pp. 215–23.
44 These details are taken from the calendar of the views of frankpledge mentioned above.
45 For similar local pressures in the Abbot of Fécamp's Hundred of Slaughter, see *VCH*, *Glouc.*, VI, p. 7.
46 For an authoritative summing up of medieval forest law see G. J. Turner, *Select Pleas of the Forest* (Selden Society, 1901). A special study of common rights in the forest will be found in C. E. Hart, *The Commoners of Dean*, 1951.
47 The Forest of Dean's fluctuating bounds are discussed by M. L. Bazeley, *art. cit.* *TBGAS*, 1910, and by C. L. Hart, *The Extent and Boundaries of the Forest of Dean and Hundred of St Briavels*, 1947.
48 The conclusions of J. Humphreys in 'The Forest of Feckenham', *TBAS*, XLV, repeated by the present writer in *Miscellany I*, *WHS*, 1960, must be modified in the light of investigations by J. West, *The Administration and Economy of the Forest of Feckenham during the Early Middle Ages* (Birmingham University M.A. thesis, unpublished, 1964).
49 Bazeley, *art. cit.*, p. 189 f. and West, *op. cit.*, p. 110.
50 Bazeley, *art. cit.*, p. 200, I, p. 39. For the equation of 'swanimote' with attachment court, see *WHS*, *Miscellany I*, p. 39.
51 West, *op. cit.*, p. 131.
52 Dean and Feckenham perambulations of the thirteenth century which give these details have been exhaustively treated by C.E Hart, *Royal Forest*, 1966, and J. West, *op. cit.*
53 *CChR*, I, pp. 116, 236, 270. *Lib. Alb.* (*Bishop*), ff. xli^v, xlii^v, xliiii^v.
54 Bazeley, *op. cit.*, p. 252.
55 *RH*, I, p. 166 ff.
56 *PRO*, JI.1/1031, m. 3.
57 *ibid.*, JI.1/966.
58 Edited by T. Wright, *Political Songs* (*CS*, 1939), and by I.S.T. Aspin, *Anglo-Norman Political Songs*, 1953.

59 *PRO*, JI.1/966, m. 5ᵛ.

60 *ibid.*, m. 5.

61 *ibid.*, m. 8ᵛ.

62 *ibid.*, m. 9.

63 *ibid.*, JI.1/1028, m. 3.

64 *ibid.*, JI.1/956, m. 44ᵛ. Nicholas of St Maur is named in the Gloucestershire list of the Parliamentary Roll of Arms. *Parliamentary Writs*, I, p. 418.

65 *ibid.*, JI.1/1032, m. 4ᵛ.

66 *ibid.*, JI.1/966, m. 8.

67 *ibid.*, KB 27/52, m. 5, 15, 18.

68 *ibid.*, JI.1/956, m. 40; *Giffard*, 229, 306, 493, 550 and *passim* (see index).

69 *PRO*, KB 27/55, m. 5.

70 *ibid.*, JI.1/1031, m. 3.

71 *ibid.*, JI.1/1033, m. 3, 4, 6.

72 *ibid.*, JI.1/1028, m. 2, 8.

73 *Giffard*, p. 540; he is described as Lord of Morton and patron of the church in the *Registrum Sede Vacante* (ed. J. W. Willis Bund), *WHS*, 1893, p. 68. *VCH Worcs.*, II, p. 350, suggests that he must have appropriated Weethley manor which was recovered after 1316 by Abbot William of Chiritone. *Ev. Chron.*, p. 289...

74 *CPR*, 1313–7, p. 429; *ibid.*, 1317–21, p. 585.

75 *PRO*, JI.1/1031, m. 1, 2, 2ᵛ.

76 *ibid.*, m. 1.

77 Robert Lyvet was lord of Haselor (Warwickshire) in 1298. *Giffard*, p. 895. Godfrey of Crombe also got the rectory of Tredington in 1295, *ibid.*, p. 450. For Weston-sub-Edge, see also *ibid.*, pp, 463, 492, 541, 544, 549.

78 *Geynesborough*, pp. 10, 82.

79 *PRO*, JI.1/286, m. 4.

80 *Registrum Sede Vacante*, p. 68.

81 *CPR*, 1317–19, p. 429; *Reynolds*, p. 178.

82 *RH*, I, p. 166 ff.; II, pp. 223 ff., 282 ff.

83 For the ban see F. M. Powicke, *The Thirteenth Century*, 1953, pp. 621–2.

84 *RH*, I, pp. 167, 171, 166–83 *passim*; II, p. 228.

85 *PRO*, JI.1/1036.

86 *The English Clergy*, 1947, p. 6.

87 *WHS*, Collectanea, 1912.

88 *Giffard*, p. 79.

89 Walter Cantilupe, Bishop of Worcester 1237–66, promulgated a set of statutes in 1240. C. R. Cheney, *English Synodalia of the Thirteenth*

Century, 1941, p. 90; *Mirk's Instructions, c.* 1400, were edited by E. Peacock for the Early English Text Society in 1868.

90 *Giffard*, pp. 70, 81, 166 ff., 176, 184, 185, 200.
91 *ibid.*, pp. 110–13.
92 *ibid.*, p. 215.
93 *ibid.*, pp. 72, 95, 174, 394, 258–60.
94 *ibid.*, p. 11.

INDEX